K THE INGMAKER

**Center Point
Large Print**

K THE INGMAKER

BRIAN HAIG

CENTER POINT PUBLISHING
THORNDIKE, MAINE

To Lisa,
Brian, Patrick, Donnie, and Annie

This Center Point Large Print edition
is published in the year 2003 by arrangement with
Warner Books, Inc.

The text of this Large Print edition is unabridged. In other
aspects, this book may vary from the original edition. Printed in
Thailand. Set in 16-point Times New Roman type by
Bill Coskrey and Gary Socquet.

ISBN 1-58547-312-X

Cataloging-in-Publication data is available from the Library of Congress.

CHAPTER ONE

THE prisoner was led through the doorway by a pair of burly MPs, who shoved him into a chair and immediately began shackling his handcuffs to the table. The table was bolted to the floor, which was bolted to the prison, and so on.

"Guys . . . no need for that," I politely insisted. And was coldly ignored.

"Look, it's ridiculous," I said, with a touch more indignation. "How's he going to break out of here, much less walk two inches from this prison without being instantly recognized?"

I was blowing hot air, actually to impress the prisoner more than the guards. I'm a lawyer. I'm not above such things.

The MP sergeant stuffed the shackle key in his pocket and replied, "Don't give the prisoner nothing. No pens, no pencils, no sharp objects. Knock when you're done."

He stared at me longer than necessary—a gesture meant to convey that he didn't think highly of me or what I came here to do. Well, neither did I—regarding the latter.

I gave him a cold stare back. "All right, Sergeant."

The MPs scuttled from the room as I turned to examine the prisoner. It had been over ten years, and the changes were barely detectable—a tad more gray, perhaps, but he was still strikingly handsome in that chisel-featured, dark-haired, deep-eyed way some women find attractive. His athlete's body had softened, but those wide shoulders and slim waist were mostly intact. He'd always been a gym rat.

His psyche was a burned-out wreck; shoulders slumped, chin resting on his chest, arms hanging limply at his sides. Not good—little wonder they had stolen his shoelaces and belt.

I bent forward and squeezed his shoulder. "Bill, look at me."

Nothing. More sharply, I said, "Damn it, Billy, it's Sean Drummond. Pull yourself together and look at me."

Not so much as a twitch. The harsh tack wasn't punching through that wall of depression—perhaps something warmer, more conversational? I said, "Billy, listen . . . Mary called the day after your arrest and asked me to get out here right away. She said you want me to represent you."

The "here" was the military penitentiary tacked onto the backside of Fort Leavenworth, Kansas.

"Mary" was his wife of the past thirteen years, and the man I was speaking to was Brigadier General William T. Morrison, until recently the U.S. military attaché in our Moscow embassy.

The "day after your arrest" had been two long and miserable days earlier, the "arrest" being the one CNN had replayed over and over, of an Army general being dragged out the side door of the Moscow embassy, surrounded by FBI agents in bulletproof vests, his face a tangle of frustration and fury. Since then there had been countless newspaper articles detailing what a despi-

6

cably awful bastard he was. If the reports were true, I was seated across from the most monstrous traitor since—well, I suppose since ever.

He mumbled, "How is she?"

"She flew in from Moscow yesterday. She's staying with her father."

This got a dull nod, and I added, "The kids are fine. Her father has some pull with Sidwell Friends Academy, a private school that caters to celebrity children. They're hoping to get them in."

Shouldn't it help to make him think of his wife and family? He was locked down in a special isolation wing and denied any contact with the outside world: no phone calls, no letters, no notes. The authorities said the quarantine was to keep him from exposing more information or receiving smuggled-in cues from his Russian handlers. Perhaps. Unmentioned, of course, was that they hoped the social starvation would drive him babbling into the arms of his interrogators.

I crossed my legs and said, "Bill, let's consider this rationally. These are damned serious offenses. I win more than I lose, but you can find plenty of lawyers who are better. I'll name some if you'd prefer."

The response was a foot shuffle. What was he thinking?

He should be wondering why I wasn't blowing ten miles of smoke up his ass. Most guys in my position would flap their arms, boast and brag, and beg and plead to represent him.

The man was a lawyer's wet dream. I mean, how many general officers do you think get accused of betraying their country? I actually checked before I flew out here—Benedict Arnold was the last, and please recall that he fled to England before he could be tried, so nobody got a piece of his action.

When Morrison didn't reply, I said, "Though, if you'd like to consider me, I know you and your wife. This is personal. I'll put my heart and soul into defending you."

I paused to let that filter in and got . . . nothing.

"Look, is there somebody else you want? Just say so. It won't hurt my feelings. Hell, I'll even help arrange it."

And indeed I would. I'd throw my heart and soul into it. I wasn't there because *he'd* asked for me, but because Mary begged me. And if you want the whole squalid truth, that left me conflicted, because she and I had once been, uh . . . how do I delicately put this? *Involved?* What do you want to bet that a lawyer was the first one to utter that particular word that particular way?

Were they in the same chess club? Or did they have a torrid love affair that lasted three incredible years?

Yes, incidentally, on the last point.

His lips made a faint flutter, and I said, "I'm sorry . . . what was that again?"

"I said, I want you."

"You're sure, Billy?"

His head jerked up. "God damn it, call me Billy again and I'll knock you flat on your ass. You're still a major and I'm still a general, you stupid asshole."

Well . . . now there was a dose of the old William

8

Morrison I knew, and never could stand. I was his wife's old slumber buddy, and trust me on this point: This is hardly a male-bonding thing. Nor would we have been pals, anyway, as he was a general and I was a major, and in the Army that's some hard frost, socially speaking. Besides, William T. Morrison was a stuck-up, overambitious, pretty-boy prick, and what in the hell was Mary thinking when she married him?

She could've done so much better. Like me.

I reached into my briefcase and withdrew a few papers. "Okay, sign these forms. The top one requests the JAG to name me as your attorney. The second allows me to root through your records and investigate your background." I held out a pen. "But first promise you're not going to use this to stab yourself or some such shit."

He yanked it out of my hand, scratched his name on both forms, then threw the pen at me. I mumbled, "Thanks."

He mumbled, "Fuck you, Drummond. I mean . . . fuck you."

Was this getting off on the right foot or what? I asked, "Have you admitted anything yet?"

"No . . . of course not. What kind of stupid asshole do you take me for?"

The man is dressed in ugly orange coveralls and is chained to a table in a high-security prison. Can this be a serious question? I said, "Keep it that way. Don't say a thing without me present. Don't hint, sidestep, deny, or evade. Guilty or innocent, your only leverage is what's locked in your head and we need to preserve that. Understand?"

"Drummond, this is my field, remember? Like I need some stupid asshole telling me how it's done? I'll run circles around any jerk-off they bring in here."

The grating arrogance I remembered so well was definitely creeping back to the surface. Was this good or bad?

Other considerations aside, I suppose good. It surely helped that some semblance of his internal spirit was flogging its way into his cerebral cortex. A moment before he'd been a suicidal husk, and if something didn't seep into that vacuum, his whole being might get sucked into nothing.

Anyway, I'd done my duty. I'd warned him, and it was time to complete my spiel. "The Army's facing a time clock of thirty days to formalize your charges and get us into court to plead. A month or so later, there'll be a trial. If you're found guilty, there'll be a sentencing hearing shortly thereafter. Do I need to tell you the ultimate penalty for treason?"

This is the kind of sly query we lawyers employ when our clients are assholes. He frowned, shook his head, and I continued, "Here's how we're going to do this. I'll get a co-counsel who speaks Russian, and I'll set up a satellite office here. Then I'll start my discovery process. You understand how that works?"

"Of course."

"Well, espionage cases are . . . different. It's going to be a real tug-of-war."

He nodded that he understood, though really he didn't understand squat. He was going to discover that his fate hung on a bunch of secret evidence the government's most tightfisted agencies would fight tooth and nail not to release, even to his attorney; that, unlike with nearly every other type of criminal case, his chances of defending himself were crippled by security rules and stubborn bureaucrats and the government's very strong desire to burn him at the stake.

I mentioned none of this to him—yet. He was already on suicide watch, and I didn't want to send him hurtling off the ledge into eternity. I stood up and said, "I better get going. I'll stay in touch."

He looked up at me with tortured eyes. "Drummond, listen, I'm completely—"

"Innocent . . . right?"

"Yes. Really, this whole thing is—"

I held up a hand to cut him off.

I wasn't his attorney of record and had no business getting into any of this yet. Later he could tell me as many whoppers as he could dream up, and I would patiently sort the exceptionally unbelievable from the barely credible, until we settled on exactly which pack of lies we'd use for his defense.

But in retrospect I should've walked out and never returned.

CHAPTER TWO

THE Pentagon is not my kind of place. The many people who work there do many invaluable things, such as making sure Congress sends enough money every month to pay me. However, the building is huge, dreary, and depressingly impersonal. Stay in uniform long enough, and you'll inevitably end up assigned there. Along the same lines, live long enough and you'll end up crinkly and farty, with a leaky bladder. I don't spend a lot of time thinking about old age. I visit the Pentagon only when I have to.

I made it up to the third floor office of the Judge Advocate General, Major General Clapper, where his secretary insisted he was in a *vitally, vitally* important meeting that couldn't *possibly, possibly* be interrupted. Her name is Martha, and it has not escaped my attention that she often repeats things when she speaks to me.

I replied, "Well, Martha, why don't I take a seat, seat while I wait, wait?"

She said, "Shut up . . . just shut up."

After a brief but chilly wait, Clapper's door flew open and a long line of glum-faced men and women in dark business suits came filing out. For some unfathomable reason all spooks have that look. Maybe all those deep, dark secrets weigh down their facial features. Or maybe they're all foul-humored pricks. What do I know?

Anyway, the instant they were gone I approached Clapper and handed him Morrison's request.

We then walked together, he and I, into his office. The door closed somewhat less than gently, and why did I suspect that an outright "Yes, you're the perfect guy for the job" was out of the question?

He jammed the request in my face. "Drummond, *this* . . . What is it?"

"Morrison's requesting me as his counsel."

"That's pathetically obvious. What isn't, is why?"

"Because he thinks I'm a great attorney, I suppose."

"No really, Drummond . . . why?"

Truly, you have to love a guy with a sense of humor like that. I don't actually love him, but I certainly respect him, and occasionally I even like him. As chief of the JAG Corps, he is akin to the managing partner of the world's largest law firm, with lawyers and legal assistants and judges strewn literally around the globe, involved in a mind-boggling array of complex cases and legal duties. It is the kind of job that breeds irritability, impatience, and bossiness. Or perhaps it's me.

My tiny piece of his vast empire is a small, highly specialized cell that focuses on what are called black crimes—which have nothing to do with racial issues and everything to do with units and soldiers whose missions are so staggeringly secret that nobody even knows they exist. It's a bigger part of the Army than most people realize, and the job of my unit is to handle its legal problems under a blanket so dense that no sunshine sneaks in, or out.

This sensitivity explains why we, including me, work directly for Thomas Clapper. We are a very troublesome bunch and quite proud of it, and I have been told on more than one occasion that I am the most troublesome of the troublesome. It's damned unfair, but nobody gave me a vote.

But, back to Clapper, I said, "I really don't know why he wants me, General. It doesn't matter—an accused man has the right to pick his own representation."

My intuition or, more likely, his expression told me that being lectured on this overriding point of law hadn't improved his mood. He asked, "Do you know who those people were that just left my office?"

"I can guess."

"No—I don't think you can. That was the inter-agency working group that's supposed to assess how much damage Morrison wrought. Those were the chiefs of counterespionage from the CIA and the FBI, from NSA and DIA and State, and a few agencies I never heard of. They climbed deeply up my ass. They are incensed that an officer of the United States Army betrayed his country in ways you can't possibly con-ceive. An Army officer, damn it . . . a general officer. They warned me that I had better not make a single mistake in handling this case." He paused very briefly. "Does that help you understand why I have reserva-tions about you?"

I nodded. Why make him explain it?

He drew a deep breath and added, "Sean, you're a good attorney, but this case is just too damned sensi-tive. I'm sorry. You're the wrong man."

Well, right, I nodded again—truly, I did agree with him on this point.

"Good." His expression turned friendlier, and a fatherly hand landed on my shoulder. "Now, you fly back out there and tell Morrison why you can't pos-sibly be his lawyer. Tell him not to worry, we'll provide one of our best."

He looked me in the eye and that fatherly hand dropped off my shoulder. "Damn it, do you have any idea what you're getting into?"

"Something about a spy case, isn't it?"

He ignored my sarcasm. This was a wise course. Encourage me and it only gets worse.

I'm not ordinarily predictable, but Clapper has known me long enough to appreciate my peccadilloes. Back when he was a lowly major, he actually instructed a dim-witted new infantry lieutenant named Drummond on the fundamentals of military law. He also happens to be the shortsighted fool who later persuaded the Army to allow me to attend law school and become a JAG officer.

You could argue, therefore, that this situation was his fault. Past sins do come back to haunt you.

Struggling to sound reasonable, he said, "Look . . . Sean . . . when the CIA and FBI first approached me with their suspicions and evidence on Morrison, I nearly choked. They've been watching him for months. They have him dead to rights."

"Well, good. All I'll have to do is strike the best deal I can get. Any idiot lawyer can do that. What are you worried about?"

Judging by his expression, a lot. "At least *try* to see this from my perspective. We're dealing with Russia on this counterterrorism effort, not to mention the ongoing oil talks and nuclear arms reductions and a hundred other sensitive negotiations. The administration doesn't want a dustup with Russia over this case. You see that, right?"

"Yes, General, I see that, but he asked for me, and he has the right to choose his representation," I reminded him, less than subtly, for the third time.

There's the old saying "No man is above the law" that applies even to two-star generals, a sort of divine provenance, or whatever. I had pushed this point as far as was healthy, and it was time to await the verdict.

He finally said, "All right, damn it. It's yours."

"Very good, thank you, sir," I replied, doing my perfect subordinate imitation, which, really, considering the audience and the moment, was a wasted effort. "Oh, I, uh, I have one other request."

"What?"

"I need a co-counsel."

"Fine. Submit your request and I'll consider it."

"Karen Zbrovnia," I immediately replied.

"No," he immediately responded.

"Why not?"

"She's already committed."

"So pull her off. You said yourself, this is the biggest case going."

"I can't."

"Yes sir, you can. Sign the right piece of paper and, poof, it happens. And I'm formally requesting you to. I *need* Zbrovnia."

His lips curled up. "Well, you see, she's already assigned to the prosecution."

We stared at each other a long moment. Karen Zbrovnia was one of the top assassins in the JAG Corps: brilliant, confident, occasionally ruthless—oh, and a nice ass, if you're the crass type who notices such things. More important for my purposes, her parents were Russian émigrés and had taught her to speak like a Moscovite.

Losing her, however, wasn't my biggest concern. I asked, "You've already formed the prosecution?"

"The prosecution nearly always comes in early in espionage cases. Zbrovnia and her boss have been approving everything for months. They have to live with the evidence, right?"

Well, yes . . . right. Was it worth noting that I also had to live with that evidence? Or how much of an advantage the prosecution had been handed after being involved in this case for months?

"You said 'her boss,' " I asked, suddenly apprehensive. "Who's in charge of the prosecution?"

"Major Golden."

It occurred to me that he had been waiting for this moment. The JAG Corps annually presents an unofficial award, a silly twist on the Navy's Top Gun, called the Hangman Award. It has rested on Eddie Golden's office bookshelf two years running, and in an obnoxiously prominent place, telling you volumes about Mr. Golden. I played a role in that award, having faced him three times, the first two of which I was carried out of court on a stretcher. I nearly got the better of him the third time, before it was declared a mistrial, which, technically, was a draw. The idea of Eddie scoring a hat trick on me was sickening.

I mumbled, "I'll send you a name when I think of one."

He nodded as I made my retreat, thinking to myself that I'd ended up with a case I didn't want, representing a client I couldn't stand, opposing an attorney I dreaded. In short, I had kicked myself in the nuts.

I drove off in a fetid mood and raced down the George Washington Parkway to the McLean exit, described in Realtors' brochures as a "leafy, upscale suburb" located right across the river from our nation's glorious capital. Between "leafy" and "upscale" the message is this: McLean is where two or three million bucks in the bank can land you.

I raced past the entrance to the CIA headquarters, took a right on Georgetown Pike, shot past Langley High School and two more of those leafy side streets, then turned into one of what those Realtors' brochures enticingly call an "elegant, highly prestigious address with old world charm." Translation—bump up the bank balance another ten mil.

The street was lined with graceful old mansions that are distinctly different from the new McMansions sprouting up elsewhere, intimating that the residents of this block pay their property taxes with old money. Old money's supposed to be better than new money, but when you have no money, like me, the distinction's a bit blurry.

I pulled into the big circular driveway and parked my 1996 Chevrolet right next to a spanking-new $180,000 Porsche 911 GT2—a glorious thing in shimmering black, a boy-toy of the highest order. I admired it for a long, simmering instant before my car door flew out of my hand and oops—a big scratch and ugly dent magically appeared.

I walked to the front door and rang the bell. The man who answered had a curious smile that flipped into a vulgar frown as his eyes fell on my face. "Drummond?"

"In the flesh, Homer, and it's a real pleasure to see you, too," I replied, with a big phony smile.

He did not smile back. The man was Homer Steele, Mary's father, a guy born with a lemon stuck so far up his ass that the stem poked out his ear. I thought I heard him laugh once at a cocktail party, but when I went to investigate, he was choking on a piece of lobster. I rooted for the lobster, incidentally.

"What do *you* want?" he demanded in a less than polite way.

"Mary. She's expecting me."

The door slammed and I waited patiently for three full minutes, overhearing a jarring argument inside. Was this fun, or what?

Finally the door opened, and there stood Mary Steele Morrison in her full staggering glory.

So let me explain about Mary.

Remember Grace Kelly . . . that alabaster skin, those scorching blue eyes, that silky white-blond hair? Remember how she walked into a room and men actually gasped? That's Mary without the slightest exaggeration. One of those Hollywood doubles agencies saw her picture in some society rag and even offered her work as a stand-in.

Two months into my sophomore year at Georgetown, she approached me in the middle of the campus quad and brazenly begged me for a date. A crowd began gathering. People were watching. I did what any gentleman would do, and then the girl started calling me all the time, making a damned nuisance out of herself, and out of pity I dated her for the next three years.

That's how I remember it.

Oddly enough, she recalls it somewhat differently.

Her father wasn't too keen on her career choice, which we'll get into later. She'd stop home on weekends, and there was always some new jerk in a Ralph Lauren sweater, perched casually by the fireplace, sipping sherry, eyeing her like a used sofa her father wanted to pawn off.

From that scant evidence, Mary deduced that her father was trying to mate her with somebody's large fortune, and that put her in a cranky, rebellious mood. The day I worked up the nerve to ask her to go see a movie, she saw the perfect candidate for the perfect plot. In a nutshell, she'd lure me home to meet Daddy Warbucks, and since I wasn't exactly what Papa had in mind, a deal would be struck—the spoiled rich kids and I would mutually disappear.

Her side of the story has going for it that it bears an almost uncanny resemblance to the facts. Homer barely glanced at me before he yanked her comely tush into his study, and the sounds of their yapping and thrashing echoed all over the house. And if you think that's not a crappy feeling, try having it happen to you.

Anyway, now as I stood in her doorway, her arms flew around my neck and she planted a kiss on my cheek. I hugged her, too, and then we stepped back and examined each other, as ex-lovers are wont to do. She smiled and said, "Sean Drummond, I'm so damn glad to see you. How are you?"

"Uh, fine, yeah, hi, gee, crappy way to meet, how are you, you look great."

Am I cool or what?

That smile—I'd forgotten how unnerving it was. Most beautiful women, the best they can do is this flinching motion of a few stingy muscles that comes across more like a favor than a feeling. Mary's smile swallows you whole.

Besides, she did look great. Her face was slightly leaner, and there were a few tiny wrinkles, but the effect was to enhance her beauty—as the poetically inclined might say, sprinkling dew on a rose petal.

She wrapped both her arms tightly around my arm and tugged. "Come on." She giggled. "I swear it's safe. My father promised to leave us alone."

"Gee, I don't know." I peeked inside. "I don't trust the old fart."

Mary giggled some more. "He has a dartboard upstairs with your face on it. He's probably up there right now."

This was a joke, right? She led me to the rear of the big house, to a cavernous sunroom built off a living room the size of a football stadium. The house was filled with ancient-looking oriental carpets, and cracked, antique-looking paintings, and leather furniture with brass studs, and all the other ostentatious furnishings meant to remind visitors of the life they can't afford.

She sat on a flower-patterned couch and I took a place across from her. The moment instantly got landlocked in the past. Twelve years is a long time, and a million questions were swirling in my mind. Unfortunately, the one that kept kicking to the surface was, Hey, why'd you marry that lousy prick when you could've had me?

Given the circumstances and all, perhaps it would be best to avoid that one. I finally announced, "I saw him this morning."

"How is he?"

"Not well. On suicide watch."

She shook her head. "Poor Bill. They called him into the office on some pretense, then he was in handcuffs being dragged out of the embassy. They deliberately humiliated him. Those bastards even invited CNN to be there."

I tried to appear sympathetic, but to be honest, I had enjoyed watching the arrest. Of course, this was before he became my client, and now I was deeply ashamed of myself. Right. Anyway, I said, "Well, he signed the request and my boss just approved it."

She tried to muster a warm smile as she said, "Thank you. I mean it. I know it's awkward. I just . . ." And suddenly that smile crumbled, and she was biting her lip.

I put a hand on her leg. "Forget it."

She laid her hand on top of mine. "We shouldn't have asked," she finally said. "What a stupid predicament."

I chuckled. "Don't worry about it."

"Sean, I have no right to put you in this position. I'm desperate . . . I have two young children and a husband accused of treason. Bill insisted on you, but I—"

"Look," I interrupted, "if you're concerned about my

feelings, don't be. Lawyers have no emotions."

"Liar."

"Liar, huh? At Georgetown Law, they caught a girl crying one day . . . She'd just learned her mother died. They threw her out on her butt. There was a big ceremony in the auditorium and they said she just couldn't cut it."

She was shaking her head and laughing. "Oh, come on."

"We're the ones in movie theaters who get dreamy-eyed when the *Titanic* goes down, counting the corpses and plotting the class-action suit."

She giggled and said, "God, I've missed you," then instantly looked chagrined, like, Oops, what made those words pop out? "Hey," she said, a *little* too awkwardly, "do you want to meet the kids?"

"Oh God, kids?" I groaned.

"It won't be bad, I promise. They're just like regular people, only smaller. Just . . . nothing about Bill, okay?"

I nodded as she left the room and went into the hallway. She called upstairs and a moment later came the thundering sound of little feet bouncing down stairs.

"This is Jamie," she said, pointing proudly at the boy, "and this is Courtney." She then paused briefly to fabricate a graceful way to explain me, the guy who would've been their father were it not for their mother's awful judgment. To them, she said, "Guys, this is Major Sean Drummond. We went to college together and, well . . . we were best of friends. He's just

23

stopped by to say hello."

They padded over and shook my hand, a pair of blond-haired, blue-eyed replicas of their mother. This was no bad thing, I must tell you, and I felt perversely gratified to see so little of Morrison's seed evident in their children. Don't ask me why; I just did.

I said to her, "Christ, your genes are greedy cannibals."

She giggled. "Bill always said I mated with myself."

Then the hard part. There's a good reason bachelors aren't supposed to have children and it's called competency. I try to come down to their level, to engage them in conversations about things I assume they're interested in, like say, Tonka trucks and Barbie dolls, and they look back at me like I'm a moron.

I regarded them with my most charming smile. "So, hey, what do you guys think of the Redskins' chances this year?"

Mary rolled her eyes, while Jamie, who looked to be eleven or twelve, pondered this a moment, then finally replied, "They need a new coach."

"You think so?"

"A new quarterback, too."

"A new quarterback, huh?"

"And their defensive backfield stinks. So does their offensive line."

"I take it you don't think much of them?"

"My grandpa likes them, so I hate them."

The timing would be off, but I stared at him and wondered if he was my lovechild. I said, "I predict you're going to grow up and become a very great man."

24

Courtney, who looked to be six or seven, had been retreating swiftly toward the protection of her mother's legs, that way shy kids do. But she was a girl—tiny and inexperienced—and thus, should still be susceptible to my charms. I flashed her my smarmiest smile. "And what about you, Courtney? Don't you like football, too?"

She looked terrifically confused as her mother reached down and stroked her hair. "Ignore him, darling. He gets awkward around women."

Courtney giggled. "You mean he's a dork?"

"Honey, we never use that word in front of the people we're talking about," said Mary, wagging her finger. "Wait till he's gone."

Courtney giggled some more. "Girls don't like football," she instructed me. "I like Playstation, though. Especially the games where you get to shoot people."

"Do they show the blood?"

"On the better ones. Some of them, the people just die."

"Yeah, I could see where that would get boring," I admitted with a knowing nod.

"I like it better when they bleed."

"I think I love you. Would you happen to be free on Friday night?"

She hugged Mary's leg tighter. "He's strange, Mom."

"I know, honey. He can't help it. Don't make fun of him, though. He's very sensitive."

I stuck out my tongue at Courtney and she broke into giggles.

"All right, you two," ordered Mary. "Back upstairs

and stay away from your grandfather. He's slipped into one of his grumpy moods."

Their obligation to meet their mother's friend completed, they scampered off with relief on their faces. I was impressed. It only took those few moments to realize that Mary was a great mother. The chemistry between her and the kids was palpable and affecting.

We sat on the couches and faced off again. I asked, "And is Grandpa ever not grumpy?"

She shook her head and rolled her eyes. "Ignore the stuffy old ass. He thinks we're idiots for bringing you into this. I told him Bill insisted on you, that he had always said if he got in desperate trouble, he wanted me to call you."

"Well . . . that's interesting."

She wisely ignored this. "Sean, he followed your legal career very closely. He really admires you, you know."

"Well, desperate trouble calls for desperate action, I suppose."

She nodded that this was so and asked, "How do you think it'll go?"

"Frankly, it's going to be an ordeal for him, for you, and the kids. When it comes to espionage cases, the government leaks everything. It's like the bureaucrats feel some obnoxious compulsion to tell the American people exactly what kind of disgusting bastard they've caught."

She closed her eyes and looked pained. "I've seen it before. I'm trying to prepare myself."

Truthfully, there was no way to prepare for this, however, I moved on and asked, "What are they telling you at work?"

Regarding this particular question, the day after we graduated, Mary disappeared into that big CIA training facility down by Quantico, Virginia, to begin the career Homer had tried to derail with his fruitless pimping. I never understood why Mary was so intent on becoming Jane Bond, however, she was the kind of model candidate the CIA dreamed of attracting—smart, polished, adaptable—and its recruiters had likely promised her a world of bullshit. Over the years I'd heard she was doing quite well, however, her world was as much smoke and mirrors as mine, so I had not a clue what she did.

She leaned back in her chair and released a big gust of air. "They haven't told me anything. They can't. I'm the Moscow station chief whose husband is accused of working for the Russians. It's a terrible predicament for everybody."

Oh my. Trying to hide my stupefaction, I asked, "The station chief?"

She nodded as I tried to absorb this news. Needless to say, this presented a whole new array of potential problems. I settled for, "So you haven't been canned or anything?"

"Not yet. I've been reassigned to a management job here in Langley without access to anything even remotely sensitive. They'll keep me packed in mothballs until this thing is resolved, then they'll quietly pinkslip me."

She explained this matter-of-factly, as though it was

just the way things worked, and why worry about it. Actually, it left a great deal to be worried about. In reply to my stare, she said, "I know . . . it's going to be the bombshell when it gets out. I'm not looking forward to it."

I pondered this a moment, then asked, "Did you have any inkling it was going down?"

"I'm his wife, Sean. I was the last person they'd say anything to."

That obviously made sense. I asked, "Did the two of you . . . uh . . ."

"Share things?"

"Exactly."

"He had a Top Secret, SCI clearance. He was the military attaché, which is an intelligence job, and I was the station chief. Leads, sources, discoveries, you name it—I held nothing back."

"Mary, I advise you to get a lawyer."

"I know. I'll be interviewing several over the next few days."

"Have you been interrogated?"

"Formally, no. I've had a few sly queries from my boss, the deputy director for intelligence, but nobody has yet sat me down for a rigorous grilling. They'll get around to it, though."

Indeed, they would. "Don't say anything. As his wife you're protected from testifying against him. Not to mention, you need to keep as much distance from this as you can."

"I'm not sure I can sell them on that. He's my husband. I'm in this up to my eyeballs."

"Legal distance, Mary. There are all kinds of possible avenues of culpability in this. Get that lawyer quickly, and if they try to question you in between, politely refuse to answer anything."

She nodded, but with an amused expression, I suppose because it's a bit awkward to get legal advice from a former lover. I recalled the warning about mixing business with pleasure, however, this was old pleasure mixed with new business so perhaps it did not apply.

I asked, "Are you mad at him?"

"Truthfully, I'm furious. I can't believe this happened. Maybe it's not his fault, and I keep trying not to blame him . . . I can't stop myself. I need someone to be mad at."

"It's natural, and you'll get past it. Say he actually did it, got any idea why?"

"Not one, Sean. Everything was going so well. We had a good life . . . we both loved our work. Did you know Bill was on the two-star list that's about to come out?"

I didn't know. "Was" would be the operative verb, however, as some guy was probably at that very moment seated in a back room putting a match to that list. The Army tends to be very grouchy about these things.

I walked across to where she was seated, bent over, pecked her cheek, and said, "I have to go. You'll be hearing from me soon, okay?"

I thought her expression looked bleak and abysmally lonely and I didn't really want to leave. What I really wanted to do, I won't go into. I asked, "You sure you should be staying here? With him?" I pointed a finger at the ceiling to show I meant you-know-who.

She gave me a forced smile and replied, "It's the best place for us. He believes in protecting his brood, and that's what the kids and I most need."

Wrong. What she and the kids needed most was to turn back the clock a dozen years, a different husband, a different father, and so on.

But, this being America, when fate deals you a crappy hand, there is one other thing you need—a lawyer. And so, here we were.

CHAPTER THREE

G IVEN that Eddie had a several month head start, speed was going to count for everything at this stage. I pulled over at the first gas station and used a pay phone to call my legal assistant, whose name, title, and all that crap is Sergeant First Class Imelda Pepperfield. She answered on the first ring, as that's her way with everything, prompt to the point of preemptive.

I said, "Hey, Imelda, me. You know that Morrison case that's splashed all over the news?"

"I heard of it."

"It's ours. Morrison asked for me, and his wife is a, uh, an old chum and she, uh, she sort of, well . . . twisted my arm."

Imelda's about five foot one, 160 pounds, a fiftyish black woman with a pudgy face, frumpy build, gold-rimmed glasses, and slightly graying hair. People who observe her only from a distance immediately lump her into that harmless grandmotherly category, one of those late-middle-aged women who use their spare time to knit mufflers and sweaters for their nephews and make chicken soup for sickly friends. One could more safely confuse an atomic bomb with a firecracker.

Imelda was raised in the mountains of North Carolina, where she acquired the affectations of a poorly educated backwoods hick she has long since outgrown, yet milks to this day to persuade suckers like me that there's some tangible reason she's supposed to salute and call me sir. What lurks behind that wicked camouflage are a razor-sharp mind, two master's degrees, and the moral ambiguity of a Mack truck. She's spent nearly thirty years in the Army, seeing law practiced and mal-practiced in all its gritty varieties, and offers her seasoned advice whenever it's asked for—or not— usually the same way a ballpeen hammer helps a tent peg find its way into the ground.

"This a bad idea," she finally replied.

"Why?"

"'Cause you don't know diddly-squat 'bout espionage cases. 'Cause you over your head."

Not many people can say "diddly-squat" and still be taken seriously. But then, I don't know anybody who doesn't take Imelda seriously. I take her very seriously. I assured her, "It's like any other criminal case. Different actors and setting is all."

"Horseshit. This 'cause of his wife?"

"Imelda, she's just an old friend. This isn't personal, it's professional . . . and please recall that her *husband* asked for me."

Without replying to that point, she asked, "You heard who the prosecutor is?"

"Golden. So what?"

"You takin' this case 'cause you hot for the wife of the accused traitor, and you goin' up against Golden, in something you don't know shit about. And now you askin' me so what?"

Imelda has a maddening habit of developing her own opinions, which can be annoying, but then I have my annoying habits, too, so it all balances out. I replied, "I'm not hot for Mary. And regarding Eddie, I'll blow him out of the courtroom." Getting back to the business at hand, I added, "I'll look into hiring an associate, and I need you to arrange a satellite office at Leavenworth."

"You better find a damned good one . . . You gonna need it."

"Thank you for your confidence in my abilities."

"Didn't say I was confident in your abilities."

She was right, however, and I next placed a call to the JAG personnel officer and asked him to run a computer search for all the Army lawyers who spoke Russian.

He called back a few minutes later with two names, one being Captain Karen Zbrovnia, previously committed. And a guy named Jankowski, whose Polish was flawless, but whose Russian was rated just shy of marginal.

This wouldn't do; I needed someone who could speed-read a Tolstoy novel in Russian without missing a single fractured nuance, assuming the Russians have such things. I therefore called an old law school chum who practiced criminal law in the District of Columbia. Harry Zinster is his name, and he is the Hedda Hopper of Washington law; sadly, what he isn't, is an even halfway competent lawyer.

He answered himself, as he definitely can't afford a secretary. I said, "Hey, Harry, Drummond here. I need a favor."

"Whatever. You got a friend who needs good representation? I've got a busy calendar but I'll see if I can squeeze him in."

Nice try—Harry hadn't seen a busy calendar since law school, leave aside that I'd never commit a friend to his feeble hands. I said, "Actually, I'm looking for an attorney who speaks Russian, and speaks it really well. Know any?"

"A few."

"I also need it to be someone who either has, or can get, a security clearance. Have I just made the problem too hard?"

"Nope. Katrina Mazorski . . . she used to have some kind of government job. She works out of her home in the District, doing criminal stuff mostly."

"You know her, or *of* her?"

"Know her, Sean, but only vaguely. She hangs out sometimes at the Fourteenth Street precinct, scrounging scraps off what the night shift drags in. We've shared a few late-night cups of coffee."

One of the things I love about Army law is that my clients fall into my lap off a conveyer belt. Spending all night in police stations begging pimps and whores and muggers for work is a part of the profession law schools don't advertise. Funny thing, huh?

I asked Harry, "Would you happen to have her number?"

"Somewhere . . ." He began opening and slamming drawers. This lasted awhile, as organizational skills were another of Harry's weaknesses. "Found it," he finally mumbled.

I thanked him, jammed in another seventy-five cents, and she answered on the first ring. I said, "Katrina Mazorski?"

"Yeah."

"My name's Drummond. Harry Zinster gave me your name."

"I know Harry."

"Well, uh, Harry told me you speak Russian. Is that speak it like you can order a beer and hot dog or like you could have a long, frank discussion with a Russian rocket scientist?"

There was a quick, harsh chuckle. "Look, I couldn't have a long, frank discussion with a rocket scientist in any language. If you mean, am I a native-quality speaker, yeah."

I noted that she had an interesting voice—deeper than most female voices, husky even. A picture formed inside my head of a woman of about thirty, elegant, mysterious, seductive. It would be too much to try to add a physical description to that picture, although one can always hope.

I asked, "How'd you learn it?"

"From my parents."

"How'd they learn it?"

"From their parents. I hope there's a point to this discussion."

"There's a point. I'm a JAG officer, assigned a case that requires me to have a Russian-speaking co-counsel."

"I see. And you're thinking of me?"

"Harry also said you used to have a government job. What did you do?"

"I was a translations clerk at State."

"Did you have a clearance?"

"Yes. A Top Secret."

This was sounding too good to be true. I asked, "Can you drop everything and come meet me?"

"I, uh . . . is this an interview?"

"It's only a temporary job, maybe a few months, and it'll involve some travel. That satisfactory with you?"

"Maybe."

I gave her the address for my office and then raced back to get ready. Imelda awarded me a testy frown, hrummphcd a few times, and threw a stack of yellow phone message slips at me. She was very unhappy with me. Granted, she was being subtle, but I could tell. I killed time returning calls.

Then came a knock at the door and Imelda stuck her puzzled face in. "Some lady here . . . says she's supposed to interview with you."

"Katrina Mazorski?"

"Same one. She ain't an attorney, is she?"

"Why?"

Imelda's eyebrows merged with her hairline, and a moment later Katrina Mazorski stepped through the portal. I had stood up to shake, only my arm froze—call it a momentary paralysis. She had on skintight, hip-hugging, black leather pants, a halter top with a black bra peeking out, maroonish lipstick, a silver bead in her left nostril, and a silver hoop poking out of her naked navel. Her hair was dark and hung straight, and her eyes were brown, or possibly green. She had wide shoulders, no waist to speak of, long, slender legs, and she was pretty—and yes, okay, sexy, too, just not in the way I'm used to girls being pretty . . . or sexy. Along the lines of Sandra Bullock pretty, only clownishly made up, with a few bangles punched through her skin.

"You're, uh, you're Miss Mazorski?"

She slid into the chair in front of my desk. "My friends call me Kate, but you're not my friend yet, so Katrina will do fine. What do I call you?"

"Sean Drummond's my name. Of course my friends call me Sean. Why don't you call me Major?"

She tipped back on the chair, grinned, and replied, "That's cool. What's the gig?"

"Gig?"

"Y'know, the case?"

We stared at each other a moment. I finally said, "I'd like to ask the questions. Silly as that might sound, I read a management book once and it said that's the way these interview things are supposed to work."

"Fire away," she said. "That's how you guys talk, right?"

I rolled my eyes. "How old are you?"

"Twenty-nine."

"When'd you graduate from law school?"

"Two years ago. Maryland . . . night school."

"And what have you been doing since graduation?"

"A little of this, a little of that."

"I don't mean to pry, but could you be more descriptive?"

"Okay . . . I spent the first few months passing the D.C. and Virginia bars and interviewing with firms. And then—"

"And did you get any offers?" I interrupted.

She appeared amused. "A few."

"What's that mean?"

"I got several invitations to sleep with the interviewers. Do you want to hear the details?"

"No, I, uh . . . let's skip that. The firm route didn't work out."

"You got the picture."

I was nodding when she asked, "What about you?"

"I'm sorry?"

She bent forward. "What about you? Where'd you go to law school? How long have you been a JAG officer? What do you expect from me?"

There still seemed to be some confusion about whose interview this was. I swallowed my irritation and replied, "Georgetown Law eight years ago. For five years before that I was an infantry officer. And I'm interviewing you to become a member of the defense team for General William Morrison."

She slumped back in her chair. "Morrison . . . the spy?"

"Same guy. Interested?"

"Uh, yeah . . . I'm interested. What do you

expect from me?"

"We'll figure that out as we go along."

She considered this a moment, then said, "Do I get involved in the criminal case or do you expect me to be a glorified paralegal?"

I have a good memory and was sure I told her *I* was interviewing *her*. I allowed a long, cold moment to pass. "This is a military case that involves espionage. The Army picked two top guns to prosecute. You said you went to U of Maryland night school, right? They have the top-drawer lawyers of the CIA and the Justice Department at their beck and call. There's going to be more Ivy League degrees trying to fry my client than you can count. So tell me . . . what can *you* contribute?"

She laughed. "I speak excellent Russian."

"Well there you have it. Married?"

"No."

"Ever been married?"

"No again."

"A U.S. citizen?"

"My mother and father emigrated ten years before I was born."

"Any limitations on travel or long hours?"

"No limitations. What's it pay?"

"I can get you one-fifty a day, plus expenses. It's no great shake, but the Army's stingy. And incidentally, that's about what the Army pays me."

"I'll take it."

"Well, that presents a problem," I politely noted. "I didn't offer it yet."

"You're going to." She chuckled. "You're definitely going to."

"Why's that?"

"Martindale-Hubbell's will tell you there's only three other lawyers in this town that speak fluent Russian. Two bill five hundred an hour and do most of their work for the Russian Mafiya. The third's facing disbarment for running an adoption scam and bilking childless couples. None of them could bribe their way into the Republican Convention, much less a security clearance. You're lucky I'm available. Now, put on a nice expression, make your offer, and quit wasting time."

I shook my head. "This may come as a surprise, but I hear there's actually lawyers outside of this city."

She shrugged. "You'll waste weeks and still not find somebody with my credentials and talents. Quit jerking me around and make your offer."

Her head was canted sideways, and she was observing me with a sort of insouciant expression. Her eyes were brown, I realized. But the more relevant thing I realized was that this woman was a bit of a ball-buster.

Actually, so what? Maybe she was bluffing about how hard it would be to find another suitable attorney. But maybe she wasn't. Time was already a bit of an issue for me.

I pondered the pros and cons and then said, "We'll try it, but conditionally. If I don't like your work, it's sayonara."

"I'll start tomorrow," she responded, "and don't worry about my work. Just try to keep up." Then she abruptly got up, spun around, and left.

The things I liked about her: She was obviously smart, self-confident, and attractive—if you like that type.

What I didn't like was that she was sassy, cocky, pushy, and looked like a Technicolor cartoon of Generation X. The appearance issue could be a problem, but more her problem than mine. What was a problem for me was that she was definitely a wiseass. I happen to admire the characteristic, however, we all know what happens when you put two wiseasses together.

But then, I'm confident of my devastating wit and, misgivings aside, would find some use for her.

CHAPTER FOUR

THE top story of the *Washington Herald* on my first full day as William Morrison's lead attorney had this to say: A knowledgeable source who wished to remain anonymous claimed Morrison was first recruited by a case officer of the KGB as early as 1988 or 1989. Mr. Anonymous knew this because those were the years when the trail of Morrison's damage first ignited. After the Soviet Union got swept into the dustbin of history, Morrison's case officer simply transferred his files into Russia's new intelligence bureaus and kept the game rolling.

Over that period, Morrison had scored some very impressive intelligence coups against the Soviets, and afterward, against the Russians, that dramatically furthered his career. He received a slew of early promotions and special assignments.

Also over that period, a number of critically vital intelligence programs had been blown and several double agents and Russian turncoats had been exposed and then brutally executed by Russia's intelligence agencies. These signs were noticed. The CIA and FBI knew they had a traitor and searched relentlessly for his identity, a search that led eventually to Aldrich Ames and Robert Hanssen, but the CIA and FBI were now forced to consider the ugly possibility that both had been tossed by the Russians to keep the spotlight off Morrison. Ames and Hanssen weren't exactly minnows—this only accentuated the scale of treason Morrison was suspected of committing.

Regarding Mary being the Moscow station chief, there was no mention. Eventually it would have to surface. It was too stunningly juicy to ignore. If Morrison was a Russian vacuum cleaner, he had not only inhaled what he discovered in his own increasingly prestigious positions, but also what Mary learned from hers.

But the tidbit that especially whetted my interest was the mention of his case officer, or, in the lingo of professional spies, his "controller." Not two controllers, or a team of controllers—the article referred to only *one* controller. In the lingo of lawyers, a highly relevant fact.

I got to the office at six, jump-started the coffee-maker, poured a fresh cup, and then ventured into my office to ponder the situation. A few minutes later I heard Imelda rumble in, and shortly behind her, Katrina. After a few more minutes I heard them chatting.

Probably Imelda was telling her to lose that damned

bellybutton ring. Probably Katrina was telling Imelda she'd have a special place in the guillotine line when the revolution went down. I heard banging and shuffling and wondered if Imelda was body-slamming her around the office.

By eight-thirty I had a general idea of what I wanted or, more accurately, needed to do. I began making calls, first to the office of the CIA general counsel for an appointment to see him. Second, to Eddie Golden's office for an appointment to see him. Third, to Clapper's office to arrange to have Katrina hired and paid, and for her Top Secret clearance to be restored.

When I walked out, a second desk had been added for Katrina, and both wall safes had their drawers opened and emptied. Imelda and Katrina had battened down the hatches, preparing for an onslaught of evidence. Smart girls.

Looking surprisingly chummy, they were seated at a makeshift table, empty Starbucks cups between them, and a crumbcake that had been reduced to its namesake.

I shrugged and started heading for the door. Imelda asked, "Where you goin'?"

"To the CIA, then to see Golden. I'll be gone most of the morning."

"You forgettin' something?"

"Let me see . . . briefcase . . . pen . . . underwear . . . No, I have everything."

"Like your co-counsel?"

"Oh, I didn't forget. They're introductory meetings. She can wait here."

"My ass. She an attorney, ain't she?"

"I might even surprise you and be useful," said Katrina, looking amused. "Hard to believe, I know."

Did I really need to explain the problem here? Other issues aside, first impressions are important in this business, especially when your first stop is the most tight-assed place on the planet. She was wearing a loose blouse, tight bell-bottoms, clogs, and a spiked collar around her neck. But on second thought, it might be worth bringing her along for the shock value. Maybe her nose bead and belly-button ring would set off the metal detector at the CIA. Wouldn't that be a thrill?

Three minutes later we were racing down the GW Parkway. Wanting a better angle on this woman, I said, "So tell me about yourself."

She chuckled and replied, "'Tell me about yourself'?" like, What kind of asshole would phrase it like that?

"It's just a question. Answer however you choose."

"However, huh? Herpes-free single white female with a law degree from a third-rate school. Likes Chanel Premier Rouge lipstick, stands in long lines for U2 concerts, and would really appreciate less condescension from her boss. Does that work?"

"Fine." However, I believe I detected a veiled message.

She said, "Quit jerking me off and tell me what you're interested in."

"It's called getting acquainted. Familiarity breeds teamwork. Says so in a management book I once read." Of course, this was the same management book that told me how to conduct interviews, so its validity was highly suspect at this point. I said, "You mentioned your parents were Russian. How come they ended up here?"

"I didn't say they were Russian, I said they taught me to speak Russian. My father was Chechen; my mother was the Russian. When they got married . . . well, the Communists didn't like Chechens or mixed marriages, and things became uncomfortable. They were smart. They came here."

"And you grew up in New York City?"

"TriBeCa, before the yuppies discovered it. It used to be a nice neighborhood before all the condo associations converted it into high-gloss hell."

"And college?"

"That would be CUNY and four years of humping dishes in Broadway restaurants with horny tourists groping my ass as I tried to balance a tray over my head. College sucked." She paused a moment, then said, "Are we done yet?"

"Almost. Why law school?"

"As in, What's a girl who looks like me doing in your profession?"

"Hey, that's a good question, too."

"If I had a rack of power suits and a Dooney & Bourke briefcase, you wouldn't ask. Meet me in court someday and I'll bust your nuts."

"I'll bet you would," I replied. Of course we both knew I was lying. "Why criminal law?"

"It's my turn."

"Who said we were taking turns?"

"Don't be an asshole," she persisted. "What about you?"

"What about me?"

"Where'd you grow up?"

"I was an Army brat. We were migrants. As soon as the bill collectors figured out where we lived, we moved on."

"Then this is legacy work for you, huh?"

"I don't think of it that way, no."

"How do you think of it?"

"As a worthy trade inside an honorable profession."

"Wow. You actually said that with a straight face." She regarded me a moment, then asked, "Why law?"

I flashed my ID to the guard at the gate of the big CIA headquarters, and said, "Because back when I was an infantryman, I had the misfortune to stand in front of a few bullets. When the docs were done putting me back together they'd made a catastrophic wiring mistake and turned me into a lawyer."

"That sucks. I hope you sued their asses off."

"Well, you know how doctors feel about lawyers. They all shot themselves."

We pulled into a guest parking space and walked over to the entrance. A young man with a sour expression met us, handed us temporary building passes, actually showed us how to put them on, and then escorted us to the elevator. You have to love these people. We went up four floors and were then deposited at the office of the general counsel, where a secretary with the face of a dried prune eyed Katrina with a disapproving stare, then starchly told us to sit and wait. For all I knew, she had a gun in that desk. We sat and waited.

A minute or so later, a guy in a nice suit poked his head out of his office and in an unwelcoming way said, "Come in." We did that, too.

It wasn't a big office, but few government offices are. He had his J.D. diploma from Boston University hanging on his wall, as well as your typical rogue's gallery of photos that showed him shaking hands with or standing beside a whole array of impressive and recognizable faces.

I took one peek at those photos, realized with a sudden, overwhelming shock how outclassed I was, stood up, and fled. Just kidding.

His name was Clarence O'Neil—he was somewhere in his late forties, and well along that road of regression from being a fairly fit, reddish-haired young man to becoming a florid-faced, stout, broad-nosed Irishman. His eyes lingered radioactively on Katrina for a few brief seconds, then he and I traded pugnacious glares, as we opposing attorneys are inclined to do. One way or another, Clarence was going to be in the background of this case, and probably was going to call a lot of the shots.

He finally leaned back into his chair, ran a hand through his unruly, thinning hair, and asked, "What can I do for you, Major? Miss Mazorski?"

I said, "We thought it might make sense to come over here and get acquainted. Maybe create some joint ground rules."

"I'm afraid I'm confused. This is a military case. It has nothing to do with this office."

I just love getting jerked around. "Let's not go there. Your Agency headed up the task force that arrested my client. You've got vaults filled with information I need. Order your people to share what the law says I'm entitled to see, or I'll walk out of this building and convene a press conference."

A nasty half-smile popped onto his face. "Every defense lawyer makes that threat. We've weathered it before, and we'll weather it again. And frankly, ever since the World Trade Center, the courts are much more sympathetic to us."

I half smiled back. We were making progress. Pretty soon, we'd half smile each other to death.

"How many of those lawyers attended press conferences wearing Army green? How many had Top Secret clearances? How many knew exactly how to embarrass this agency to get what they want?"

He stood up and walked around his desk to position himself in front of me. He got less than a foot away and looked down at my face. It's the oldest intimidation stunt in the book. You either stare at his groin like a pervert or up at his face like a supplicant.

I opted for the supplicant option, in case you're interested.

"Listen, Drummond, your client betrayed this country in ways too horrible to contemplate. Sure, you're only doing your job, and believe it or not, I admire that. But when you learn everything your client did, you'll want to strangle him. He's responsible for more havoc than you can imagine. We're still trying to assess the damage, but it's probable we'll add murder to the crime of treason."

In an outraged tone, Katrina said, "Murder? That's bullshit."

He pinched his nostrils and stared over at her. She was shrewdly trying to provoke more information from him. Smart girl . . . nice move . . . very commendable.

Unfortunately, Clarence didn't get to this level by being stupid. He went across the room and stared out his window. "William Morrison not only gave the Russians the names of agents and turncoats, he also exposed the inner workings of our foreign policy deliberations and helped shape our responses to Russian acts that would turn your stomach. In the history of espionage, there's never been one like him."

When neither of us responded, he continued, "Your client's a master of duplicity. He worked right under our noses for over a decade and fooled everybody. For three years Mary Morrison headed up the task force responsible for finding the traitor. He slept beside her every night, so forgive me if we seem reluctant to share sensitive information. There'll be no orchestrated effort to stonewall you—hell, I've already assembled twenty attorneys to cull through the evidence, but don't you get on your high horse, Drummond. It won't sell."

I tried to listen to his every word but was having some difficulty coming to terms with that one nasty zinger he'd let slip. Mary Morrison had been in charge of the molehunting task force—she'd been sleeping with the man they were now convinced was her prey. If Morrison was in fact a traitor, she'd been cuckolded in ways that almost defy the imagination.

I stood up and Katrina followed my lead. "Mr. O'Neil, thank you for your time, and I look forward to getting your team's products at the earliest possible date."

A self-satisfied smile erupted on his face and remained there as I fled out his door. Score: Clarence one, Drummond zero.

Back in the car, Katrina said, "Gee, you handled that well."

"Thanks."

"I wasn't serious."

"I know."

"Am I missing something here? What was that about his wife?"

"Mary Morrison was the CIA station chief in Moscow. You know those Washington power couples you always read about? Bill and Hillary. Dole and Dole. The Morrisons were *all that* in the world of supersecret agencies. Oh, and incidentally, I had a fling with his wife in college."

Sometimes, say things quickly enough and it doesn't register. She frowned, however, and remarked, "A fling, huh? She wasn't the one who talked you into defending her husband? Tell me this isn't so."

"The relevant point is that *he* asked for me," I said, partially answering her question, and partially not.

"Then you and he are acquainted also?"

I nodded, and she asked, "How well acquainted?"

"More than I want to be."

"Why's that?"

"He's a jerk."

"He's a jerk?"

"You're right. Let me amend that. A social-climbing, ass-covering, arrogant, self-serving, mealy-mouthed jerk."

"Are we having objectivity issues?"

"What's not objective? The subject's a jerk and all else flows from there."

Wisely, she decided on a different tack. "I was under the impression you guys promoted capable people to such high ranks. Don't tell me Hollywood had it right all along?"

"I never said Morrison isn't capable. I worked with him once, back when I was in the infantry. Back before he met Mary, even."

She leaned against the door and said, "Tell me about that."

"I was a team leader of a unit that was ordered to take out a terrorist cell that was planning to murder some American diplomats in Israel. Only our intelligence agencies intercepted a few of their messages and somebody decided to preempt it. Morrison was the liaison officer from the intelligence community. I had no complaints there. He knows his job."

"What part did you have complaints about?"

"Him. He was bossy and abusive to my people. He started telling us how to prepare for the mission, how to plan it, how to cut eggs. I told him to back off, and he rudely reminded me he was a lieutenant colonel and I was a lieutenant. He started angling to come along. I said no, he wasn't part of the team, wasn't screened, wasn't trained. It was dangerous for him, and dangerous for us."

It wasn't hard to guess where this was going. "But he went anyway?"

"Some general who was a buddy of his pulled strings. He ended up on the plane."

"And did it cause a problem?"

"I suppose that depends whose side of the story you listen to."

"I believe I'm stuck with your side."

"We landed on the coast twenty miles north of Beirut, then worked our way by foot down to the Shiite quarter of the city. We were all dressed up like Arabs, our hair and mustaches dyed black, our skin tinted. Morrison kept bossing my team around. We exchanged words a few times, and he got testy, so I got testy back. I couldn't figure out what his game was. I assumed he was just a guy who wanted to have a war story to tell his grandkids. I underestimated him."

"How so?"

"The target turned out to be different. Wasn't anybody's fault, it just was. We used our night-vision goggles to stake it out and saw nearly twenty guys, instead of the six we'd been told to expect. The whole mission had been rehearsed down to the minutest detail, and I had only eight men. Morrison insisted we had to call it off. I said we'd just replan it on the fly. The terrorist attack was scheduled for four days away, so it was then or never. He kept insisting, and that's when I figured out his game. He was a plant. The intell folks were scared about what would happen if their information turned out to be wrong and the mission got bollixed. He was their bureaucratic stopgap."

She nodded like that made sense. "And . . . ?"

"We gagged and hog-tied him, took down the target, and picked him up on our way out."

"And you have hard feelings? Have I missed something here?"

"Indeed so. We went back to Bragg and he went back to his intelligence unit in Maryland. A few months passed and my team was ordered to attend some ceremony. On the appointed day Morrison arrived with his general officer buddy, then some guy was reading the citation for Morrison's Silver Star for gallantry in action. He got credit for the whole operation—planning it, leading it, even courage under fire during the takedown."

"I see." She stared out the windshield while I spent the rest of the drive to Golden's office wondering how I was going to compartmentalize my feelings toward the lousy prick I was defending.

The address I'd been given turned out to be a big, modern office building on 14th Street, a few blocks from the White House. We took the elevator to the twelfth floor, the doors slid open, and there stood two fierce-looking badasses with Uzi submachine guns pointed at our chests. Eddie has a real sense for how to orchestrate a warm welcome.

I grinned somewhat awkwardly. "I'm Major Drummond, and this is Miss Mazorski. We have an appointment to see Major Golden."

The one on the right whispered something into his lapel, and another guard instantly appeared, only this guy wasn't carrying an Uzi, just a big black pistol in a shoulder holster even an unpracticed eye could detect, since he had his jacket off so you'd be sure not to miss it.

"Damn, guys, nobody told me this was a gun party. I would've brought mine and we could all whip them out and play who's-got-the-biggest-gat."

Nobody smiled. Katrina said, "Don't antagonize them. I'm not sure they've been fed yet." Which was much funnier than what I said, but then, in certain situations, I don't mind being upstaged by my underlings.

The new guy hooked a finger and led us through a series of corridors, past a number of offices droning with quiet activity. Whatever agency this was, it obviously owned the full top floor of this building. Eddie had to be in heaven. He was all ego anyway, but blow a little fairy dust into it, like his own armed guards and dozens of special assistants, and he'd become Dumbo the Flying Elephant. I was seriously not looking forward to this meeting.

We were eventually deposited in a big empty conference room and ordered to wait. So we waited. And more of the same.

Our appointment was for eleven, and at twenty after, the door blew open and he entered, followed by ten or eleven fawning assistants. They just kept coming and coming, and the only one I recognized was Karen Zbrovnia, who wore her Army uniform, unlike Eddie, who sported an exquisitely tailored blue wool suit.

So. A bit more about Eddie: Picture Robert Redford before he got old, wrinkled, and splotchy, toss in more persuasive bullshit than William Webster, and then add the generosity, grace, and selflessness of Jack the Ripper.

Eddie is all this, and so much more. He is to Army law what Babe Ruth is to baseball, the holder of more records and awards than there ever was. At least that's what someone once said about Eddie, and to show he believed every word of it, he made it a practice ever after to send autographed baseball bats to everybody he beat in court. Lots of us have those bats—I have two of them—and we all privately dream about someday bashing Eddie's beautiful head in with them.

He rounded the table and approached, squinting and offhandedly saying, "Drummond, isn't it? Haven't we met before?"

This was Eddie's trademark greeting to all opposing attorneys, his lousy way of saying, Hey, you're so insignificant I barely recall we ever met.

"Yeah. And who are you? I'm supposed to meet with some asshole named Eddie Golden. He here yet?"

It was a very stupid thing to say, and Eddie immediately chuckled like this was just so damned amateurish, so adolescent, but he's so magnanimous he'd just take it in stride instead of stuffing it down my throat with some snappy comeback. Which, really, was a snappy comeback.

Admiring chortles erupted from his fleet of admirers. I swiftly said, "Uh, this is my co-counsel, Katrina Mazorski."

"Jesus Christ, Drummond. Where'd you find *this* one?" He laughed, igniting another broadside of yuck-

yucks from the gallery.

Katrina calmly weathered this, folding her arms and waiting patiently for the laughter to subside to giggles. She grinned. "You're very funny, Eddie."

"I know."

" 'Where'd you find *this* one?' That's what you said, right?"

"That's what I said."

Her grin disappeared. "The implication being what, Eddie?"

"Choose your own implication," he replied, ever the cocky prick.

"I can't. Help me out here. 'Where'd you find *this* one?' What's the implication? Why did everybody laugh?"

The background chortling died. It suddenly struck Eddie what everybody else just realized. "There were no hidden implications."

"There had to be, Eddie. I hope it wasn't sex discrimination. What? Where'd you find this skank? What gutter did she crawl out of? What?"

"I just meant . . . like, where'd she come from? Virginia? New York?"

She put a hand to her chin. "And that's funny?"

"To some folks . . . apparently."

She gave him a threatening look. "I don't think it's funny. Do you think it's funny?"

"Uh, no, I guess not."

She spun away and faced me. She winked, and did this little jerky gesture with her hand. Now that was funny. At least, I thought it was very funny. Eddie didn't and he sulked the whole way back around the table.

I waited till he was seated before I said, "So who are the rest of your distinguished colleagues?"

He stopped sulking and produced a raw grin. "A few members of our interagency prosecution team. I obviously couldn't fit everybody in this room—hell, I can barely fit them all on the three floors assigned to my task force. Hah-hah-hah. So I handpicked a few key members to sit in."

This was a very shrewd way of saying he had a whole legion of lawyers behind him, which I already knew, but leave it to Eddie to reinforce the point.

He pushed back his chair, leaned on the two rear legs, and put his feet up on the table, soles facing me. In Asia, that gesture's considered an unforgivable insult. He casually looked down and began playing with his fingernails, like he was digging dirt out of one of them, which was farcical because Eddie never collects any dirt under his nails.

"So, Drummond, you requested this meeting. Why?"

"I just thought we should all get introduced."

"We're already introduced. You and I met in court twice already. What's next?"

Which was another clever move, because it threw the onus of carrying this meeting on my shoulders. I replied, "A few procedural points. Have you decided what charges you're going to bring?"

"Not yet. Your client committed so many crimes, over such a long period of time, we may take our full thirty days to decide on the full range. For the time being . . . just treason."

And that confirmed my first suspicion. The deal was this: Eddie would stall till the last minute and then fire the full barrage of charges at our doorstep, forcing us to scramble around in confusion under a precariously short deadline to decide how we wanted to respond to a slew of unexpected disclosures.

"Okay, fine." I worked up a menacing expression, then said, "I spoke with O'Neil and he said you have a group of attorneys clearing evidence for release to my team. I'll tell you what I told him. If I don't start seeing that evidence early, I'll start holding press conferences. I'll also lodge a request for dismissal on the grounds of obstruction of justice."

Eddie looked up from his fingernails for the very first time. "That would be really stupid, Drummond."

"Not from where I sit. Is it true you and Captain Zbrovnia have been working for months with the team that caught my client?"

"They've been exposing us to various details along the way," he replied evasively, back to studying his fingernails.

"Then you've had plenty of time to consider your evidence and build your case. No judge is going to have sympathy for you. If I don't get charges and evidence in a timely fashion, I *will* lodge that request for dismissal and you'll have to explain to a judge how you wasted months of preparation before the arrest."

Eddie turned on that big flashy smile. This was all so much fun. "Won't work, pal. Nobody's been pushing harder to get it cleared than I have. I've got a file drawer filled with memos and requests to show any judge that's interested. Isn't that right, everybody?" he asked his admirers. They all began nodding furiously, like, Yeah, really, nobody's pushing harder than the boss here. He's just such a fabulous guy. Don't you just love him? We sure do.

Eddie continued, "The sooner you see how this went down, the quicker you'll realize the deep shit you're in. I've never seen a stronger case. And please, plead innocent, because I'm really, really looking forward to shoving it up your ass."

I worked hard at keeping my face perfectly bland, although from the expressions across the table I think I came up short. Before this got worse, I stood up. "I think we've accomplished everything we can today. I'll be waiting for that evidence."

Outside in the car, I turned to Katrina. "Well? What did you think?"

This being her first real dose of the big leagues of law, the poor girl seemed shell-shocked. She simply stared out the windshield for a while.

"He definitely won that round," she finally said.

"Other than that?" I growled.

"He seems very, very good. And they seem very, very convinced they have an ironclad case."

I chuckled. "Prosecutors always try to make you think that way."

She went back to staring out the windshield. As did I.

CHAPTER FIVE

I T took three oversize vans to transport Imelda, two enlisted assistants, Katrina, our supplies and materials, and of course me from the Kansas City Airport north to Fort Leavenworth. The drive took fifty minutes, along an interstate and then a series of hilly, winding roads past small farming towns.

As there were no spare offices on post, we were assigned a set of quarters along what is known as Colonel's row. This had its advantages, as these quarters are big red-brick Victorian houses constructed at the turn of the century, with wide verandas, living rooms with grand fireplaces, and full kitchens and dining rooms. There were enough bedrooms to spare us the need to stay in hotels, and enough nooks and crannies downstairs for offices and conference rooms. In Imelda's typically competent fashion, she had already arranged for temporary furniture to be delivered and phones to be turned on, so that by ten that night we were in business.

An hour later Katrina and I slipped out. It was late, but I wanted her to get a quick introduction to our client. We'd ask him a few simple questions, then return in the morning for the heavy stuff. It wouldn't inconvenience him any. Prisoners in solitary know no time. They live in an infinity of boredom.

He was led into the interview room and the MPs went through the lock-him-to-the-table routine again. He seemed more aware than last time. Grumpy, but aware.

I said, "General, this is Katrina Mazorski, who will serve as co-counsel. She's a lawyer and she speaks Russian."

He studied her for five sullen seconds before he exploded. "You're shitting me."

I had started to open my lips when Katrina held up her hand to shush me. She calmly said, "What part of that confused you?"

He rolled his eyes and said to me, "Christ, you stupid bastard. My life's on the line, and you hire some groupie slut from a rock concert."

"Ahh . . . it's my looks that bother you?" She smiled. "That's *so* surface. How about this? I got my law degree from U of Maryland—night school, no less. And I've only spent two years practicing law. Can you believe it? I can barely believe it. Now you can piss in your pants."

He and I both stared at her in shocked disbelief. Like I needed this. She was going to give him a heart attack. She continued, "Consider this, however. I've won ninety percent of my cases and was top of my class at U of Maryland. No, it's not Harvard Law, but if Harvard hadn't been so damned expensive that I had to turn it down, who knows?"

He started to say something, she held up a hand, and said, "I have an IQ of 170, rate a 4.0 on the State Department Russian fluency exam, and I kick ass in court. Relax and have faith in Major Drummond's judgment. He doesn't tell you how to interpret satellite photos or whatever the hell you do, so why are you questioning his judgment in attorneys?"

I looked at Morrison, and his jaw was agape. I said, "How you doing, General?"

"Huh?"

"How you doing?"

"Shitty."

"That's prison for you. At least you don't have some three-hundred-pound cellmate named Bubba who wants to give you a colorectal exam."

He stopped staring at Katrina and faced me. "I have no television. They won't give me anything to read. I just sit in my cell and go fucking crazy."

"Right . . . that's their game. They want you so freaking lonely and bored you'll turn diarrhetic when they interrogate you."

"And what are you going to do about that?"

"About what?"

"I'm a brigadier general in the United States Army, asshole. That's supposed to mean something. Get off your stupid ass and do something."

"Like what?"

"You tell me the answer to that. Get me a fucking TV. Get me books. Get me a cellmate, something, anything to keep me from going mad."

"The Chief of Staff of the Army couldn't get you a TV. This is part of the process."

He began cursing and shaking his head like this was absolutely deranged. I allowed him to vent a few more seconds before I interrupted, "We're going to ask a few questions. Nothing too intense, just a few start points."

"Drummond, God damn it, you're not listening to—"

"Question one," I interrupted, affirming that he was right. "Did you betray this country?"

"What? No . . . of course not. It's complete horseshit."

"We're your lawyers. Our conversations are protected and we need to know the truth to properly defend you. Did you betray your country?"

His face lurched forward and the veins stuck out in his neck. "Damn it, you asshole, I just told you. I never betrayed my country."

"Why'd they arrest you?"

"I don't know. Damn it, I don't even know what I'm being charged with. How the hell do they expect me to defend myself when I don't know what they're saying I did? Huh?"

"The full range of charges hasn't been filed yet. This morning's newspapers say you began working for the Soviets in 1988 or 1989, that you transferred your loyalty to Russia when the Soviet Union collapsed, and you continued feeding them information through all these years. They say Ames and Hanssen were tossed to protect you. They say you're the vilest mole in the history of espionage."

This blunt soliloquy was intended to make him back down and stop climbing up our asses. I might've been more gentle had he not called me an asshole three times in one minute.

His eyes bulged. "Who's saying this?"

"Unnamed sources leaking things in a torrent. And nearly every day leading up to the trial there'll be a fresh revelation. And by the way, the CIA's general counsel mentioned they may add murder to whatever charges they settle on."

He was furiously shaking his head. "Oh, God damn it, no! This is so wrong. I didn't betray anybody. I didn't murder anybody. Nineteen eighty-eight? How did they come up with that?"

"We haven't seen any evidence yet."

"Get the fucking evidence, Drummond!" he shrieked.

"I've lodged requests with the CIA and the prosecutor. I'm not hopeful, though."

"Why? They'd better produce something. What kind of fucking country is this? What kind of idiotic lawyer are you?"

Katrina soothingly said, "You need to get ahold of yourself. This is all part of the game."

"It's not a fucking game, bitch!"

"We'll get the evidence." She calmly said, "Your arrest put us on a treadmill. Right now, they control the pace. We'll look for a way to reverse that."

"And what the hell am I supposed to do in the meantime, huh? You assholes don't know what it's like in here."

I said, "We'll spend time tomorrow getting background. I'll want to start back in 1988. I'll need to know what you've been doing all these years."

"Read my fucking record."

"I did."

"Then what the hell is there to talk about?"

"Job titles don't help." I added, "We need to know what you were doing, what you were working on, what you were exposed to. Then, when the evidence does come, we'll have something to work with."

He kneaded his temples and stared miserably at the table. I looked at my watch. It was nearly eleven-thirty. I said, "Tonight, think carefully about your actions over the past ten years. We'll begin our questioning first thing in the morning."

"I'm innocent," he grumbled.

"Then fight to prove it. Get mad. Fight for your honor. Fight to see your family again."

He looked up as though I'd just jarred his memory. "How's Mary?"

"Fine. I stopped by her father's house yesterday. She asked me to tell you she loves you." Although that wasn't really true, because now that I thought about it, she hadn't said that. I added, "One more question . . . that father of hers, Homer?"

"What about him?"

"How can you stand that son of a bitch?"

He looked confused. "What are you talking about? Homer and I get along fine."

Of course. Why had I even asked?

Once outside the prison and heading toward the car, Katrina, looking somewhat disapproving, said, "Your bedside manner sucked."

"My manner was fine. You don't get it."

"What don't I get?"

"He needed the shock treatment."

"They teach you that in law school?"

"Our client is drowning in self-pity. Hard to detect, I know, but the clues were there."

"And the shock treatment is supposed to . . . what?"

"To sober him to the realities of his situation."

"But it has nothing to do with your dislike of our client?"

"Not a thing," I replied, halfway believing myself. I asked, "And what about you? Was all that true? Everything you told him in there?"

"Everything?"

"Did you actually turn down Harvard Law?"

"I never applied. That's the same thing, isn't it?"

"And your IQ and won-lost record?"

"I might've gotten them mixed up."

"Oh shit. Please tell me you really speak Russian."

She smiled. "Are you questioning my integrity?"

CHAPTER SIX

AT 8:00 A.M., William Morrison was shackled to the table as Katrina flipped on the tape recorder she'd thoughtfully brought along. As with the night before, Morrison appeared moody and disgruntled, and like my whole life before this moment, I could barely stand to look at this pompous, bullying jerk.

I began, "Okay, General, start with this. If you're innocent, why do you think they arrested you?"

"I told you, Drummond, I don't fucking know. I never betrayed this country . . . I swear I didn't."

Katrina placed a hand on my arm and interjected, "We're your attorneys. You've got our presumption of innocence. Help us think this through."

"All right. Maybe somebody was jealous of me."

Actually, I knew him, and he didn't have my presumption of innocence, so I said, "Jealous enough to do this?" punctuating my words just so.

"Maybe . . . why not? Sure."

Katrina quickly said, "Okay, it's a possibility. Can you think of others?"

"I was framed."

She asked, "By who?"

"If I knew that, I wouldn't be sitting here, would I?"

"Oh, Christ!" I exploded.

Katrina looked at him, then at me and asked, "Are you two enjoying this?"

I tried to look innocent. "Enjoying what?"

"This shit has to stop," she said. "Why don't I step out of the room so you two can pound the crap out of each other?"

Morrison said, "He needs to remember my rank. I won't put up with his disrespectful attitude. He's exploiting my position."

I replied, "Oh, horseshit."

"You," she said, pointing at Morrison, "you asked him to be your attorney. Why?"

"I needed a JAG officer."

"There are hundreds of JAG officers. You asked for him."

"I was fucking desperate."

"So desperate you asked for the guy who used to date your wife? Help me out here."

"Okay, because he's a prick . . . a first-rate prick. In a situation like mine, that's what you look for. A real bastard."

"It sounds to me like you know him well." She began

whirling an arm through the air, like she was reeling words out of his mouth. "Because you were with him in Lebanon and know he's not a guy who'll take no for an answer? And you know he's tough and resourceful and smart, right?"

I smiled and nodded. That was me all right. No question about it—the girl had read me like a book.

"You're overstating it."

"Which part did I overstate?"

"All right," he sullenly conceded. "I read about a few of his cases. I know he's a good lawyer."

"And you." She wheeled that finger in my face. "Could we be having a macho pissing contest here?"

Now Morrison was smiling, and I replied, "Hell no."

"Eddie Golden's going to love you two." She looked at him and explained, "He's the stud they picked to prosecute you. Wait till you see him. The military has nine men on death row, and he made the reservations for four of them. You're on his calendar as number five."

This background had come from Imelda, I realized. She faced me and said, "And he's got a six-month head start on you. Not to mention all those people he's got working under him. So cut the shit."

Wow. Morrison and I stared at each other.

Nobody spoke.

I finally asked, "So, sir, did you have any indication you were under suspicion?"

He replied, "Good question, Major. No, my first indication of this whole thing was the day they arrested me in Moscow."

"You saw no signs, nobody hinted . . . ?"

"Never."

"Where were you assigned in 1988?"

He stared up at the ceiling. "That was the year before I got married . . . Washington."

"Doing what?"

"Working at the CIA."

"Isn't that an unusual place for an Army officer to work?"

"Yes and no. Each year the Army selects a few officers to work in other intelligence agencies." He couldn't stop himself from adding, "It's a plum job for elite officers."

Did I really have to put up with this? "And where were you working in the CIA?" I politely inquired.

"Soviet Affairs."

Having already reviewed his record I knew he was a Soviet Foreign Affairs officer, had been sent by the Army to the language school in California, then for a graduate degree in Russian studies at Harvard, and then spent six months at the Russian Center in Garmisch, Germany. Presumably, Morrison did well at his training, as the Army tries to hide its dunces and uglies rather than assign them to other agencies.

I asked, "Did you have access to knowledge that would've been helpful to the Soviets?"

"I saw everything."

Katrina said, "Describe everything."

"Military assessments, what you'd call spy reports, the most sensitive satellite shots and electronic intercepts. If I asked for it, I got it."

I asked, "Was this material controlled?"

"There were safeguards. You'd get a paper with a control number stamped on it, so you had to keep the original. The office copiers had control methods, too. But sneak in a camera and take a picture, and nobody would ever know."

"Like Ames did?"

"Exactly."

Katrina asked, "Did you have any dealings with the Soviets?"

"Not then, no. I got occasional invitations to cocktail parties at the Soviet embassy, but I always reported those contacts to the Agency."

I leaned forward. "Did you ever go?"

"Are you kidding? I knew why they were inviting me."

"Why?"

"To see if I was vulnerable."

When I didn't reply to that, he continued, "They first try to establish social contact with a target. They charm you. They probe to see if you're disaffected, or need money, or are vulnerable to flattery or sexual overtures. They make their try, and if it works, the game's on. If it doesn't, they invite someone else to the party."

Katrina asked, "Did you know any Soviets?"

"A few. Mary's job put her in much more contact than mine. That rubbed off, though."

I asked, "Why? What was Mary doing?"

He stopped and leaned back in his chair. "Wait a goddamn minute, Drummond. I'm not dragging her into this."

I drew a deep breath and very nicely said, "Neither am I, General. But yours wasn't just any marriage. There are all kinds of possible intersections we'll need to sort out."

He considered this. "You're not going to involve her in this?"

"She's already involved. She's interviewing lawyers. Would you prefer I learn these things from Eddie Golden in the courtroom?"

A truculent scowl shifted into place. "Okay, okay. But you better be damned careful with what I tell you about her activities. You got that?"

Surely, this was the appropriate moment to remind him that I used to sleep with her, too. Okay, right . . . perhaps not.

He said, "Mary was a case officer. She was controlling some assets."

Katrina said, "Like spies . . . agents . . . targets?"

"All the above. Mary was in a cell that worked the Soviet embassy and the large contingent at the UN."

"And how did that bring *you* in contact with Soviet citizens?"

"It didn't. I knew who she was meeting with, though. I'm only warning you about this in case any of those people were exposed."

"How about 1989? What were you doing then?" Katrina asked.

"That was the year the disintegration began. Suddenly all the intelligence agencies were critically short of people."

"Why?"

"Because Eastern Europe and the Soviet republics were coming apart at the seams."

"Tell us about that," I said.

"We called it the Big Bang. It happened so fast that Gorbachev's own apparatchiks couldn't understand it. Neither could we. Over fifty years we'd built this massive intelligence kingdom to watch the Soviet Union. Presidents and their advisers became spoiled. The thing we were watching moved half an inch and legions of analysts immediately wrote thousands of papers to explain why. We were experts at watching water freeze."

Katrina scratched her head. "What did that have to do with you and your responsibilities?"

"The White House was screaming for information, and we couldn't keep up. I was rushed through the Georgian desk, then the Azerbaijani desk, and then the Chechen desk."

"Doing what?"

"Producing assessments. I was flying to those places, interviewing officials, meeting with country teams, trying to get a handle on it."

I suggested, "And meeting Soviet citizens?"

"Of course. I went to Moscow five or six times that year and I met with plenty of Soviet officials in the republics."

"Did you form any special relationships?" I asked, slyly homing in on the one relevant fact I'd learned from the news releases.

"What do you mean?"

"Did you form any long-term bonds with Russians?"

He suddenly looked very nervous. He rubbed his lips with a finger and was obviously struggling with something. Uh-oh. He replied, "Drummond, I, uh, I can't discuss this with you."

"You have no choice. Besides, I'm not only your lawyer, I'm an officer with a Top Secret clearance. And Katrina had her Top Secret restored last night."

He studied our faces. "You don't get it. I could get court-martialed for *whispering* this name."

"No shit?" said Katrina, in every regard an appropriate sentiment.

Still we had to weather thirty seconds of hand-wringing, heavy breathing, and idiotic indecision before he said, "Have you ever heard of Alexi Arbatov?"

"No."

"Alexi is currently the number two man in the SVR, one of the two agencies that split out of the old KGB . . . the one with responsibility over external affairs." He paused in a transparent attempt at melodrama. "I met Alexi that year . . . I cultivated him."

"Cultivated?" Katrina asked.

"It means I didn't succeed in fully turning him. But I got him halfway there."

"And halfway there is . . . what?" I asked.

"Alexi sometimes passes me information. It's always his choice and usually his volition. In our jargon, he's an uncontrolled asset."

"He still is?" I asked.

"Yes. I was his controller. Eventually we brought in Mary also. I was assigned as the military attaché in Moscow and she was assigned as the station chief to put us right next door to Alexi."

I was gaping, mouth hung open, the whole nine yards. Morrison was claiming he'd "acquired" the number two guy in Russia's most important spy agency. That's like owning the deed to the Empire State Building: You see all kinds of things from a really great vantage point.

Obviously impressed, I said, "Holy shit."

And he replied, "Now, asshole, do you see why Mary took me over you?"

Actually, I'm just good at mind reading—what he really said was, "You're understating it. I brought home the biggest intelligence catch the CIA ever heard of, and look what those bastards have done to me."

We stared at each other for a while, a sort of awkward pause, contemplating the possible ramifications of this news.

I finally asked, "How did it work?"

"Alexi wouldn't let others be involved. He knew better than Mary and I did how penetrated we were. He made it a stipulation."

Katrina deduced that my interest in this topic was something more than idle curiosity and decided to join the play, asking, "Weren't there safeguards or something?"

"Alexi insisted on one-on-ones, but every time we met, the Agency required me and Mary to write extensive reports. It's a standard procedure."

"Explain how that works," Katrina said.

"You compose it immediately afterward to reduce the risk of memory lapses. You try to recall everything that was said, the target's mental state, the general mood."

"Who gets copies of these things?"

"Arbatov was so critical, and so sensitive, that distribution was limited to the deputy directors for intelligence and operations. Oh, and a psychiatrist."

We both looked and were in fact confused, so Morrison added, "Part of our responsibility was to sustain his willingness to feed us, to handle whatever psychoses or neuroses he was experiencing. There are tremendous undercurrents of guilt and fear for a man who's betraying his country. The shrink would comb through our reports, look for hints of problems, and advise us how to handle him."

I found this curious and asked, "And was this Arbatov stable?"

"He had his reasons and he thought they were good ones."

"And what were those reasons?"

Morrison was hunched over, toying with his manacles, and from my perspective, he appeared evasive. Conceivably, he was merely nervous about disclosing such sensitive information. Or conceivably there was something more here.

He finally replied, "I think Alexi selectively gave us things he considered . . . What's the best way to put this? If Russia was doing something he felt was morally repugnant, he'd report on that. But, for example, he never gave us the names of American traitors, like Ames or Hanssen. He gave us no counterintelligence information."

"Did he ask you for information?"

The ugly frown on Morrison's face implied that he finally realized where this line of query was heading. "Fuck you, Drummond. Of course we discussed things. I always included my responses in my reports, though. I never told him anything that was a betrayal."

"You're sure?"

"Mary and I were given firm guidance about what we were allowed to disclose. I never went outside those boundaries."

Sensing we'd reached an impasse, I said, "Okay, were there others like Arbatov?"

"For me, no. Mary had others, a lot of them, but my principal duties didn't involve controlling assets."

"Who brought Mary into it?" Katrina asked.

"He did. After 1991, I had a number of jobs that didn't allow me to properly control Alexi. He suggested Mary."

I considered this and concluded that from Arbatov's perspective it made sense. It kept it all in the family and limited his risk of exposure. I said, "Think hard. Were there any other Russians you stayed in contact with from 1989 to the present?"

"None," he immediately replied, leaving me wishing he'd at least spent a few seconds scouring his memory.

The molehunters were focused on a trail of espionage that led all the way back to 1988 or 1989. How they came up with those years I didn't know. I did know this, though: The anonymous leaker said there was only one controller, and by extrapolation that controller had to be acquainted with Morrison from the very beginning.

So maybe they thought that guy was Arbatov—or

maybe someone Morrison wasn't telling me about. I looked over at Katrina and her eyes were locked on Morrison's face. The intensity of her stare surprised me. Set aside her appearance, her ball busting, and her sarcasm, and what you got was a deceptively sharp and determined woman.

I said, "Okay, General, that's enough for now. Start mentally organizing the years 1990 through the present. We'll come again and begin with those years. Okay?"

Morrison nodded but looked troubled.

I said, "What? You got something you want to add?"

"I, uh . . ." He hunched over, as if in pain. "Listen, Drummond. About Arbatov . . ."

"What about him?"

"I'm not saying Alexi's connected to this or anything . . ."

"But?"

"Well, it, uh, it might be a good idea to look at him closer."

"And how would I do that?"

"Talk to Mary. See what she thinks."

I said that we would, and we then departed, leaving our client chained to the table.

CHAPTER SEVEN

KATRINA and I cloistered ourselves in the living room of our grand office quarters. I had brewed a fresh pot of coffee, tossed a few logs in the fireplace, and lit a big fire before we settled down in righteous style to ponder our next steps.

I wanted to start with her impression of our client. Lacking a past history with him, she might've detected things I was blind to. Doubtful, but worth checking.

She was still getting comfortable as I said, "Well, isn't he every bit the asshole I warned you he was?"

Always helpful to predispose a witness, right?

She replied, "He, at least, has a good excuse"—intimating, I think, something about me. She added, "It's this arrested and being charged deal, I suppose. Funny what sets some people off, isn't it?"

"Not hah-hah funny, no. He's even more insufferable than I remember him. How could that be possible?"

"You tell me. You know him."

I struck a thoughtful pose and stroked my chin. "How does anyone get that way? . . . Spoiled rotten from birth . . . everything always fell in his lap. He—"

"Good Lord." She shook her head and said, "Just give me the facts and I'll make my own conclusions, okay?"

"Okay . . . the facts. He's forty-nine years old, was born in Westchester, New York, the son of some big Pepsi bigwig. Had a typical rich kid's upbringing, went to Andover, became probably the only Yale graduate in modern history to enter the Army, and, as the saying has it, went on to do great things—depending on your perspective, obviously."

She leaned back onto the cushion and asked, "And how did he meet his wife?"

"I don't know how he met his wife. I wasn't there," I answered, sounding, I suppose, a little annoyed.

"You have a problem with that topic?"

"Me? No . . . What gives you that impression?"

She picked at a nonexistent piece of lint on the couch. "You're sure you don't have a problem with this topic?"

Actually, my problem is with nosy, prying women. I let that thought lie, though, and replied, "They met at work, dated a few months, and got married. Okay?"

She pushed a stray strand of hair off her eyebrow. It obviously wasn't okay, but she seemed to conclude it was the best she was going to wring out of me. She was right, incidentally. She asked, "Do you believe he's guilty?"

I folded my hands behind my head and stared at the fire. I hadn't forced myself to consider it. For one thing, I'd been on a whirlwind since Mary first called, and for another, it's not a question most defense attorneys want to answer about a client. The preservation of ambiguity has almost irresistible appeal in our line of work.

I finally suggested, "It doesn't exactly fit with my view of him."

"Now that's enlightening."

"Look . . . he just doesn't fit."

"You can be very annoying."

"Okay, for those who need lengthy explanations, Morrison doesn't fit the crime." Ticking down my fingers, I added, "He's a pathologically ambitious prick. He's an oily bastard and an inveterate bully. But a traitor? I could be wrong, but they've got the right kind of man for the wrong kind of crime."

"Trying to cram an oval into a round hole?"

"That works for me."

"Did you attend the wedding?"

"Damn it, what is it with you?"

She looked down her nose. "It was a perfectly innocent question. Am I missing something here?"

Innocent, my ass. I replied, "Why do you want to know?"

"Until a minute ago, it was idle curiosity. Now I'm wondering if there's a tar pit here."

"There's no tar pit here. I was invited, but, uh, I . . . I was too busy to attend."

"Too busy?"

"Exactly."

"Not too bothered? Too busy?"

"I was in Panama, helping track down some asshole named Noriega."

"You're serious?"

"The wedding invitation was in my P.O. box when I returned from the war. It'd been sent a month before."

She said, "Boy, that sucks." And she was right; it did suck. Then she asked, "Would you have gone?"

The woman was like a dog with a bone. Stubbornness can be a virtue. At the right place and time, it can also be a king-size pain in the ass.

Anyway, the right and proper thing to say, obviously, was, Well, yes, absolutely. All's fair in love and war, and so forth. I wouldn't have sat in a front-row pew, where I could hear their lips smack when the preacher got to that "man and wife" part: I would've been there, though, the classic good sport, rooting for the bride and wishing her everlasting love and happiness with the idiot she chose.

I was fairly certain that lie wouldn't sell, however.

"I don't know," I said, and tried my best to sound convincing, while sensing from her expression that I was wasting my time.

Having squeezed more out of that response than I wanted her to, she asked, "Can you adequately defend him?"

"I won't know that until we hear the full charges and see the evidence."

"Nice try. Deal with your compatibility issues."

"Oh . . . that. Yes, I can represent him."

She sipped quietly from her coffee and let that one drop off a cliff. I said, "Can *you* adequately defend him?"

"It's going to be a challenge. This whole world of the Army and espionage is completely foreign. I've been handling street criminals."

"And what makes you think this is different?"

"It *is* different."

"Why?"

"The people I've been defending have miserable, hopeless lives. I come from the street and can get into their heads. People who work in espionage are different."

"Not really. Just think greed, larceny, jealousy." I smiled and added, "And since we're delving into my personal life, what about yours?"

"What about it?"

"You're what—twenty-nine and still single?"

"And you're what—thirty-nine and still single?"

"In the event you're not aware of it, age is irrelevant with guys."

For some reason, this struck her as hilarious. She slapped the pillow and nearly choked to death. "You're a piece of work."

My smile widened. "I just want to know who I'm working with." Okay, I know. It sounded lame even to me.

She smirked and said, "Then let me help. Do I have a boyfriend? No. Have I ever? A few. Am I desperately seeking? Not. Did I miss anything?"

Like I needed this. "No. That's fine, thank you."

"Maybe you want a description of what I'm looking for?"

"Fine. What are you looking for?"

"Definitely not some chest-thumping meathead who spends his weekends knocking down six-packs and screaming obnoxious things at the football jocks on his TV. Masculine, but the right kind of masculine—the kind that knows the difference between a flute and a piccolo."

This sounded more like a dickless canary than a man to me, although I do know the difference between a flute and piccolo: Spelling.

She continued, "Good-looking . . . but the right sort. California beach boys are a turnoff. Back hair is a turnoff. I'm inclined toward the dark-haired, worldly, charming types."

Now she was talking. Mouton Cadet, '67, anybody?

I suggested, "And now I suppose you want to know what I'm looking for?"

"I already know." She glanced in the direction of the fireplace and said, "Our client's wife."

That didn't even dignify a reply, but I gave her a finger in the air anyway.

We moved on to researching the cases of the Walkers, Ames, and Hanssen. The ever-resourceful Imelda had found a trove of material that covered everything from the trial procedures to some well-written synopses of the strategies used by the prosecutors and the defense. In separate folders were materials on the Wen Ho Lee case, which were vastly more hopeful, from our perspective, since the defense slipped the willie to the prosecutor for the whole world to see. But then, there were distinct differences between the Lee case and ours—like our defendant was white and couldn't accuse anybody of racial discrimination; he didn't have a charming daughter to run around and hold free-my-daddy rallies; and in Lee's case, when forced to put up or shut up, the government suddenly coughed a few times, looked mortified, and admitted it had caught a fairly severe case of evidence deprivation. If O'Neil and Golden were to be believed, the government's dilemma regarding our case wasn't an evidence shortfall but a swamp so vast and murky that an army of attorneys could barely slog through it.

By midnight, drool was spilling out my lips. I stretched and mumbled, "I've got to get some sleep."

Katrina's beaded nose was stuffed in a big folder. The girl had endurance, having been in the office at six that morning and she was still going like a choo-choo eighteen hours later, while my gas gauge bounced off empty.

In my bedroom I slipped out of my clothes and was asleep almost immediately. I'm a light sleeper, however. The problem with old Army quarters is creaky stairs, as well as a complete absence of modern insulation and noise abatement buffers. At three-thirty, I heard her footsteps on the stairs. I alternately cursed and prayed she'd move her skinny ass a little faster and then rush through her ablutions and let me get on with my sleep.

Then I swore I heard cabinets opening and shutting downstairs. I quietly slipped out of bed and tiptoed to the door. I paused to briefly consider my quandary. Definitely there were at least two different sets of noises out there, possibly three. I needed to see why, although *sneaking* quietly down those stairs was out of the question.

I chose the other way and plunged down so fast that I nearly tripped over my own feet. And at the base of the stairs, that was exactly what happened. Sort of. I flew through the air and crashed face first into a wall. Except I hadn't tripped. Something had shoved my back and helped me along.

I recovered my senses and spun around just in time to get a hard, booted kick in the center of my chest. I made a loud "ooof" sound and sank to my ass on the floor. The lights were out but I saw a large figure looming over me.

Oddly enough, the next thing I saw was the face of a young female medic waving one of those smelly things under my nose, saying, "He's coming to."

I heard Imelda say, "That nose look broken."

I heard the medic reply, "Yes, I think you're right."

I noticed that the back of my head seemed to have a big dent in it, and my face hurt, and my chest ached.

The medic squeezed my nose and looked at me with tender eyes. "There, there, Major . . . you're going to be fine. Just a few bruises, a little blood, and maybe a broken nose."

I replied, "Ouch, damn it. Let go of my nose."

Which she did. And that made me happy. I wedged my way up the wall and got unsteadily to my feet. A stretcher rested by the door, where two more medics were waiting to load me aboard. They looked terrifically relieved to see me standing. Lazy bastards.

"What the hell happened?" I asked.

Imelda adjusted her glasses on her nose and said, "We came down when you got knocked 'round. Heard the door slam and saw two men runnin' away, only nobody got a good look at them. They was dressed in black and wore hoods."

"Was anything taken?"

"Didn't check yet," Imelda admitted, suddenly sheepish that she'd been so busy attending to me that she'd failed to see what might have been stolen. It wasn't like her to commit such a breach of duty.

After fibbing to the medics that I'd eventually come over to the dispensary and let a real doctor check me out, I helped Imelda and her two assistants look around. To the best I could tell, nothing had been touched—no open drawers, no ransacked boxes, no sign of burglary at all. Very strange. We all ended up in the living room. I asked, "Did anybody see anything missing?" and instantly felt like an idiot—how do you see something that's missing?

Heads were shaking all around when I felt this odd flip-flop in my stomach. "Katrina, the tapes. Where are they?"

I had blurted out the question, and the enormity of the possibility hit us simultaneously.

She rushed upstairs and I hobbled after her. She hurried to her purse and flung it open on the bed. Among assorted other female debris, the tape recorder and two tapes spilled out. A common sigh of relief escaped from both of our throats. And, in fact, I was starting to walk out of the room when Katrina said, "Wait."

She picked up a tape, stuck it in the recorder, and pushed the play button. Nothing. Not a sound, just empty tape. She withdrew that tape and inserted the second one—ditto. She flipped the tape over, fast-forwarded, and reversed. Not a sound. She handed me the recorder, and I stuffed it in my pocket with a loud curse.

Our client was not going to be very happy with us. I was not very happy with us. But Uncle Sam was going to be unhappiest of all, as somebody had just stolen a tape that contained the name of America's top foreign asset, a name I had very stupidly allowed to be placed on a tape I even more stupidly failed to secure.

CHAPTER EIGHT

T HE team that descended on our building reminded me why so many American citizens go live in the woods and mumble about black helicopters and paste I LOVE GUNS stickers all over their rusted old pickups.

The FBI agents came up from Kansas City. The CIA folks flew in from Washington, apparently on a very fast jet, because they and their FBI buddies were streaming through the front door some two hours after I called to report the incident. Not that you could tell them apart—they all wore cheap-looking gray and blue suits, complemented by that glum, dour expression that distinguishes a government employee from the rest of humanity.

They went over that house with a fine-toothed comb, took foot molds and fingerprints of my entire team, and inventoried everything we had and a few things we didn't. They canvassed the neighborhood for witnesses and asked every colonel's wife who resided on that row if she had happened to be staring out the window at three o'clock that morning. All this was accomplished with Prussian efficiency and New Yorker manners, which is to say the worst of both the old and new worlds.

When all this was done, the head of the team, a CIA guy named Smith—if you couldn't guess—pulled me into an upstairs room for a come-to-Jesus meeting, as we say in the ranks.

He had a tough-guy look about him, a slouchiness of the face, a well-defined musculature of the body. He stuck a cigarette between his skinny lips, lit it up with a Zippo, then flipped the lighter shut with a harsh jolt of the wrist, badass style. He puffed a few times and fixed me with a withering glare. "So, Major," he began, "how long you been in?"

"Thirteen years."

"You've been briefed on security procedures before? You've signed those little forms that say you understand your duties and obligations?"

"I have."

"Still, you made a Top Secret tape and left it lying around a room?"

"I did," I confessed, my lawyer's instincts screaming I shouldn't, but my conscience seeing absolutely no way around it, considering the circumstances.

A trail of smoke eked from his nostrils. "That's a real dumb-shit move, buddy. A first-rate dick-up."

"I could say I had no idea burglars would break in and steal it. But that doesn't make any difference, does it?"

"Nope."

"So what are you going to do?"

He took another drag from the cigarette and seemed to ponder that question. That moment dragged on much too long. Eventually he poked his lit cigarette toward my face. "First, I'm gonna report this to my superiors. I'm sure they'll then report this to your superiors. I don't know how they handle these things in the Army, but in the Agency you'd be looking at doing some time."

I stuck my hands in my pockets and glumly nodded. This is pretty much how the Army handles these things, also. "So I'm in pretty big trouble?"

"The loss of that tape, that's a fuckin' catastrophe."

He had a point, but I wasn't done trying. "You know, technically, the tape was guarded. I did try to stop them and was overpowered."

"You had no safe. You weren't armed. And, uh, you were asleep. I wouldn't try goin' that route, I were you."

I shuffled my feet a few times. "Yes . . . you're right . . . unless . . . well, there might be one other extenuating circumstance."

"Yeah?"

"It's a really odd thing. I hesitate to bring it up."

"Go ahead," he said. "Try whatever lawyer bullshit you want."

"Right." I scratched my head and replied, "The thing is, who knew we'd made any tapes? Miss Mazorski and I didn't tell anybody . . . not even anybody on our own defense team."

"Yeah, so?"

"So, whoever did the theft knew we'd made them, and even that the tapes were in her purse. Don't you find that suspicious? I sure do. And they even brought blank ones along to replace them. If I hadn't walked in on them, we might never have known those tapes were taken. But of course, they were stomping around and making all that noise."

"So?" He drew another long drag and stared at me

with a fathomless expression.

"So who could possibly have known we made those tapes?"

"You tell me."

"No, you tell me."

"I haven't got a clue," he replied, with all the intense insincerity that response deserved.

"Well, I do. You wired our interrogation room. You listened to everything we said."

He coolly looked around for an ashtray, didn't see any, so he walked over and opened the window. He flipped his burnt-down butt outside, faced me, and said, "That's a serious charge, Drummond. Can you prove it?"

"It's circumstantially obvious."

"To you, maybe."

"And to any reporter I tell the story to, maybe."

He reached into his pocket and pulled out another cigarette. Otherwise he appeared as cool as a brick of ice. He said, "Drummond, you got a coupla problems here. You and your client, you been discussing things way outside your security sphere."

"And how would you know that?"

"I hear these things. And as to whether anybody wired your interrogation room, I'd be willing to bet that if you were to go over there right now, you wouldn't find any trace of wire."

"And how do you know *that?*"

"Call it good gut instincts."

"I see. What do you intend to do?"

"Like I said, report your very serious security violation to my superiors. What they do with it's up to them."

"Very fine," I said. "Then I'm sure you won't mind if I make a few calls to the *New York Times* and the *Wall Street Journal*."

"Actually, I do. That'd be a real stupid idea," he said, struggling to appear unimpressed.

"Stupid from where you stand . . . from where I stand, it's brilliant."

"No, really, Drummond . . . do that, and God knows what might happen to you."

"Oh, goodness. Did I just hear a threat?"

"Just say I got good intuition, too. But listen here, pal, there might be a way around this makes everybody happy."

"And what might that be?"

"Well, you got a client that did a lot of damage to this country and don't exactly deserve your loyalty or sympathy. You're a soldier, right? We need to know what your client gave away. Lives . . . our country's security could depend on this. All we want is your guarantee that if he was to tell you something he disclosed to the Russkis, you'll let us know. It'll be quarantined from this little game you lawyers are about to play. Strict firewalls between us and the prosecuting team, I swear."

Well, goodness gracious. What was I hearing? The theft was an attempt to blackmail me into becoming their stooge. And the noise and fracas was a trigger to make sure I knew. And the ass-kicking? That was just the fun part, I guess—for them, anyway.

"All I have to do is tell you whatever he discloses to me?"

"Simple as that."

"Or you'll report the security violation to my bosses?"

"Right again."

"Sounds fair . . . just one problem."

He took another puff off his cigarette. "And that would be?"

"This." I withdrew Katrina's tape recorder from my pocket and held it up to show it had been running.

The thing with smartasses like him—they can't believe anybody can out-smartass them, until the evidence is jammed right under their noses. Looking quite annoyed, he said, "Drummond, you lousy bastard, give me that tape."

"Well, that would be stupid, wouldn't it?" Actually, regarding stupidity, I wondered for just the merest fraction of a second if Mr. Smith had been authorized by his bosses to use deadly force in pursuit of this blackmail. If so, the easiest thing for him to do at this instant was yank out his gun, blow a hole in my head, and walk off with that tape. From his bewildered expression I supposed he was wondering the same thing.

"Drummond, you can't do that," he finally blurted.

"Well, yeah, I can. Military judges don't take kindly to government agents who mug an Army lawyer and attempt blackmail. I'm an attorney, Mr. Smith. Trust me on this. I have very good intuition. I have good gut instincts."

Smith and I did not share the same sense of humor.

"Listen up, asshole, Morrison's a worthless fucking traitor. Give me that tape."

"No."

Mr. Smith could've benefited from a few more gallons of brainjuice, but the realization suddenly struck him that I wouldn't be tossing threats back and forth if a solution to this quandary wasn't possible. He broke into a smug grin and said, "What do ya want? What can I do?"

"Get your bosses on the phone."

"Don't go there, Drummond. You got no idea who you're fuckin' with here. These guys, they don't like to be bothered by pipsqueaks."

We played eye tag for a moment until he came to the right conclusion, which was this: I could and would screw him into a wall.

He angrily yanked out a cell phone, stalked out to the hallway, and punched in a number. I heard him whisper furtively into the mouthpiece. I looked out the window and politely let him make his explanations in privacy. I thus had to imagine what his bosses were saying when they found out the thug they sent out to blackmail me was now being blackmailed himself.

He eventually walked back in with a very sour expression and handed me the cell phone. In my most wiseass tone, I said, "And to whom am I speaking?"

An older voice replied, "Major, this is Harold Johnson."

This was not good. "I've heard of you before," I said, which was true, because Johnson was the deputy director for intelligence, the number three guy in the

Agency, and something of a legend in the secret agency community.

"I don't know what that asshole Smith did, but I apologize nonetheless. Trust me when I tell you he's something of a wild card. He sometimes approaches his job with too much . . . shall we say, enthusiasm?"

Idly rubbing the big lump on the back of my head, I replied, "No kidding."

"Now what's this problem he's caused?"

"I'm not sure what problem you're referring to, sir. Where he wired the interrogation room where I met with my client? Breaking and entering into my legal offices? Stealing legally protected tapes? Maliciously mugging an officer of the United States Army? Or the attempted blackmail? Which one's your favorite? It's the mugging that really pisses me off."

"Jesus, what was that asshole thinking?"

"And do you believe he *admitted* all that on tape? Hard to find good help these days, isn't it?"

What I'm sure he wanted to say was, "Up yours, Drummond," only that would've killed the mood here, and he was an old pro. He replied, "Well, listen, I'm terribly, terribly sorry if he did all that. Nobody told him to. Believe me."

"Of course not," I said, following my line in the script.

"Now, what do we have to do to get this cleared up?"

"Why, sir, the first military judge I run into's going to get it all cleared up right nicely for us."

"That's not a very good idea."

"Convince me of that."

"Because Morrison's the biggest traitor I've ever heard of."

"Well, you know, you're probably the fiftieth person who's told me that, only I have yet to see a single shred of evidence. And I have yet to get an inkling of cooperation from the prosecution or your Agency."

"That can be corrected."

"Can it?"

"Yes. I, uh, I didn't realize you were having a problem about this. I can have truckloads of evidence on your desk by nightfall."

"That's a good start point."

Showing what a diligent listener he was, he asked, "And what's a good end point?"

"Your guarantee there'll be no more attempts at wiring our interrogation rooms. And no more break-ins to my offices or attempts to find out what we're discussing."

"Done."

"Oh, and a television for my client, with satellite cable that gives him all those late-night dirty movies. He's a very lonely man, you know. And books and writing materials."

"Drummond, you're pushing it. There are very sound reasons for denying him those things."

"Undoubtedly true. But I have this tape. And if I use it, he'll be watching all the cable TV and reading all the lurid thrillers he wants in less than a week."

"Yes . . . I suppose."

"Good. We've got a deal. Only—not that I don't trust you—I'm holding on to that tape."

A roguish chuckle resonated through the phone. "No. Mr. Smith leaves with that tape. It's a matter of common trust here—you don't trust me, and I don't trust you."

"How about I send the tape to my boss, General Clapper, where it'll be in neutral hands?"

"That works for me. Now put that asshole Smith back on."

"Certainly, sir. And it was a pleasure speaking with you."

"The pleasure was yours, Drummond. All yours."

Not really. I tossed the phone to Smith, whose face looked like an overripened tomato. My own face looked worse, what with my swollen nose and the fact that both my eyes had started to blacken. I wondered if Smith was the guy who did the job on me.

He snapped the cell phone closed, wounded-badass style, gave me a perfectly arctic glare, then marched stiffly from the room.

When I got back downstairs, all the blue- and black-suited storm troopers were gone, and Imelda was looking at me inquisitively. "They gonna boil your ass?" she asked, well aware of the stiff penalties for losing classified materials.

"In fact, some Agency bigwig called to thank me for putting up such a valiant battle in defense of our country's security. He said I'm a real good guy."

Imelda mumbled, "Tell 'em to talk to me."

It occurred to me that I had just won a round. However, a case like this can last fifteen or twenty rounds, and to be lulled into complacence can be fatal.

Regarding my conversation with Johnson, I was still a little shaky. A man does not rise to such an exalted position in the CIA—where backstabbing, one-upping, and conspiracy are art forms—unless one is ruthlessly persistent. I had the sense we would meet again, that I had just tipped my hand, and the next occasion would be a bit more artful.

CHAPTER NINE

THE dents and scratches on the side of the black Porsche had disappeared when I parked right next to it. Image is all-important to Homer Steele, and I couldn't begin to imagine how much trouble and expense he'd gone through to make those scabs and bruises disappear. Actually, I spent a very pleasurable moment trying to imagine it, because that was the whole point, right?

Katrina's eyes widened as she got a good glimpse of the house and neighborhood. "Nice little shack," she murmured.

"Yes, it is. But inside that big palace lives a mean, nasty ogre."

"Don't tell me. You and her father, you got a thing, too?"

"We got a thing, too," I admitted.

She leaned against the car door and adopted a wearied look. "Don't you have any friends?"

"That are alive?"

She chuckled and asked, "Okay, what's the father's story?"

This was a fair request, all the more since nobody should have to meet Homer without fair warning. Actually, to be perfectly accurate, nobody should ever have to meet him—period.

"Homer's his name," I explained, "and the fact he sired Mary is biologically incredible. There's been big money in the Steele family going back to the dinosaurs. Root hard through our country's economic history and you'll find a Steele with his hand out at every turn. One bankrolled the first steamship. Another supplied the boots to the Union Army. Another . . . look, if you want the full anthology, ask Homer. It's his favorite topic of discussion."

"So he's rich? So what?"

"The way they stay rich is they keep marrying their pile of money to other piles of money, a sort of long family tradition. The first time I came, he shook my hand and his opening words were, 'Well, young man, what's your father do?' I said, 'Well sir, he sells used cars.' His head flew back. 'Used cars,' he snorted. Just like that. The words actually popped out his nostrils."

Katrina somehow found this funny.

I continued, "Anyway, Mary's mother died when she was young. She was their only kid, and the thought that the last family eggs would cross-fertilize with me drove him nearly crazy. He badgered her continuously. Then he banned me from the house. When all that failed, he hired private detectives to tell me to stay away from her. Oddly enough, that very same night someone took sledgehammers to my car."

"And what did you do about that?"

"I had it towed away."

"You've never heard of the police?"

"You've never heard of evidence?"

"Did you tell Mary?"

"I didn't have to. We were leaving for spring break in Florida the next day. We were going in my car."

"And what did she do?"

"She rented a chauffeur and a big black limo and filled it with champagne and imported beer. We kept it the whole ten days, and she charged it all to her father."

I threw open my door, and oops.

Katrina said, "You're striking that car."

"Damn, you're right." I did it again.

She peered at me with an odd frown, obviously wondering what kind of vindictive, juvenile jerk she was working with.

I rang the bell and we waited about forty seconds. That's why I don't own a big house like this. Someone knocks on your door, and it takes forever to hike your way from the back parlor to the front entry.

Suddenly, Homer was staring at me with that squeamish look some women get when a big, nasty cockroach prances across their kitchen counter. I said, "Good afternoon, Mr. Steele. My associate, Miss Katrina Mazorski. Your daughter's expecting us."

His eyes took in Katrina's outfit, which today consisted of a short skirt and an old cardigan over what looked like a camisole. He appeared to be on the verge of vomiting.

His eyes shifted to my Chevrolet. "Is that where you parked the other day?"

"I'm sorry . . . I don't understand."

He spun around, slammed the door, and stomped off to get his daughter. Was this fun or what?

A few moments later the door opened and there stood Mary, wearing jeans and a simple white sweater that came down to her thighs, looking like an ad for *Casual Living* or some such thing.

I said, "Hi, uh, Mary, this is my associate, uh, uh, uh, Katrina Mazorski," experiencing this sudden odd difficulty, a sort of mental paralysis.

Mary and what's-her-name shook hands, and then Mary bent forward, squeezed my arm, and pecked my cheek. "God, you're a sight for sore eyes. Please, come in."

She led us through some long hallways to the sunroom in the back. We got ourselves seated, and I could see Katrina's eyes watching the two of us, obviously trying to take the temperature of our relationship. Behind that sarcastic, laid-back, cocky playfulness was more curiosity about things that were none of her damned business than was good for her, or me, or whatever.

Mary bent forward and studied my face. "Sean, what happened to your nose? And your eyes?"

"I . . . well, I walked into a wall," I said, which was true; I did walk into a wall—full speed—with a little help. Only I wasn't about to mention the rest of the story to either Mary or her husband. I had my reasons and believed they were sound.

She reached over and squeezed my nose. "You must've been moving pretty fast. Your nose looks broken."

That squeezing hurt like hell, but I'm a guy, and she's a good-looking girl, so I smiled, which looked pathetically stupid, as my eyes welled up with tears.

"I guess. Anyway, we spent yesterday with your husband."

"How is he?"

"Angry, but better. He thinks he's been framed."

At first, she didn't reply. She appeared shocked, then curious, then asked, "By whom?"

"He claims to be completely baffled by the whole thing. Mary, he's just throwing darts in the dark . . . Believe me, we defense attorneys hear it all the time." Especially from perps who know they're guilty as hell, I politely failed to mention. "Anyway, we went back over his career. The papers are claiming his betrayal began back in '88 or '89."

She was shaking her head. "I read the articles. It's ludicrous. It would mean he started within months after we married. It's impossible, believe me."

"The articles also mentioned he had a single Russian controller over all those years. We therefore reviewed what he was doing, looking for contacts he made with Russian citizens."

"That's a logical approach, but I'm sure you discovered it was hopeless. Our whole careers were centered around Russians."

I nodded and then paused for a brief moment. "Mary, he told us about Alexi Arbatov."

Her eyes suddenly widened and her whole body convulsed forward. "Oh my God. Sean, he should never have mentioned that name. You have no business knowing about that. What in the hell is Bill doing?"

"Defending himself. Don't worry, Katrina and I have proper clearances. Your secret's safe," I insisted, conveniently forgetting to mention that little incident about the tapes.

"Your clearances are meaningless. Knowledge about . . . about him is the tightest compartment in the Agency. Less than ten living people know about him. Forget that name. Please."

I allowed Mary a polite interlude to realize that the cat was out of the bag, so to speak. I had expected her to be uncomfortable, however, she appeared to be almost distraught.

She finally burst out, "You'll have to be read on to the compartment."

I chuckled—she didn't.

"Sean, it's not funny. This is the most sensitive secret in Agency history. You'll have to be read on"—she glanced at Katrina and insisted—"both of you."

"Mary, we're not going to be read on. We'll never be allowed to mention anything about this again. This guy Arbatov's the only Russian your husband knew all those years. He might be a link to what's going on here."

"Oh God, Sean, can't you see what Bill's doing? He fed you that name because he knew how much it would frighten the Agency. I want him to be innocent, but this is dangerous."

"Look, what I hoped was, we could have a long, candid conversation about Arbatov. This could be important for you, too. You were meeting with him also."

"Don't you understand? . . . I *can't* speak with you about . . . well, about this topic."

"And why can't you?"

"I take polygraphs. I'm subject to prosecution. If I mention that name, I could go to prison. I have two young children. You see that, don't you?"

I suddenly did—with a clarity that brought a rush of blood to my face. Merely bringing this up, I put her in peril. But then, her husband had to know that, too. So why had that conniving asshole sent me to ask Mary about Arbatov?

While I tried to reason through this, Katrina swiftly asked, "Didn't Bill take polygraphs also?"

"No. As an Army officer he was immune from that."

I abruptly stood up and mumbled, "Listen, we've got to get going. We've got all kinds of things that have to get done."

Said less adroitly, it was time for a clumsy exit to match the even more clumsy mistake I'd just made. Nobody argued with me. No surprise there, right? Mary politely followed us out and at the doorway, put a hand on my arm and said, "I'm sorry I disappointed you, Sean. I want to help. Please believe that. I have to think of the children, though."

"It was my fault."

"It was not. Outsiders have no idea what it's like to be hooked up to those detectors. I know one girl who literally begins shaking about a week before her annual sessions." She laughed. "Wouldn't you love to be a fly on the wall at her confessions?"

I appreciated that in her typically gracious way she was trying to take the sting out of my embarrassment. But the only thing that would help at that moment would be to get my hands around her husband's throat.

Mary smiled at my co-counsel and said, "Katrina, it was a real pleasure meeting you. I really wish it was under better circumstances."

"Likewise. Listen, sorry about your husband. How are the children handling it?"

"They still don't know. I'm trying to keep it that way. We've canceled my father's newspaper subscriptions, and the cable TV hookups have been disconnected."

"They don't know?"

"I told them he's on a trip. Maybe it's a mistake . . . they've been yanked away from their school and home and friends in Moscow. They're only kids. How much do you inflict on them at once?"

Then I received a perfunctory peck on the cheek, and we were off.

Once we were settled in the car, Katrina studied my face for a moment. "You think it was deliberate, don't you?"

"He had to know."

"Maybe he was using you to sound her out. Maybe it was a loyalty test. Or maybe he's just desperate."

"Or maybe he's just an asshole," I opined, putting the car in drive and peeling out of the driveway. I didn't think it was any of the three reasons she just suggested. I thought he was trying to make me look like an idiot in front of Mary. And I walked right into it. From a personal standpoint, it pissed me off. From a professional standpoint, I found it alarming. This case was difficult enough without my client arranging emotional ambushes to show he's the better man.

Back at my office, one of Imelda's assistants was in the process of signing for a huge shipment of boxes. Three uniformed guards stood beside a delivery van, and a fellow in a gray suit blocked my doorway. Either FedEx was becoming very security conscious or I was looking at Eddie's first evidentiary dump.

I walked up and introduced myself to the guy in the gray suit, who flashed a badge I didn't recognize, identified himself as Herbert Something-or-other, and then coldly demanded, "Where are these documents going to be secured?"

I regarded the stacks in the back of the van and wondered myself. My office contained only two wall safes, and there were enough boxes to fill at least six. I told him I'd order more safes before we left that night.

"That won't be satisfactory," he snarled. "I'm not permitted to leave until I've ensured all the proper precautions are in place."

Given that this guy was sent by the same fellas who'd broken into my office that very morning, this was two feet short of hilarious. I pointed at a chair and said, "Make yourself comfortable."

Katrina and I then walked in and started cracking open boxes. We yanked out folder after folder after folder. I knew this drill. When Eddie got the call from Johnson to start releasing evidence, he and his legions began stuffing boxes with as many papers as they could lay their hands on. The vast majority of this stuff was meaningless garbage intended to exhaust and frustrate us.

Did I mention yet that Eddie's a complete prick? Aware it was only me and Katrina on my team, the more of our time he could waste, the better.

Unfortunately, I had no solution to that. Katrina and I therefore dutifully stayed till midnight, speed-reading through folders and struggling to sift the important from the trivial. It was a high-risk game. Eddie's folks surely kept a log of everything, and the odds were we'd get to court and Eddie would unleash some critical piece of evidence, and we'd scream, "Hey, objection, we never got that"; and Eddie would smile and hold up that log and say, "Yeah, then how come this says it was sent over to you on November 20?"

Someday I'm going to piss on Eddie's tombstone.

At midnight I told Katrina I'd walk her out to her car. The little guy in the gray suit was seated fastidiously beside the entrance; American tax dollars at work.

I turned to Katrina. "Ain't this better than pushers and dealers and whores?"

She ignored my question. "What happened to you two?"

"What two?"

"You know exactly what two."

Oh Christ. Could I just shoot her and put an end to this crap? Not with a witness by the door, obviously, so I said, "I never really knew. I swear. Please . . . let that suffice."

"Never knew? The chick's a babe, Sean. The perfect

woman, the type who gives men messy dreams. And you have no idea?"

So much for that. "I don't. We dated my last three years in college. Came graduation, we both got busy. I went into intensive training, and she went into intensive training. I went on deployments, and she went on deployments. We saw each other a weekend every two or three months or so. I came back from Panama, and she'd turned into Mrs. Morrison."

"Did you intend to marry her?"

And how did I know it would lead to this? Guys are not really into this post-affair psychoanalytic crap. Take me—you date a girl, and it works or it doesn't. One or the other mumbles the marriage word, and the other either says, "Okay, I've got nothing better to do" or "actually, I'd rather have a sulfuric acid enema." Then you either shuffle to the altar or go looking for the next prospect, without any lengthy claustrophobic pauses in between.

I admitted, "Maybe."

Fortunately, we'd gotten to her car, a beat-up, clapped-out Nissan Sentra that probably had 200,000 miles on it the day she bought it from a used-car dealer. I opened her door and she had to climb in. I watched her drive off.

What did she think about all that? Probably that I'd been an idiot who waited too long. Or maybe that I was one of those intractable bachelors who're afraid of losing their monopoly on the big-screen TV, letting Mr. Dickie feast wherever he wants, keeping their greedy grips on their own paychecks. Truthfully, I have some of that strain in me.

But that wasn't it. I had always wondered about Mary.

CHAPTER TEN

WAS pulled out of the shower the next morning by a phone call from Katrina telling me to turn on my TV. It was only seven, and Eddie was standing on the front steps of that big office building on 14th Street, flanked by three gimlet-eyed prosecutors, as he read from notes on a lectern:

". . . investigation that has spanned seven months of intensive work from hundreds of dedicated people from the Army, from the FBI, and from the CIA. We have carefully considered the spectrum of charges we could bring against General William Morrison and settled on the following: two counts of murder in the first degree; treason; conduct unbecoming an officer; adultery; perjury; and lying in an official investigation. These charges have been signed off by Lieutenant General Halter and filed with the military court of the Military District of Washington."

Eddie looked up and stared right into the camera, somehow avoiding that smarmy smile of his, somehow maintaining that all-American-boy-with-a-toothache expression. "Are there any questions?"

Of course there were questions, hundreds of them, because all you could hear was the stormy sound of journalists howling in that toxic way they do.

"No," Eddie charmingly replied, "we don't yet have

a hearing date, but we expect expeditious treatment. The court is aware of the high level of public interest in this case. The only thing holding us up right now is the defense, who incidentally have already received a great volume of evidence and been given ample time to consider their case. I certainly hope they don't stall."

I screamed, "You rotten bastard!"

"Good point," Eddie said to another unseen questioner, not to me, and judging from his suddenly broad smile, I guessed the reporter was female and gorgeous, because this was Eddie's come-sleep-with-me look. "No, we have not offered a deal. That matter is still under contemplation."

One of the three attorneys on Eddie's team hastily stepped forward and leaned into a microphone. "I'm very sorry. That's all the time we have for questions today. Thank you all very much."

Eddie gave them all a look intended to say, Gee, I really wish I could stand here and do this with you all day, because you're reporters and I love you very, very much. And I hope you love me, too, except I'm a very busy man, maybe the busiest man in America, since, as you must acknowledge, I have a most important job to perform for the American people, whom I also love more than mere words can convey.

He backed away from the podium and allowed himself to be escorted back up the stairs to his building, his shoulders slightly hunched from the terrible burden he was carrying, his legs moving with the bounce of a man with a purpose. It was a scene straight from *Masterpiece Theatre.*

Katrina was still on the phone and I heard her say, "Well?"

"What an asshole."

"Any other thoughts?"

"They've loaded the docket."

"To be expected. What about that deal mumbo-jumbo?"

"Exactly right," I said.

And we both knew what this meant. Eddie's hedged ambivalence meant he *was* going to offer us a deal. And *I* knew why, and *he* knew *I* knew why, if you can follow that convoluted trail. Since the CIA was desperate to know everything Morrison supposedly gave away, and as blackmailing had been tried and failed, a deal was their only resort. The moment Harold Johnson got off the phone with me, he must have called Eddie and twisted his arm right out of the socket.

And Eddie being Eddie, he therefore chose to air the full slate of charges in a public forum, trying to harden his eventual negotiating position. The way the protocols work, when the *only* folks who know the full panoply of charges are the prosecution and defense teams, backroom deals are made in a painless vacuum. The prosecutor can trade away charges and reductions, and nobody's the wiser. But once the public knows, the prosecutor's hamstrung. The public has visibility into the hand he was dealt, and if the defense walks off with too big a pot, they get pissed. Thus Eddie was putting us on notice. He had deliberately given away his free hand, a slick way of pressuring us not to ask for too much.

So this was another of those good news/bad news things, the good part being that Eddie had still lost a lot of leverage. We now knew that the CIA wanted him to get a deal, and that's a pretty big gun to have stuck at the back of his head. The bad news was that any day, Eddie was going to call for a meeting, knowing damn well that Katrina and I were caught on that proverbial horn of an excruciating dilemma. We didn't know whether our client was guilty or innocent. We didn't know how strong Eddie's case was, or how weak our options were.

All we knew for sure was that Eddie would walk into the room and say, "Here's the deal—take it or leave it." If we said leave it, Eddie would march into Harold Johnson's office and say, "Gee, I tried my best to get a deal, and they told me to stuff it. Sorry, Chief, their call." Which was exactly what Eddie wanted, because only by going to court could he become the most famous lawyer in Army history. And did I fail to mention that Eddie is a very ambitious prick?

The sum of which meant that we were now at his beck and call. The hourglass had just been turned upside down, only we didn't know how many grains of sand it contained. When he did call, we'd better know a hell of a lot more about our options than we did at that moment.

By the time Katrina and I arrived at my office another delivery truck was idling beside our door and three guys were hauling out more boxes. Eddie has impeccable timing.

Herbert, in his now-wrinkled gray suit, was still

seated by the door, looking severely depressed and exhausted. As it was, I could barely get into my office, so many containers were strewn around.

Katrina was holding two large cups of Starbucks and two slices of crumbcake. She frowned as she handed me a cup and a slice of cake. "Look at this. We're going to need more attorneys."

"Two is more than enough." Perverse as this sounds, I have an aversion to lawyers. They can be okay in ones and twos, but in flocks they get to be insufferable.

Her eyes wandered across all the cardboard and she said, "Think again. They told me a different crew is loading another truck right now."

"Then we'll bring Imelda back from Kansas."

"You'd do this to her?"

It could take three weeks to wade through this mess, and as was already stated, more was coming.

"She can handle it," I replied.

Katrina gave me a disapproving frown and asked, "What's the plan for the day?"

"Back to Leavenworth. The plane leaves in an hour."

"Go solo. I'm going to start wading through this."

"Wrong. You have a calming influence on our client."

"That's ridiculous."

"Why?" Not for the first time was I noticing that Katrina had both a stubborn and an independent streak—a very noxious combination.

"You're big boys. Handle it."

She was right, of course. I should be able to converse civilly with my own client. I still said something that sounded like "up yours" as I went into my office and called Clapper. I bitched and moaned and explained my predicament. He joyfully chuckled, because Eddie was his fair-haired boy, his legal Adonis, his most lethal hired gun. Clapper loved it when Eddie pulled one of his stunts, and he particularly loved hearing about it from whining complainers like me. I swore I'd someday walk into Clapper's office with Eddie's ass on a platter.

I warned Clapper that if I got a bunch more shipments I'd need another lawyer. He chuckled some more. It just made his day when his pet peacock terrorized the opposition.

I caught the flight to Kansas City, made it to the prison shortly after noon, Kansas time, and Morrison was already shackled to his table when I walked in.

He looked surprisingly chipper as he said, "Good afternoon, Major."

"You got your TV and books?" I guessed.

"And a satellite dish. Drummond, you might be a decent lawyer after all."

Well, we all know the old saying about how easy it is to make a starving man believe he's in the midst of a feast. I fell into the chair across from him, withdrew the tape recorder that had so recently salvaged my career, lovingly caressed it, flipped it to record, and said, "Go back to 1990. The last time we spoke you were chasing assessments in the Caucasus. What came next?"

He withdrew a few sheets of notepaper, and I was pleased to see my contribution wasn't limited to providing entertainment for him. "In late 1990, I was shifted to the Policy Planning Bureau at State."

I said, "I'm not familiar with it."

"It's the internal think tank of State. I was working with a few other Sovietologists to help manage the changes."

"And still handling Arbatov?"

"Some of the time. I'd gotten busy and that was the year he asked me to use Mary as my surrogate."

"Busy with what?"

"To start with, separatist riots in Georgia were threatening Gorbachev's grip on power. The conservatives in his government were furious with him, believing his perestroika policies had incited the unrest. Gorbachev tried to mollify the hard-liners and sent the KGB in to handle the protests."

"I recall something about some massacres, right?"

"Correct." He looked up from his notes and said, "It was a regrettable move, because it incited more riots and protests. It also undermined Gorbachev's image as a great reformer. It was the beginning of the end for him. Boris Yeltsin was rabble-rousing in the streets about how it was time for real change."

"And what position did you take?"

"I wrote a few memorandums predicting Gorbachev was through. I recommended we open channels with Yeltsin."

"And how was this perceived?"

"Like I shit in the swimming pool. The Bush people had crafted their whole Soviet policy around Gorbachev. They were focused on unifying Germany and were convinced they needed Gorbachev's support to accomplish that."

"So . . . what? How did that impact you?"

"Suddenly a lot less actions were flowing into my in-box, and people stopped inviting me to meetings, the usual bureaucratic signs of a fall from grace. You know the funny thing? It served me in pretty good stead when Bush lost the election."

"How come?"

"Because the new team read my memorandums and liked what I'd written. They also felt Bush had blown it. By cozying up to Gorbachev, he'd poisoned the well with Yeltsin. Like the Chicken Kiev speech."

"And what was the Chicken Kiev speech?"

Morrison frowned, put out that he had to explain this. "In the midst of all the upheaval, Bush actually flew to Kiev and gave a public address urging the Soviet peoples to rally around Gorbachev and stay within the Soviet Union."

"Tell me this is not so. George Bush?"

"Ironic, isn't it? On the cusp of winning the cold war, our President is in Ukraine beseeching the enslaved to stay in their chains. I was outraged. I sent up several stiffly worded memorandums."

I said, "And what happened when the new team came in?"

"By a stroke of good fortune, somebody found my memorandums and showed them to the President's old college roommate, an academician who'd written several books on the Soviet Union and the cold war. He was made an Assistant Secretary of State, and as things later turned out, the White House turned over all the former Soviet states to him."

My eyebrows shot up. "Are we talking Milton Martin?"

"Yeah, Milt. He brought me in and interviewed me. I made a good impression and he offered me a position."

"And what position was that?"

"His special assistant."

"You were Martin's special assistant?"

"That's what I said."

"Right. That's what you said." I very curiously asked, "And what did that involve?"

"Well, Milt's problem was he hadn't spent any time in government. He was vulnerable. Since I had considerable Washington experience, the idea was that I'd represent him and his views in Washington, which freed him up to travel as much as he needed."

I kept nodding my head and tried to take this in. The title of Assistant Secretary of Anything is ordinarily a fairly banal position in Washington. Secretaries of Something are walking gods. Deputy and Undersecretaries of Whatever are mystical creatures with lethal wands. But there are so many *Assistant* Secretaries that they're like bunnies in the forest, living in the shadow of the redwoods, groping silently around the roots and hoping not to get stepped on.

Milt Martin was an exception to the rule. Actually, *the* exception. He'd been one of the President's best chums since they'd roomed together in college, and even the Secretaries of Something trembled when he walked into a room. In Washington, image trumps all, and whether he did or didn't, everybody believed

Martin had the power to pick up the phone and call his old roomie and say, "Yo, boss, you know that jerk you hired to head the Treasury Department? Well, he pisses me off. Fire him."

Nor did I have to wonder how those critical memorandums worked their way into Martin's office. Morrison had few equals as a bureaucratic panderer—I'd seen him in action and knew this firsthand. He'd likely found a slick way to have somebody bring them to Martin's attention.

I said, "And how long were you Martin's assistant?"

"Four years."

"Did you travel with him?"

"Not in the beginning. After a year, though, he said I was too indispensable. I handled everything: his correspondence, his speeches, his position papers."

"Were you still reporting your contacts with Russians?"

"Shit, how could I? On a trip I'd meet hundreds of Russians. I'd be in conference rooms where they were coming in and out. Afterward there'd be a big reception or a dinner with dozens of guests."

"That's not good. The prosecution can say you had constant contacts that afforded you ample chances to betray secrets."

"I was rarely alone. I was almost always with Milt."

"And he was preoccupied. And he trusted you. He wasn't watching to see if you were passing microfilms or documents."

"And what do you expect me to do about that, Drummond?"

"Nothing." I rubbed my temples as I contemplated the ease with which Eddie could show Morrison's opportunities for treason. "It's a vulnerability we have to be aware of. What happened next?"

"After the President was reelected, I told Milt I needed to move on. I explained how the Army worked, that I needed new, increasingly more important positions in order to get promoted."

"And how did he take that?"

"You know, he said he'd been thinking the same thing. He suggested a position on the National Security Council staff."

"And you said?"

"Are you kidding? It was perfect. He and I shared a very close personal relationship, were in sync on the issues, and we both knew we'd be watching each other's backsides."

"And what did your new duties entail?"

"I headed up the former Soviet Affairs part of the staff. I was the guy who prepared all the interagency policy papers, who briefed the President before trips, who coordinated our positions toward all the former Soviet states."

I felt a headache start to pulse. Ordinarily an impressive résumé is just that: impressive. In his case, it was an anchor tied to his feet. In trying to ascertain what he'd been privy to, I'd learned that for ten years he'd seen everything. I mean, think of what damage Ames and Hanssen had done—both low-level spooks—and all the excitement they'd caused.

I asked, "And what was Mary doing during all

those years?"

"Several jobs. She was in Analysis, doing the same kind of work I'd been doing. But when the Ames affair broke, a number of Soviet specialists were caught in the backlash. People who had nothing to do with Ames were beartrapped by other improprieties—cheating on taxes, drinking too much, all kinds of things. Everybody got scrutinized, and the result was a bloodbath. Those who survived became even more valuable because the ranks of trained Sovietologists had been thinned so much."

"And Mary was one of those survivors?"

"Oh, better than that. Mary helped handle the investigation."

"Tell me about that."

"She was the one who discovered that some of the betrayals attributed to Ames couldn't have been done by him."

"How'd she uncover that?"

"By correlating the events and assumed disclosures against where Ames was at the time, what he had access to. She realized he couldn't possibly have done all the damage being blamed on him."

"And that meant . . . what? Another mole?"

He nodded. "So the Agency put her in charge of a small, very sensitive compartment to find the other mole. It had to be handled quietly, because people on the Hill were so angry about Ames that they were actually talking about disbanding the CIA. The Agency was scared."

"The CIA's general counsel intimated you had

knowledge of her activities. Did you?"

"Of course. She was my wife, and I was cleared to know everything she was doing."

"So you knew about her efforts to find the mole?"

"Actually, I was part of those efforts."

My headache lurched toward a ten on the Richter scale. I drew a deep breath and said, "Please describe that."

"It started with filters to see how many employees had access to the knowledge that had been betrayed That turned up a large group, hundreds of people. So Mary came up with the idea to try a few entrapments: We laid bait for the mole. We designed a few operations and distributed some classified assessments to see if any were leaked to the other side. And I was the guy pushing the bait through the system."

"And then what happened?"

"Causes and effects were built into each entrapment. We watched for the effects, but we never saw any."

"And what came next?"

"After several years, they decided to move Mary. She'd had her chance and come up short, so they moved someone else in."

I shook my head while he waited for the next question. Frankly, I already had enough to think about. He and his wife had lain in bed at night talking about how to catch the mole the government now believed was him. His increasingly important positions gave him access to the most sensitive secrets imaginable, and because he was an Army officer, he hadn't been subjected to the lie-detector tests CIA people take on a regular basis.

As much as CIA people hate them, the truth is that years of passing those tests bends the benefit of doubt in their direction. To the best I could see, my client had no counterweights to sway the benefit of doubt even remotely in his direction.

I got up and began packing my papers in my briefcase. I said, "One last question."

"What's that?"

"At Golden's press conference this morning, he added a charge that confused me. Adultery. What can you tell me about that?"

In the Uniform Code of Military Justice, adultery's still considered a crime. It's rarely prosecuted unless the act occurs between two members of the same unit, in which case it affects the general climate of order and discipline, which is one reason why it's on the books. Or for when a general officer sleeps with a subordinate, in which case it's viewed as an abuse of power. Or when somebody's being court-martialed for other crimes, and you add it to the list of charges as a way to say "screw you."

He finally said, "I don't know what he's talking about."

"You're sure? I'd hate to get broadsided by some nasty little disclosure here."

He paused to think a moment, then said, "I had a secretary once who claimed I'd had an affair with her. It was horseshit. The whole thing was thoroughly investigated. There was no substantiation. She was lying."

"And you think they're just rehashing some old

garbage to add to your charges?"

"It's the only thing I can imagine. It happened five or six years ago. I was vindicated."

I nodded and said, "Fine." Then I leaned across the desk. For obvious reasons, I'd been saving this confrontation for the end. "Last point. If you ever involve me in anything that compromises Mary again, you'll be looking for a new attorney."

His head reared back. "What the hell are you talking about?"

"When you sent me to ask Mary about Arbatov, you knew damn well the position that put her in. If you weren't my client I'd knock your ass through that wall."

He didn't look at all embarrassed or chagrined. But neither did he try to make any excuses or defend himself. He simply nodded as I walked out.

CHAPTER ELEVEN

MY late flight back to Washington arrived at eleven. I rushed straight home, climbed into bed, and stared at the ceiling for two hours.

The reason, in a word, was Eddie. I finally had an inkling of his strategy, and it frightened the hell out of me. He was working diligently to make his six-month advantage decisive. He had the momentum and virtually a one-way street on knowledge. Even in the hands of a perfectly average attorney those would be almost insurmountable advantages. Eddie, however, was the Babe Ruth of Army law.

If I didn't find a line of defense, and damn quick, I'd be trapped in a fog of ignorance when Eddie called with his deal. Even if Morrison did everything they claimed, I obviously couldn't admit that to Eddie. I needed something plausible—not necessarily persuasive, just . . . plausible. So what did I have?

Morrison claimed he was framed, and no matter how overused that line was, or how suspect, it still represented a usable alibi. The problem was, it was a possibility that cut two ways. Framed by someone on our side? Or by someone on Russia's side? And why? Because Morrison knew something and needed to be taken out? A plain and simple grudge? For sport? No small details, these.

It was even possible that this was a particularly excruciating instance of mistaken identity. The government knew it had a mole; it just pinned the tail on the wrong donkey. How do you prove that?

The last possibility was that Morrison had done some sloppy things that were being blown extravagantly out of proportion. Give or take a little, that's exactly what happened to Wen Ho Lee. Depending on how incriminating those things were, it could still be a catastrophic problem. Did he just forget to close and lock his safe a few times when he left the office at night? Or did he accidentally leave a bundle of Top Secret documents lying on Boris Yeltsin's desk?

There could be other possibilities, but these were the three that passed the stink test, which, as a wise old law professor of mine defined it, simply meant they stank less than other theories. When operating on conjecture and instinct, this is what legal theology boils down to.

Katrina was in the office when I arrived the next morning, and pacing in the corner was the inimitable Imelda, blowing bubbles with her lips and inspecting the boxes cluttered all over our office. Imelda is very protective of her domain and, like most career Army sergeants, has a tendency to be maniacally prickly about neatness.

She stopped pacing and flapped her arms, threateningly. "Who made this friggin' mess?"

"Eddie. He's got a couple of hundred lawyers and investigators cramming every piece of paper they can get into boxes. We've gotten three truckloads already. We expect more."

She kicked a box. "Asshole."

Exactly. I then led her and Katrina into the office, where I briefed them on what our client told me the day before. I articulated the possibilities I'd pondered, and both nodded frequently, interrupted occasionally, and shook their heads dismally when I was done.

Imelda said, "And you got no notion what's in them boxes?"

Katrina said, "I've been going through them for two days."

"Findin' what?" Imelda asked.

"They were tapping Morrison's phones and had bugs in his office. Thousands of hours of recording transcripts are in these boxes. The few I surveyed confused the hell out of me. I don't know shit about embassies or attaché duties."

This wasn't good news. "Anything else?" I asked.

"Four or five are stuffed with financial background information, going back two decades, mostly IRS and bank records. The Morrisons filed jointly and used a professional tax preparer. They kept copies of their tax records going back ten years."

"Anything interesting?"

"Possibly, but it doesn't fit."

"What doesn't?"

"He filled out an insurance form in 1989, the year they were married. His net assets were estimated at around five hundred thousand dollars, including equity in Morrison's townhouse in Alexandria and what the investigators assumed was a very sizable wedding gift from Homer Steele."

"That's a lot of net worth for an Army officer," I said.

Katrina politely ignored this absolutely useless observation. "They made a spectacularly good investment in a brand-new company called America Online, back in 1992. Ten thousand shares. They sat on it, and that block of stocks, after multiple splits, is now worth nearly two million dollars."

"And what do the investigators assume to be their total net worth today?"

"Four million, give or take a hundred thousand."

"Wow," said I, shaking my head—yet another unremarkable observation.

Katrina said, "There was a questionable addition. In 1997, they supposedly inherited nine hundred thousand dollars from some source. It was listed on their joint tax return."

"And we don't know where it came from?"

"I don't. But you might. Maybe Mary lost a grand-parent?"

"If there was a miracle after I dated her. Her grand-parents were already dead. Her father was older when he married, and they waited a while to have a child."

"Morrison's parents?"

I said, "Maybe."

She said, "Hopefully."

I pondered this new input and said, "Even aside from their investments, they probably bring in close to two hundred and fifty thousand a year from their combined paychecks. Eddie's going to have a bitch of a time proving greed was the motive."

Imelda said, " 'Less Morrison had bad habits."

"Not him," Katrina corrected. She added, "One whole container is filled with charge card summaries. Mary was the big spender. Some of those bills from upscale women's clothiers were huge. Your kind of girl, Sean. A regular clotheshorse."

"Define huge," said I, not all that nicely.

"Sometimes five thousand dollars."

"Mary's a professional woman," I replied in her defense. "Impressions are important in her line of work."

"Of course they are," she responded. Then she said, "The point is, nothing jumped out at me, and I doubt anything jumped out at them."

I added, "And you have to figure, Mary's father is sit-ting on a big pot of gold, and she's an only child. Instead of all the hassle involved in treason, Bill could've just bumped off the old bastard and ended up filthy rich overnight."

"We should all be so lucky," Katrina agreed.

"So, let's not waste more time on money," I ordered, and they both nodded. This might not sound like any great leap forward, but when you're facing infinite possibilities, anything that ushers you into the realm of the finite is a huge relief. If Eddie tried to claim Morrison sold his loyalty, I felt fairly confident we'd stick that where the sun never shines.

I looked at Imelda. "Get the evidence and inventory under control, then start wading through it."

Katrina said, "Some of the tapped phone conversations are in Russian. Dog-ear those and give them to me."

Imelda blew some bubbles, flapped her elbows, and stomped out to get started. Katrina shot me an anxious look. She said, "That's a lot of boxes to go through. And there's more coming."

"It'll be a cakewalk for Imelda," I assured her with the kind of bold self-confidence that comes only when it's someone else doing the work.

I then shooed her out of my office and called a think tank up in New York City. I made an appointment to be there at three o'clock, and then called and booked two seats on the shuttle.

CHAPTER TWELVE

THE Society for International Affairs, or SIA, is one of those stodgy old institutions everybody always wants to join as it means you have become part of the Establishment. It was founded back in 1917, according to the shiny brass plaque tacked on the wall beside its entrance, and is a collection of out-of-job diplomats, former power-wielders, and lots of folks with big money who like to make one another's acquaintance.

The ex-government people like the rich people because they pay the foundation's bills, allowing the ex-government folks a cushy, prestigious, well-paid nest while they wait for some political patrons to fight their way back into power and give them new important-sounding jobs. The well-heeled bill-payers like the arrangement because it gives them tax writeoffs, and the ex-government types introduce them to people in power overseas, who then help the rich people get richer.

At least this is my understanding of how this kind of nonprofit organization works, which does beg the question of why it's called a nonprofit, because frankly it strikes me that all kinds of people profit wildly from it.

Anyway, it's housed in a granite-faced mini-mansion on Park and 54th, and the receptionist inside the door asked if we were expected, and, if so, by whom, to which I politely replied that the "whom" was Mr. Milton Martin, former roommate of a guy who no longer wielded power.

He asked us to wait, which we did, till a fairly attractive, mildly buxom young woman in a conservative blue flannel business suit came down to retrieve us. Her name was Nancy, she pertly informed us with a manufactured smile, and wouldn't we care to follow her up the marbled staircase?

We took a left on the second floor and ended up in a large suite at the end of the hallway, Katrina asking Nancy things like what does SIA do, and how long had she worked for Martin, and our escort was saying, "You're so lucky to have caught him in today. He's in such demand. He's always traveling. He's so intelligent and accomplished, and he has such great contacts over there."

The "over there" obviously being the former Soviet states, because after all, Milt Martin spent eight years managing every tiny particle and pinnacle of our relations with that vast foreign group of lands. And Nancy was wasting her sales spiel on us—we couldn't afford to rent two minutes of this guy's time.

I mumbled, "Yeah, we're just damned lucky."

She nodded that indeed we were. "If you'll wait a minute, I'll see if he's free."

Which I assumed to be an oxymoron, because what Milt Martin was doing since he was no longer a government employee was renting his thick Rolodex to the highest bidder and reeling in the lucre as fast as he could. The word "free" had slipped out of his vocabulary, dictionary, thesaurus, whatever.

I spent my minute studying the assortment of photographs placed strategically on the walls, showing Martin in a variety of poses with a variety of faces I mostly didn't recognize, aside from a shot of him and Yeltsin playing tennis. The rest I presumed to be the potentates of the other countries created out of the Big Bang. There were also plenty of brass plates and other trinkets that foreign leaders like to present to one another to show folks back home how internationally esteemed they are.

Why had I flown up here to meet with this guy? Well, he had worked beside Morrison for four of the years he'd supposedly committed treason and might be able to shed some light on that. But principally because the first thing every aspiring defense attorney learns is to test the credibility of his client. The problem with our profession is that their lies become your lies. That can be okay if you know they're lying. It can be less than okay if you don't but the prosecutor does.

Adding to that, Morrison's veracity was all the more crucial to us because Eddie was hogging the important evidence, so all we had to go on were Morrison's insights.

My clever ulterior motive—the only real lead Morrison had given us thus far, aside from Alexi Arbatov, was Milt Martin. Martin was about to become a barometer to Morrison's integrity, and along the way we'd twist his arm to become a character witness, since he'd obviously liked Morrison enough to make him special assistant and get him a job in the White House. It never hurts to have a world-famous figure say what a great guy you are.

Nancy came back out and primly ushered us into Martin's office. Over the years, I had seen plenty of pictures of Martin in the newspapers and watched him doing his thing on the talk show circuit, but that still didn't prepare me for him in the flesh.

He had the biggest nose I'd ever seen. The rest of his

features were fairly tiny and ordinary, making his schnozz seem even more extravagantly gigantic. He wore large-rimmed glasses in an obvious effort to deflect attention from his nose, but it was futile. It looked like the Eiffel Tower bent over sideways. If the man sneezed, we'd all be dead.

He popped up from his chair with a big frothy smile and stuck his hand out. "It's a pleasure to meet you both. You're obviously Major Drummond, and you're obviously Miss Mazorski. Please, call me Milt."

Knowing our names and acting effused to meet a pair of complete strangers is one of the oldest diplomat's tricks in the books. It is meant to impress and I was, as intended, impressed. This guy was best buddies with presidents and an array of foreign muckety-mucks, and to be treated as the high point of his day was seductive.

I said, "Mist—uh, Milt, thank you for agreeing to meet with us on such short notice. General Morrison told me you two were very close."

He gave me a surprised glance. "Close? I wouldn't say we were close. No . . . definitely not close."

I took a step back. "Well, isn't that odd? He gave me the impression you were nearly Siamese twins."

He appeared perplexed, then suddenly relieved, almost amused. He said, "Why don't we sit? Nancy, perhaps our guests would like something? Coffee? Tea?"

"Thanks, nothing," I said, and Katrina waved her off also. We ended up around a big glass table. He smiled at Katrina and said to her, "Please don't take offense, but you don't look like a conventional attorney."

"Who'd want to?"

"Good point." He chuckled and asked, "So what can I do for you?" He was still smiling, although truthfully, it was damned hard to tell because his nose nearly hid his lips.

I tried to stop staring. "We know you're busy, so we won't take up much of your time. We only have a few questions."

"Questions? I'm afraid I'm confused. The investigators have spent hours with me . . . I told them everything I knew."

That shouldn't have surprised me, but it did. Anyway, I said, "Right, but they're from the other team. They don't share that knowledge with us."

"Of course." He nodded. "Ask anything you wish. Whatever I can do to help."

Katrina said, "Could you start by telling us what you told the investigators?"

"In abbreviated fashion, I told them Bill worked for me a few years, that he was a capable officer, diligent, hardworking, moderately intelligent. I had a generally favorable impression of him."

I gave him a curious look. "Didn't he travel with you, handle your correspondence, represent your views in the interagency arena?"

His head was shaking long before I finished. "That's a terrible exaggeration. True, he was my special assistant, but only after he implored me. He said the Army wouldn't release him to work for me unless he had an important-sounding title. I was new to Washington and easily hoodwinked." He scratched his cheek and added,

"Well, what's in a title anyway, right?"

This from a guy whose own former title nowhere near conveyed the havoc he could wreak with one simple phone call. However, it did fit with my impression of Morrison, shamming and finagling for every ounce of prestige.

"So Morrison didn't do all those things?" Katrina asked.

He half-chuckled. "I hate this term, but Bill was a bag carrier."

I asked, "Were you personally close?"

His expression became mildly abashed. "I hope this doesn't sound boastful, but I received weekly invitations to the White House, from heads of state, from every ambassador in Washington. I count among my closest friends the most powerful people in our capital. Bill was one of many people who worked for me. I was friendly toward him, but professionally friendly . . . not personally friendly, if you understand the distinction."

Put that way, yes, I did understand. Martin moved in a rarefied world, and, really, why would he befriend a guy like Morrison? Indeed, in any world, why would anyone . . . but, I digress.

Katrina said to him, "Didn't you help Morrison get a job on the NSC staff?"

"Yes, that's true. When the investigators came by, they even showed me copies of the letters I sent to the National Security Advisor recommending him. But Bill worked under me for four years, and frankly, I tend to be loyal to people who work for me. It can be a fault, but there it is. And truthfully, I was, well . . . relieved to see him go."

I asked, "And why's that?"

"He was becoming, um, what's the right way to couch this? He was telling people around town how important he was to me. The word kept filtering back. He was exaggerating our relationship and his importance in our government. From your questions, it sounds like he's still doing it."

Indeed, it did. I asked, "Did you trust him?"

"Yes, actually. His exaggerations bothered me, but it's an unfortunate trait of many people in Washington. I never suspected him of something like this." He paused and gave me a rueful grimace. "I probably should have, shouldn't I? I feel so stupid now. I was a fool."

"One more question." I tried to look endearing, friendly, whatever, and asked, "Would you agree to testify to his character?"

"I, uh . . . well, I don't think I can do that."

"I don't mean to be difficult, but when he stopped working for you, you sent letters of recommendation to the National Security Advisor. You thought highly enough of him to believe he should work in the White House. Assume he's innocent of these charges. Assume it's all some big foul-up. Would you still refuse to testify?"

He looked confused. "I, I don't think I can. I've already agreed to testify for the prosecution. I don't think I can testify for both sides."

I traded quick glances with Katrina, who was obviously thinking the same thing I was. I said, "I see."

He held up both hands in helpless acknowledgment. "They approached me weeks ago. I told them I don't have any knowledge of Bill's treachery. They said that's fine. They want me to testify on his tendency to exaggerate."

Katrina asked, "And when was that?"

He looked at the ceiling. "Two weeks ago. A Wednesday, I believe. If it's important I can have Nancy pinpoint it exactly."

There was no need. We knew enough. Eddie hadn't missed a beat. Aware that once they arrested Morrison he'd get a lawyer, and that that lawyer would root around for friendly character witnesses, they'd swept up as many as they could before the defense ever had a chance, before the arrest even happened.

I suppose I looked deflated. Martin peered at me and said, "Look, if there's anything else I can do to help you, please let me know. My position in this whole affair is embarrassing. If Bill is vindicated, I'll be elated. He worked for me . . . I helped him get his job in the White House. You understand?"

"I understand."

He was shaking his head. "I still find it hard to believe Bill did this. He certainly never struck me as the type."

On our way out, a flock of guys in turbans and robes were waiting by Nancy's desk. She was busy saying, ". . . to have caught him in. He's really a very busy man . . ." And so on.

As soon as we climbed into a cab for the ride to La Guardia, Katrina said, "Nice guy. That nose, though. If he could carry a musical note, he'd be rich."

I chuckled. "He is rich. A smart guy, too. You never read any of his books?"

She shook her head.

"I never did, either. He wrote a few best-sellers that caused a big stir in conservative circles."

"And would you happen to know what the stir was about?"

"If I recall, one revealed a bunch of dirty CIA operations in Vietnam, and another poked holes at our cold war strategy. Anyway, he speaks Russian, has lots of prestigious degrees, and was held in very high esteem in Russia. They say he could twist their arms to do things even the President couldn't deliver."

"He impressed me." Katrina then said, "But was he telling the truth, or just trying to get his distance from Morrison? Which one speaks with forked tongue?"

I reminded myself to quit underestimating her. Without prompting she'd figured out the purpose of the interview.

I replied, "You heard what he said. Morrison's at the very least an exaggerator."

"But who wouldn't want to crawl as many miles from him as they possibly could?"

"There's that. He must feel like the elephant that got raped by the butterfly."

So what was the truth? Was Morrison his indispensable right hand or a distant groom with an inflated title? Truthfully, the exaggerations fit with my view of Morrison. However, I didn't want to be swayed by my prejudices and I knew how to find out.

The moment we landed back at Ronald Reagan Airport, we rushed back to the office. I called Mary, but of course, Homer answered, and I said, "I need to talk with your daughter, the girl I tell everybody in Washington I used to sleep with."

I heard the gagging sound in his throat as he threw the receiver down and fled. I couldn't believe I was getting paid for this.

Mary finally came on and started with, "Hi, Sean. Listen, please, you've got to stop taunting my father. He said he thinks you're putting dents in his car, but I insisted it couldn't be you. I told him you're not that immature or vindictive. He's not as young as he used to be."

I chuckled. "All I do is say my name and he gets all red and puffy. Between you and me . . . I don't think he likes me."

I could hear her sigh.

"Listen," I said, "I just got back from New York, where I met with Milton Martin."

"Bill's old boss."

"Right. A most delightful guy. Now, Bill told me he used to be Martin's Cato. He said the two of them were inseparable, the Siamese twins of the State Department. Martin said that's a big, nasty lie. He said your husband was a bag handler, a factotum with an inflated title, who went around exaggerating his value to his boss and blowing so much hot air it eventually got embarrassing. He said that's why he kicked him upstairs to the White House. I'm just trying to see which one's the dirty rotten liar."

The line was quiet so long, I finally said, "Mary, you still there?"

"Sean, I don't know what the truth is."

"You don't?"

A pained, even resentful tone crept into her voice. "Bill has a few flaws. Everybody does. I have to be frank with you about this, though, because I brought you in, and I don't want you having illusions. Bill wasn't always truthful about things. He's very ambitious. He wasn't above taking credit for things he had little to do with."

"Isn't everybody like that?"

"Bill is . . . more like that than others. I used to warn him about it, and he always insisted that's how the game's played in Washington. The meek never inherit the earth, not in D.C., he would always respond. He even took credit for some of my work. It was maddening, but what could I do? He was my husband."

"So he wasn't close with Martin?"

"He told everybody he was. I really don't know, Sean. It's, uh, well, it's possible Bill thought it was truer than it was. He's very vain. He could fool himself about his own importance."

Note how tactfully she couched it. She was his wife, and therefore wasn't going to blurt out the obvious—the man was a lousy, lying, self-inflated weasel.

"Okay." I paused, and then said, "One other question. Your 1996 tax form listed an inheritance of nine hundred grand. Where'd that come from?"

"That was the year Bill's mother died. She and her husband were well-to-do. His father died back in 1994 and everything passed to her. When she died, the estate passed to Bill."

"His father was a Pepsi exec, right?"

"Yes. His name was William also. I adored him. In fact, he was the one who got Bill interested in the Soviet Union in the first place."

"How so?"

"You may recall that Pepsi was the first big Western conglomerate to open operations in the Soviet Union."

"That somehow escaped my notice."

"Way back in 1961, the co-founder of Pepsi, Don Kendall, actually met with Khrushchev and talked him into letting Pepsi build a few plants. It was a big thing at the time, the first American corporation to get a foothold in the Communist capital of the world."

"And this had something to do with Morrison's father?"

"Bill's father was in charge of the whole operation. He oversaw the construction of those first plants, marketed the products, oversaw the whole thing. It was his life's work."

"And did he speak Russian?"

"Fluently. He made countless trips over there. He even had an apartment in Moscow and another in Leningrad. When Bill was younger, he took him over a few times."

I was getting a truly sickening feeling. If Eddie and his goons got wind of this, it spelled big trouble. The conclusion was inescapable—Morrison's father was the perfect conduit for the Russians to make their payments.

Perhaps I'd been hasty overruling greed as a motive. Even if it wasn't Morrison's motive, the Russians would probably have insisted he take some cash. In every spy novel, spymasters invariably try to use money as the hook in the fish's gullet. Then, if Morrison got cold feet, they could blackmail him into staying in the business.

But how to channel those payments? Well, there's always the rub.

Aldrich Ames made himself vulnerable when he began driving to work every day in a flamboyant new Jaguar sedan. That car should have brought all kinds of suspicions in his direction—it didn't, but it should have. Hanssen had better sense and lived frugally, while he had the Russians open a Swiss account, and buy him diamonds, and stockpile his earnings like a squirrel saves his stash of acorns for winter. The problem with that tack is that you don't realize the benefits of your crime. There you are, slaving away and betraying your nation's secrets, but where's the instant gratification we Americans are so well-known for?

The problem is hiding or justifying those big lump-sum payments, because anytime a check larger than $10,000 gets cashed, federal law requires the bank to report it. And pretty soon the federal government's knocking on your door, wanting to know why you're not paying taxes on hidden income, and why there are no W-2 statements accompanying all those big payments. But if the payoff gets shuffled through your father's account, probably one that was with a Russian bank in the first place, and lands in *your* lap as an inheritance, you've bypassed that scrutiny.

Money may not have been Morrison's main motivation, but who's going to turn down free cash when it's offered? Not me: I rummage through public pay phones for wanton quarters.

I said, "Well, thanks."

"Okay. Listen, I'm just telling you Bill has some fairly serious warts."

"Right." Maybe bigger warts than either of us knew.

"Sean, I, uh, I'm sorry."

"Don't worry about it. It's not your fault."

It didn't help when I got back to my apartment that night and the late news revealed the newest government release on Morrison's crimes. According to that voluble unnamed source, he'd not only given the Soviets the names of two of their agents whom we'd turned—both of whom were recalled and executed—but he'd also provided the Russians with our negotiating position toward the North Koreans on the nuclear issue, which the Russians had then generously passed along to the North Koreans.

A commentator came on and claimed that armed with that information, the North Koreans were able to persuade us to build them two nuclear plants for power generation while they continued building a nuclear bomb in a secret underground facility, which that secret document informed them we did not know about.

True or not, it sounded awful. I drifted off to sleep dreading the next nasty revelation. With Eddie, they'd only get better.

CHAPTER THIRTEEN

W E caught the early bird to Kansas City the next morning. As the few leads Morrison had passed us failed to pan out, it was time to consort with our client again to see if we could coax something more useful out of him. Less technically, he'd screwed me, and I was going to put his nuts in a vise.

Katrina drew her usual assortment of stares and ogles as we boarded and passed down the aisle to our seats. This morning's ensemble included hip-hugging, skintight, bell-bottomed jeans that were torn at strategic locations and a black spandex long-sleeved shirt that had only one shoulder and sleeve. The shirt came that way, too, and I'll bet she paid full price.

No sooner were we belted in than Katrina pulled out an MP3 player, jammed a pair of earphones in her ears, cracked open a copy of *Rolling Stone* magazine, and stuffed her beaded nose inside. Overhearing the low throb of some kind of music, and with a profound sense of mature superiority, I dug into a newspaper filled with screechy articles and poisonous editorials about the pathetic bastard I was representing. I was tired and surly, and the flood of damning publicity heightened my gloomy mood. I was chewing with a vengeance the peanuts the stewardess brought me.

Katrina eventually yanked out her earphones, leaned over, and whispered, "You're attracting attention. In case you haven't heard, people are spooky on airplanes these days."

I popped another fistful into my mouth.

She looked slightly amused. "I think you need to get laid."

"I'm already getting screwed, thank you." An old line but appropriate to the occasion. I waved the newspaper at her. "One asshole's killing us with leaks while the other's got us chasing our own tails. I spoke with Mary last night, incidentally. She said her husband wouldn't know the truth if he tripped on it."

"Is that why I get the impression you're going to create a big, nasty scene when we get there?"

I replied, "Any day, Eddie's going to call with his deal. What do we say? 'Gee, between your hogging all the key evidence, and our client telling us a bunch of big fibs, we're a little confused.'"

"And kicking his head in is going to help?"

"It will make me feel better."

"I see." She stared at me a long moment, as though I were a bottle of nitroglycerin she'd better not shake too hard. Then she put the earphones back in, somehow leaving me the impression we weren't in mutual accord here.

Morrison was already shackled to the table when we arrived. Without the slightest ado, I announced, "We met with Milt Martin. We're experiencing a credibility crisis here. He said you were a lackey. He said you bullshitted everybody in town about what a bigwig you were. He said the most important thing you ever did for him was shine his shoes."

Morrison looked up in utter shock, more or less the

expression I had hoped to elicit. Only a dose of emotional electrocution was going to jar some honest words out of his mouth.

He finally sputtered, "That prick. That lying bastard."

Obviously, it was time to turn up the voltage. I walked across the room. "This morning's papers say you gave the Russians the names of two guys they called home and shot. And you gave them our negotiating positions on the North Korean nuclear issue, which they then helpfully provided their old chums in Pyongyang."

"That's bullshit, Drummond. God damn it, listen to me. I didn't even have access to the North Korean stuff."

I straddled the chair across from him. "The prosecutors wouldn't have told the press unless they had substantiation. We need to know what that evidence is. We need any decent leads you can give us. But you know what we really need?—quit lying to us."

His lips were trembling, and his eyes were wild and wet, on the verge of tears. The veins were sticking out of his neck, from the pressure of blood boiling with frustration.

"God damn it, I *am* telling you the truth, asshole! I'm not making this up."

Katrina suddenly bent across the table, between us. "Would you two mind if I stepped outside?"

I said, "What?"

"The testosterone level in here is killing me."

I shook my head. "You think you can do better than me?"

She looked at me and replied, "Which part? Pissing off our client? Trading insults? Getting nothing done?"

A big, satisfied smirk was on Morrison's face.

"All right, smartass," I said, "proceed."

She dropped into the chair next to me. She studied our client and he studied her back. She said, "We can do better than this, right?"

He nodded.

"Good. You say Martin lied. Who can verify that?"

He considered this, then said, "My secretary, Janet Winters." He paused. "I'm not sure she'll help, though."

"Why won't she?"

"She was the one who claimed we had an affair. She was, well, she was bitter when it was over."

"Why?"

"I was fighting for my career. I had to hire a civilian lawyer who specializes in these things. She lost her security clearance and was fired."

Being a lawyer, I had a fairly good inkling what he was talking about. As did Katrina, who tried to look unruffled, but it wasn't hard to guess her position, her being a woman and all. There's some unwritten sister-hood code that in these kinds of things all the benefit of the doubt anatomically flows to the side with boobs.

Morrison sensed it, too. His new buddy was slipping away. He awkwardly said, "Look, the lawyer said it was the only way. I'm not proud of how it went down. She was my secretary for three years, and I, uh, I probably let it get too close. But she was lying . . . Christ, I never slept with her."

"Why did she claim you did?" Katrina asked.

"She fell in love with me. She started asking me out. I stopped by her apartment once or twice when I came back from trips, just to pick up things, and she was all over me."

"Did Mary know?"

"She was the one who told me to get rid of her. When I tried to fire Janet, that's when she brought the charges. Do you see why I had to defend myself?"

Rather than dwell further on this point, Katrina swiftly said, "Okay, is there anyone else who can confirm what you were doing?"

"Ask Mary, my wife."

I shook my head.

"What, Drummond? Why are you shaking your head?"

"We talked. She said she had no idea," I replied, discreetly withholding that part where she described him as Walter Mitty in green drag.

"I was important," he insisted with a shocked look, completely unaware how asinine that sounded.

Rather than waste more time on that debatable point, I changed tacks. "Alexi Arbatov. Shift back to him. Where'd you two meet?"

"In Georgia, after the second massacre."

"Did you approach him, or did he approach you?"

"Neither. The Georgians held a big funeral for their slain countrymen, and we both ended up there."

"Why?"

"It was a good place to test the temperatures. Coincidentally, Alexi and I both thought we'd melt in with the crowds, to see how serious it was becoming."

"And what? You ended up next to each other?"

"Well . . . yes, exactly. Then, before I knew it, I was being harassed by a group of KGB goons demanding to see my papers and asking what I thought I was doing there. Alexi pulled them off to the side and explained that the Soviet government didn't want any serious incidents with the Americans. He told them to back off."

"Just like that?"

"No, not just like that," he angrily responded. "They knew who he was."

"Why's that?"

"Because he was Yurichenko's protégé."

"And who was Yurichenko?"

"Not *was*—who *is* Viktor Yurichenko."

"Okay . . . who *is* he?"

"The head of the SVR, the agency responsible for external security."

"And Arbatov was his buddy?"

Morrison was shaking his head, unable to believe he had to explain these things. "At the time, Yurichenko was the equivalent of a three-star in the KGB. The man was legendary. He'd joined the KGB late in the Second World War, and there were rumors he put Kim Il Sung in power in North Korea."

"That's nice to have on your résumé. How'd Yurichenko do that?"

"Kim Il Sung spent the Second World War hiding out in KGB training camps in Siberia. Yurichenko was his controller, and when the war ended, he accompanied

Kim back into the country, then orchestrated the Soviet support that allowed Kim to elbow everybody else aside."

"That's ancient history. Let's go back to Arbatov in Georgia."

"Well, we began talking. It took a while, but I made him feel comfortable, and he began to open up. He said Gorbachev was a fool for sending in the KGB to batter these poor wretches. The old system was dying. Gorbachev couldn't point his finger toward a new future and keep his feet planted in the past."

I said, "So you figured he was a pretty good guy?"

"Drummond, Alexi was serious. And he told me his boss, Yurichenko, felt the same way."

I gave him my you're-full-of-crap look. "This guy Arbatov sidles up next to you, a couple of KGB thugs threaten you, he steps in to save you, then he starts talking about what a hash this whole Communist thing is. You don't see where that might look suspicious? Where some folks might even conclude he was worming his way into your confidence?"

"It wasn't like that. I swear it wasn't."

I shook my head. My oval-into-a-round-hole theory seemed to be springing some very nasty leaks. With this guy it was axiomatic that every step forward was two steps back. I could feel the frustration welling up in my chest, and sensed that if I didn't immediately invent an excuse to leave, I might be facing a murder charge.

Walking to the car, I said to Katrina, "Incidentally, you did a good job back there. That good cop/bad cop stunt was very convincing."

"Think so?" she asked.

"Oscar material."

"Then I should thank you for making it easy."

"What's that mean?"

"You seem to enjoy pissing him off."

"I'm trying to get the truth. It's for his own good."

"Arbeit macht frei," she replied.

"Meaning what?"

"It was on a sign that hung over Auschwitz concentration camp. It means 'Work will set you free.'"

I was sure she was sending me another of those subtle messages, but I'm a very black-and-white, meat-and-potatoes sort, so it went clear over my head.

"Well, anyway," I said, "you try to track down Miss I-got-screwed-by-my-boss-and-all-I've-got-to-show-for-it-is-this-unemployment-check. I'll see what I can come up with on our other big lead."

We drove back to our fancy digs and got back to work, which for me meant investigating Alexi Arbatov, which wasn't going to be hard, since I knew exactly where to start my research.

When I mentioned I used to be in the infantry, I meant I used to be part of something called the outfit, which is one of those units in the United States Army you never heard of. It does super-sensitive, spooky little things like follow Noriega around before you invade him, or infiltrate the Iraqi capital a few days before the Gulf War air campaign to knock out the central computers that control their entire air defense system—things like that.

I spent five years in that unit before two or three bullets did enough damage to my internal organs that I could no longer run marathons—which was frankly a relief—or stay in the outfit—which frankly wasn't.

This was why I went to law school, but it also left me some fairly good contacts in the intelligence community. For example, this was where I first met Morrison. Aside from that, I had fond memories of the outfit.

I called Lieutenant Colonel Charlie Becker, who used to be the intell officer of our little unit, and had moved on to something bigger and better called the National Intelligence Council, or NIC.

I said, "Hey, Charlie, Drummond here."

And he said, "Hey, Sean. What you doin'?"

"Still a JAG guy. In fact, I'm defending a guy named William Morrison. Know him?"

"I know him. He's a prick. Want my advice?"

"Sure, Charlie, what's your advice?"

"Sandbag him. Do your worst job and let the bastard fry. I never liked him anyway, but that fucker dishonored our uniform and doesn't deserve to breathe."

I perhaps failed to mention that Charlie Becker's a very tough guy who doesn't mince words, an unusual quality among military intelligence officers, who, fairly or not, are considered somewhat effete by the more manly combat branches. They are broadly regarded as wimpy, overintellectualized types who are very adept at saying infuriatingly ambivalent things such as, "On the one hand this, and on the other hand, that." Charlie was an exception to this rule. He could bench almost four hundred pounds and used to be an

All-America heavyweight wrestler at the University of Wisconsin. Charlie could kill me with his spit.

I said, "Well, I took this oath when I became a lawyer and—"

"Yeah, yeah, I know. Can the horseshit. How can I help you defend the traitorous bastard?"

"I need two profiles. Two Russian spy guys. One's named Yurichenko, and the other's named Arbatov."

"Viktor and Alexi," he said in his subtle way, letting me know he was leaps and bounds ahead of me. He added, "There's always lots of requests on both of them, so I could ask and not draw attention. Especially Yurichenko."

"You know about him?"

"Does a Catholic know about the Pope?"

"No kidding?"

"I keep a blown-up picture of him above my desk. When I grow up I want to be just like him."

"So you like him?"

"Like him? The man's a walking plague. He's the best you ever saw. I hate his guts. I wish he was on our side."

Coming from Charlie, this was high praise indeed, because he has very rigorous standards. I gave him my Washington office address, and he promised to bring over the files within a few hours. I told him to hand-deliver them to Imelda, and by the time I landed at Ronald Reagan Airport and drove over to my office, she had the two very important files Charlie had brought over.

I tromped into my office and opened Yurichenko's

first. Viktor Yurichenko was estimated to be somewhere in his mid-seventies. Since no foreigner had ever laid eyes on his KGB file, this estimation was based on the fact that he joined the KGB in 1944, when he was anywhere from eighteen to twenty-two years old. He was a spymaster's spymaster—those were the exact words used in the file, and human intelligence files aren't like book reviews, so it's rare to see any kind of tribute. Nobody was too sure exactly how many incredible operations he'd pulled off, although, in addition to that stunt in North Korea, he was believed to be responsible for recruiting Castro, for helping North Vietnam win the war, and for penetrating the CIA and FBI on countless occasions. I saw why my old buddy called him a plague. He sounded like a one-man cold war.

Yurichenko was a chess aficionado, which had brought him to numerous international events, where he was known to sit in the back row and critique the moves of the likes of Bobby Fischer and Gary Kasparov. Several times the CIA had positioned agents in his vicinity; they swore Yurichenko had predicted every move the players would make, within seconds after their opponents moved. Yet to the best anyone could tell, he'd never participated in any international chess events himself. He seemed content to sit on the sideline and observe others.

When Boris Yeltsin disbanded the KGB back in 1991, it was widely thought that Yurichenko would be near the top of the blacklist, having been the mastermind of so many cold war intelligence coups that he was virtually a poster boy for the old system. Recall that Yeltsin was disbanding the KGB to show the West and his own people that a new day had dawned, that the bloody-handed practitioners of dirty tricks were no longer employable by the new state. To everybody's surprise, Yeltsin made Yurichenko the head of the SVR, the Russian equivalent of the CIA.

One source reported that Yurichenko had smelled what was coming and had secretly approached Yeltsin long before the breakup. For several years he had provided Yeltsin with insights about what was happening in the world, in addition to early warnings about Gorbachev's efforts to squelch Yeltsin and his movement. In short, Yurichenko had ingratiated himself with the upcoming leader, although whether from ruthless self-interest or a genuine belief that the old system was so rotten it should collapse, nobody was too clear about.

He'd kept a generally low profile since taking over the SVR. He'd visited the United States three times to attend seminars and meet with each new CIA chief who came to office during his reign. The assessors suspected that he merely dropped by to get firsthand impressions of his competition; this, about the same guy who sat in on all the big international chess championships to observe the players. I wondered if he was as good at predicting the moves of our past three CIA chiefs. Or maybe the past ten?

He was described as a meticulously neat man who dressed like an old world diplomat in tailored three-piece wool suits. Two Agency psychiatrists had sat across from him at one marathon meeting and tried to assess him. They had walked off with wildly divergent impressions. Both agreed he was highly intelligent, but one considered him a cold fish, while the other thought he was charming. One found him uncompassionate; the other insisted his conscience was highly evolved. One said he had an enlarged ego; the other said he was humble to the point of subdued. And so on. Either the two shrinks had split personalities themselves or Yurichenko was an incredibly deceptive chameleon who could convince two simultaneous and highly skilled observers he was showing two different colors.

I stared at the photo Charlie had kindly tucked into the packet. The shot must have been taken covertly, because Yurichenko had that relaxed, unposed look. He was seated alone in a chair in what looked like a hotel lobby. He had snow white hair and thick white eyebrows, wore old-fashioned gold-rimmed spectacles, and had ordinary, moderately attractive features. Hundreds of tiny creases were cluttered around his mouth and eyes, giving the impression of a sense of humor. He looked like a skinny Santa Claus, sans that big beard and those long locks. He had never married and had no known children.

I opened the packet on Alexi Arbatov. This time I began with his photo—I wanted a physical impression of the guy who perhaps bagged my client like a three-legged deer.

He had dark hair, dark eyes, and features that somehow managed to seem both sharp and soft: sharp, like he had a lot of brainjuice and didn't miss much; soft, like friendly, but not pretentiously so. It was what you would call a beguiling face—damned handsome, only the reassuring, drag-this-boy-home-to-meet-Mama kind of handsome. There was a mole on his left cheek. I was reminded of John Boy Walton, everybody's favorite boy next door.

He was thirty-six years old and had attended Moscow University, the Soviet Union's Harvard, graduating when he was only fifteen years old, a record that had never been surpassed. He had received a master's in something called American studies, followed by a doctorate in political science. It was believed that Yurichenko considered him like the son he always wished he'd had. They were inseparable.

A very interesting point there. Yurichenko and Arbatov had been sidekicks forever. In other words, Alexi Arbatov was Yurichenko's henchman, the guy who handled key assignments.

Take recruiting and controlling the most valuable spy in Russian history: That would be a key assignment, wouldn't it?

Right. I read on, and Arbatov, like his boss, had been observed and analyzed by several CIA psychiatric profilers. He fell well outside their standard template for clandestine operators. He appeared to be fastidious, altruistic, nearly monastic in his habits. He was a vegetarian, which is about as rare in Russia as tulips in wintertime. Even more unusual, he was a teetotaler who rarely consumed more than a glass of wine. It's a wonder the Russians gave him a passport.

"Magnetically charming," claimed one observer. Despite his obvious intelligence, not bombastic, nor arrogant, nor overbearing—none of the standard traits found in your typical clandestine operator. "Surprisingly shy and tactful" was how the observer summarized him.

All of which added up to a manner that would endear him to an overambitious, egotistic officer who thought he was smarter than anybody. It wouldn't have been a fair match: the poseur against the boy wonder. Poor Morrison would never have felt the hand that slipped into his pocket. If the CIA was even half right about Arbatov, putting Billy Morrison in his proximity was like sending a Little League team up against the Green Bay Packers. They don't even play the same sport, for Chrissakes.

In short, were I on the task force investigating Morrison, I'd be completely fixated on his relationship with Arbatov.

CHAPTER FOURTEEN

KATRINA had no trouble tracking down Miss Janet Winters. The State Department's personnel office gave her the forwarding address, which was in Rosslyn, Virginia, a ten-minute drive from my office.

Katrina wisely made the call to Janet, since the instant the poor woman heard a male voice identify himself as an attorney for Morrison, she'd probably invite us over so she could mow us down with a twelve-gauge shotgun. Incidentally, near the head of my list of ways I don't want to die is being slain by the jilted paramour of a complete jerk-off.

Katrina sweet-talked her and wangled an invitation. It turned out Janet lived in a red-brick townhouse she shared with a few other professional women, a common enough arrangement in our capital's anthropology, where young people nest together until they either find suitable mates or enough cash to hibernate alone.

We knocked, the door opened, and an extremely attractive woman in her early thirties stared at us. She took in my uniform, and that didn't make her the least bit happy. Then her eyes fell on Katrina's costume, which consisted of floppy camouflage pants and an OD halter top, obviously chosen for my benefit. I ordinarily like cheeky women. You can push it too far, though.

We ended up in a sparsely furnished living room that, like all collective nests, was a hodgepodge of jointly owned furniture assembled in one room. Where the male variety of these nests normally comprises a big-screen TV surrounded by three or four ratty old lounge chairs and a beer-stained rug, the female variant somehow manages to nearly always look tidy and tastefully decorated, despite the clashing striped and flowered and paisley couches and chairs. Women are so impractical that way.

Katrina sat on the striped couch, and I was starting to sit next to her when she quickly scooted her fanny over, exiling me to one of those flowered side chairs. She was shrewdly arranging the social setting for the best psychological effect, so she and Janet could have a confidential, chiquita-to-chiquita chat, which I believe to be much wimpier than a mano-a-mano, bare-knuckled discussion.

Janet wore jeans and a sweatshirt with the words UNIVERSITY OF GEORGIA curled around a picture of a snarling English bulldog. She had long honey blond hair, a classically pretty face, and a sleek, slender body. She struck me as the type you'd want to have an affair with. I'd want to have an affair with her. But we were here to find out if Bill *did* have an affair with her.

She began playing with the hem of her sweatshirt, betraying her anxiety, and Katrina gave her a warm smile and asked, "That shirt yours or in honor of a boyfriend?"

"Mine."

"No kidding. What year did you graduate?"

"Nineteen ninety-two. I majored in political science."

Katrina smiled sweetly. "Is that why you took the job at State?"

Janet stopped playing with the edge of her sweatshirt. "I wanted to be a Foreign Service officer, but I was having difficulty with the tests."

"Hey, got that," said Katrina, instantly sympathetic. "I worked at State, downstairs in Translations, trying to scramble up cash for law school. I had lots of friends trying to do what you did, though. It's a bitch of a test, isn't it? I knew one friend, took it six times and never passed. And I mean, that woman was smart as hell."

Janet shook her head. "You want irony? I took it twice and failed. The third time was just before this thing with Bill. I was notified afterward that I passed, except I lost my security clearance and was disqualified."

Katrina, her new buddy, shifted to a distressed frown. "Wow, that sucks. What are you doing now?"

"I'm a paralegal in a small firm downtown. Not exactly what I hoped to do with my life."

"You must be royally pissed at Morrison, huh?"

"I'd hate to be in the same room with her. I'd probably strangle her."

Katrina shot me a quick sideways glance. "Her? Uh, I thought her husband was behind it."

Janet broke into a throaty chuckle. "Him? He's just spineless. She hired the lawyer and detectives who sabotaged my life. I mean, okay, I was having an affair with her husband. I'm not proud of it. He was miserable in that marriage, though. She made his life hell."

Katrina nodded sympathetically, like, Well of course he was miserable. Married to Mary, with her money, looks, and class, who wouldn't be? Poor, poor Bill.

"How'd she find out about you?"

"He sent some gifts over to my apartment . . . some lingerie, some jewelry. And do you believe this? . . . the idiot charged it. She saw the receipts and hired a detective to track me down. Then Bill came into work one morning and asked me into his office. He looked like hell, like he hadn't slept all night. He said he had to fire me. She ordered it."

"And what did you do?"

"I said, no way. Transfer me, but don't fire me. I knew I'd done well on the exam the last time. It would ruin me."

"And he said . . . what?"

A harsh chuckle erupted from the back of Janet's

throat. "He offered me money. I told him to stuff that money up his wife's ass. He'd told me dozens of times he loved me. Why was he letting that shrew ruin his life? Our lives? You know what he said?"

"What?"

"For the children. That old line. It was bullshit. He was a miserable father. He ignored those kids. They were so much like her, he hated being around them."

"Then what happened?"

"I protested the firing. There was a hearing, and those high-priced lawyers and detectives had testimonies from the first guy I ever slept with to every affair I ever had. Look, I'm no nun, but I don't go around throwing myself at married men, either. They made me sound like pathetic trailer-park trash."

Katrina was again nodding in her sympathetic way, like, Aren't men just the biggest cads? What in the hell was God thinking when he gave them such a big role in reproduction? She said, "Hey, I have to tell you. Bill doesn't come off sounding very good."

"Well, yeah, he was spineless . . . but I don't blame him. That wife of his is like Lucrezia Borgia. You have no idea."

Uncomfortable hearing Mary described in such thorny terms, I swiftly said, "So you didn't think Bill was an honorable person?"

She shot me a noxious look. "I didn't say that."

"No?"

"This whole thing in the news is hogwash. Some-body's made a terrible mistake."

"Really?"

"Yeah, really."

I scratched my jaw inquisitively. "What were his duties in that office? He says he was Martin's right hand. Was that true?"

"Was it true? The guy was at the office every morning at six and didn't usually go home till ten or eleven at night. Martin showered work on him."

Katrina and I exchanged another glance. This had suddenly become much more interesting. "Give me some examples of the kinds of things he did for Martin."

"You name it, he did it. He wrote nearly all of Martin's memorandums and policy recommendations and messages. I typed them, so I know. He represented Martin at meetings with State, or with the White House, or with the CIA. A lot of Martin's work depended on intelligence, and Bill collected it, summarized it, and kept it flowing."

"No kidding? Martin said Morrison was a low-level flunky with a puffed-up title."

She violently shook her head. "What a lie! He depended on Bill for everything. Not that I'm surprised Martin denies it."

"No?"

"His ego's bigger than his nose. He thinks he's the new Kissinger. Well, he's not nearly as bright as he thinks he is. He knew nothing about Washington. Bill kept him from being fired. He made him look good."

I looked at Katrina and she was gazing back at me with an expression I couldn't quite fathom.

Katrina said to Janet, "I can't thank you enough. If

something evidentiary from those years turns up, we may need you to testify. Would you be willing?"

"Of course. I hope his wife is there. I've waited a long time to tell her what I think of her."

On that note, we bid our farewells and departed. In the car I turned to Katrina. "Well?"

She looked away. "Mary has a hard touch."

"Yeah, well, what would you do if you caught your mate cheating with his secretary?"

"It's irrelevant. Wouldn't happen."

"How come you're so confident?"

"I'm fantastic in bed. My men don't wander."

"Well, then, notionally speaking . . . say your husband *was* cheating?"

"Remember John Bobbitt?"

"Could any man forget him?"

"Of course, I wouldn't toss it in a field where they could find and reattach it. I'd put it in the garbage disposal and grind it into mush."

"Wouldn't a simple divorce suffice? Less wear and tear on your disposal."

"Well, afterward, I suppose. He'd be worthless. Why keep a dickless man?"

And Mary has a hard touch? I finally said, "Put her on the witness list, but she's a last resort."

Katrina stared out the windshield. "Of course. They'd tear her to pieces on the stand."

They would indeed, which meant all we had so far was one character witness of questionable reliability and infinite vulnerability.

CHAPTER FIFTEEN

A "SOURCE close to the investigation" revealed that night that Bill Morrison had provided the Russians with eight years' worth of technologies that had been submitted to the Commerce Department for export licenses, and were subsequently denied.

The "source" explained that it was the most catastrophic industrial espionage leak ever. When companies submit requests to Commerce for permission to export their latest inventions, they include detailed blueprints. And when the experts at Commerce's office of export licenses deem a particular technology too strategically sensitive, or too militarily valuable, they stamp "not exportable" on the request and order the company to never, ever let any foreign power see how that product is made.

The "source" said that Morrison gave the Russians hundreds, if not thousands, of blueprints of outrageously sensitive technologies ranging from radar systems to vital software codes to more powerful microchips, to you name it. It was "impossible to quantify the damage," opined that anonymous source.

I formed a mental picture of Eddie slumped back in his blue wool suit as he smugly spun this latest horror story for his admiring audience of reporters. The bastard was having the time of his life. Would it be too much to ask that he just keep his mouth shut and unload this in court, like any decent lawyer?

Nor did it escape my notice that Eddie's leaks were spewing out faster and faster. There was a hidden message in this—he was trying to get it all out before he offered his deal, an indication it wasn't far off. Not a good development.

I picked up the phone and called his office.

A youngish-sounding female secretary answered. "Office of Eddie Golden, chief counsel of Counterespionage Team One and chief prosecutor in the Morrison case."

My, my . . . Dumbo the Elephant had invented not one, but two grand titles for himself.

Raising the tenor of my voice, I said, "Yes, yes. I don't wish to bother Mr. Golden, as I'm sure he's ridiculously busy, but could you please inform him the Sexually Transmitted Disease Clinic at Fort Myer called. And . . . well . . . we really need him to drop by right away."

The secretary said, "I, well, uh, I'm sorry, you have the wrong man. This is the office of Major Eddie Golden."

"Oh no, dear, he's the one. An utter slut. The man's in and out of here so often we're thinking of renaming the clinic after him. Thank you very much," and I hung up.

I can be so infantile. And with any luck, he was having a fling with the secretary who answered, and the next time he passed by her desk she'd knee him in the nuts.

Sleep came more easily that night, knowing I'd at least struck one small blow for freedom. Unfortunately, it had a short half-life, because at three-thirty my phone rang, and a deep male voice identified himself as the commandant of the Fort Leavenworth Disciplinary Barracks. Sounding curt and hurried, he informed me I had better get my ass out there real quick because my client had just tried to commit suicide and was in the hospital in critical condition.

He hung up before I could respond. Very funny. Eddie Golden can be such a sly, sly devil. Like I'd fall for this and rush down to the airport and catch the early bird to Kansas City.

When I couldn't fall back asleep, I finally had the operator put me through to the commandant's office. Sounding like he was talking to a three-year-old dolt, he repeated every word of it.

I caught that early flight and rushed into the dispensary at 9:30 A.M. Imelda had somehow arrived ahead of me and was in the waiting room, pacing back and forth like an English sentry.

I breathlessly asked, "Is he still alive?"

"So far," she dryly observed.

"What happened?"

"Seems some dumbass had a TV set brought into his cell. He opened up the back, yanked out some sharp objects, and slashed his wrists. Guards found him at the twenty-minute check, laid out in a big puddle of blood."

I felt my face flush. "So it was close?"

"Not *was* close, *is* close. Docs been runnin' in and outta there all mornin'."

I fell into a heap on a nearby couch. I stewed. I hate to sound selfish, but if Morrison died, I'd be front-page

164

news by noon, the Dr. Kevorkian of military law.

My bosses would be both happy and furious with me. They'd be happy I provided my client the tools to save the government the time and expense of weathering the trial and appeals process before it executed him. There'd be no big crowd of folks holding a candlelight vigil outside his death chamber, no fussy editorials about the morality of executions, no question about whether he got a fair trial, because he had carried out the sentence himself.

And they'd be furious because to pinpoint and repair the damage, the government needed to know everything he gave to the Russians. Corpses don't speak.

And so I waited in selfish agony for a doctor to come out and tell me he was dead. Or alive. Or still hovering in that testy netherworld in between.

At 9:50 a chubby, grim-faced surgeon approached. "Major Drummond?"

"Unfortunately," I dolefully admitted.

"General Morrison is resting peacefully. It was damned close. He lost so many pints, he had a minor infarction."

"But he's going to be okay?"

"He should be. But whatever idiot let him have a TV should be shot. What were they thinking?"

Yeah, what were they thinking? I asked, "Can I see him?"

"If you'd like. Make it quick, though. We have him on tranquilizers, so he'll be in and out."

He led me down a few hallways to a door with two MPs standing beside the entrance. Inside, Morrison lay in bed with two or three IVs pumping various fluids into his body, his head turned sideways, his face ashen and flushed, like his new blood hadn't yet worked its way to the surface.

I sat on the edge of the bed. He mumbled, "Shit," which fairly well summarized our common view—him because he was still breathing, and me because that meant I was still his attorney.

I said, "That was really, really stupid."

His eyes narrowed. "Yeah . . . I lived."

"You'll make it through this."

"Yeah? How?"

"You just do."

He stared at the wall and said, "Drummond, a week ago, I was . . ." He stopped and took a deep breath. "Shit, did you know I was on the two-star list?"

"So what?"

" 'So what?' " He rolled his eyes in disbelief. After a pause, he asked, "What are my odds?"

"At this stage, we don't know."

He turned and looked at me, his eyes haunted. "I saw the reporting on TV. I've already been convicted."

"You saw a bunch of Beltway assholes throwing around opinions. It takes ten officers and a shitload of evidence to convict you."

He thought about this a moment and then asked, "How could this have happened?"

"Well, either you did what they're claiming or somebody's made a really big mistake."

"You don't believe me, do you?"

"Let's just say I met your former secretary yesterday.

And you might recall I was at your award ceremony for the Silver Star."

He turned away again, refusing to look me in the eye.

For good measure, I added, "And on a more personal note, you're an asshole for cheating on Mary."

"So I fucked up, Drummond. Nobody's perfect."

"Mary is. She didn't deserve that."

He let loose a raw chuckle. "You stupid asshole. She's not perfect. Christ, you have no idea."

"Wrong. I have a very good idea."

"You weren't married to her. You have no idea what a bitch she can be."

This conversation could only go downhill from here, aside from which he seemed to be on the verge of losing consciousness, and there was pressing information I needed out of him. I said, "When you worked for Martin, what was your relationship with Commerce's export control office?"

His eyes were closing. "Huh?"

I squeezed his arm. "The export control office. The guys who say whether U.S. companies can export their crap to foreign countries."

"I never worked with them. They're part of Commerce."

"I see." I pondered this a moment, then took a shot in the dark. "Do they have some sister office in State?"

"The Office of Munitions Control?"

"Right, those guys." I guessed that's what I was talking about. I mean, other than guys like Morrison who spend most of their careers in Washington, who in the hell knew where all the tentacles of government flow and interlock? No wonder the Republicans want to cut the size of our federal institutions. At least then, when a new team comes to power every four years, they don't spend their first two studying wiring diagrams and trying to figure out who all those frigging people are and what they do.

The befuddled look was still on his face. "I didn't do any work with them. Why?"

"Last night's release said you handed over hundreds of requests that were turned down by that office."

He shook his head, although I sensed his mood had shifted from outrage to resignation.

I added, "They said you turned over blueprints, tech assessments, the works."

He started that mirthless chuckle again. "Christ, who'd ever think of giving them the rejects from that office? It's ingenious."

"Ingenious?"

His head flopped over, he faced the wall again, and explained, "Those requests go all over town. Commerce, State, CIA, DOD, NSA, everybody has a whack at them. It's a big veto ring." He took a long, labored breath. "Dozens of offices . . . hundreds of people are involved—you'd never know who did it."

"So the leak could've come from any number of sources?"

"Of course."

I touched his shoulder. "Okay, listen, I promised the doc I wouldn't stay long. So you promise me something."

"What?"

"No more of this suicide crap. If I'm going to work my ass off on your case, I don't want any more late-night phone calls about your health."

I couldn't see the expression on his face or the look in his eyes. "Okay."

"I'll stop by again later. I may need some help on something."

"Okay," he said again, and I inspected his suite to be sure there were no sharp objects or other deadly instruments within reach. Unless he used his IV lines to hang himself, he appeared to be safe for the time being.

I returned to the house on Colonel's row, drafted a press release, and told Imelda where to send it. Not that anybody was likely to feel sympathetic about Morrison's attempt. Most folks would shake their heads and ask, What the hell's wrong with this picture? That bastard can figure out ten different ways to betray his country but can't figure out how to snuff himself?

I next made some calls to Washington, because if I didn't start making headway on this case, I'd be attending my client's funeral instead of his trial. I slipped back into his hospital room later that afternoon, got what I needed, and then flew back to D.C. I called Katrina as soon as I returned and told her to pack her bags for Russia.

CHAPTER SIXTEEN

'D never been to Moscow, a city that in a perverse way was once the American soldier's version of Mecca, the capital of the empire that kept most of us employed for about fifty years. It was where revolutions and wars were bred, where devious plots for global domination were hatched, where bushy-browed men in outdated, frumpy, ill-tailored suits stood on reviewing stands and watched the largest military machine in the world march by, the same military we all thought would someday, inevitably, come marching against us.

My first introduction to Russian efficiency was the two hours after we landed, as we waited on the runway while ground crews scoured around for the mobile steps that would allow us to deplane. Katrina stoically endured this, I assume because she had Russian blood and was genetically inured from this form of brutal inefficiency. A typically spoiled American guy, I petulantly cursed and moaned the whole time. I'm not graceful in situations like this.

We took a taxi from the airport to a hotel in the center of Moscow that would've been considered a fleatrap in New York City, or even Fargo, North Dakota, but I had been told was a five-star by local standards. The lobby was crowded with floozies and whores in cheap, glitzy clothes, and guys wearing black jeans and black leather jackets, all of whom seemed to be chatting on cell phones, and none of whom looked the least bit like choirboys.

After another twenty minutes wasted ironing out the problem that the hotel had somehow lost or misplaced our reservation, Katrina and I took an elevator up to the fourteenth floor and our side-by-side rooms. My room reeked of tobacco smoke and stale sweat, was barely larger than a broom closet, and the TV in the corner looked like something built in the 1950s. I was impressed—imagine all this luxury for only $280 a night, American.

I threw my bag on the bed, punched the remote, and the screen flickered to life, sound at full blast, showing a girl and three guys doing things that give multitasking a whole new complexity. I frantically punched at the remote to try to flip the channel, or turn down the sound, or turn the damned thing off—it was hopeless. The only thing that worked was the on button, and the girl on the screen was making loud noises intended to convey what a great time she was having, although frankly, I wouldn't want to trade places.

Katrina's room and mine had one of those connecting doors, and it took forever to find the TV button that turned the damned thing off, Russian sets having different knobs and symbols from ours.

I yelled through the connecting door, "Gee, my TV was preset on that channel."

I heard her chuckle. "It's cool. If that's what turns on you older guys, doesn't bother me."

Older guys? I chuckled to show I could take a joke. Bitch.

An hour later, I was showered and changed, and the phone rang. A chipper-sounding United States Army captain named Mel Torianski informed me he was in the lobby, and I knocked on the connecting door and yelled for Katrina to meet us downstairs when she was ready. After she assured me she would, I left and found the elevator.

Torianski was a studious-looking sort, skinny, narrow-shouldered, and bespectacled, a poster child for the military intelligence corps. We did the handshake thing as he said, "Welcome to Moscow, Major. I'm a deputy attaché."

"Lucky for you, Mel. You're at the embassy, huh?"

"Yes sir. Two years now."

"I guess you knew the general pretty well?"

"As well as a captain gets to know a general," he replied with an anguished expression. No need to explain further.

The elevator door opened and out stepped Katrina, although at first I didn't realize it was her. *Rolling Stone* magazine had turned into the *Wall Street Journal*. Gone were the SoHo slut clothes and cartoonish makeup, replaced by a tailored blue business suit with a short skirt that showed long, tantalizing legs, matched with high heels, the sum of which was a female butterfly that could make all the little male butterflies get petrified wings. The only residue of her more natural self was the bead in her nose, and oddly enough, mixed in with her conservative apparel and toned-down makeup it seemed quite sexy, a sly hint that underneath that buttoned-down business suit lurked something more brazen.

I cocked my head and she smiled. I whispered, "My, but don't you look nice."

"A Dooney & Bourke goddess, huh?"

I swallowed my curiosity and introduced her to Captain Mel Torianski, who was checking her out like a hungry man eyes a slab of tenderloin on a hook. He was a horny little wimp, at least. He had a government sedan parked outside that we all three walked out to, and along the way to the embassy I asked, "So Mel, how's the embassy taking the arrest?"

He stared straight ahead, no doubt pondering whether he should confide these things to Morrison's lawyer. He finally said, "We've got lots of visitors from Washington. You know what I'm saying here, right, Major?"

I guessed I did. The way these things work, after a spy's caught, since the government has already gone to the considerable trouble to form a big investigation team—and everybody's getting bored and antsy—they shift into what's called the damage assessment phase. Said otherwise, a witch hunt to see who else might be knowingly or unknowingly implicated, the general rule of this phase being that if you shoot everyone, you can be damned sure you get the guilty parties.

I said, "So a bunch of glum-faced guys in black and blue suits are running around the embassy?"

He nodded miserably. "A huge team flew in four days ago. We're all being interrogated repeatedly, and these aren't nice guys, if you know what I mean."

I knew exactly what he meant. I asked, "So what'd you think of Morrison?"

"Truthfully?"

"No, Mel, I want you to lie to me."

That got a nervous chuckle. "Uh . . . right. He treated us like garbage. It was all about him. You won't find many folks who worked for him that have nice things to say. I doubt you'll find any."

Well, no surprise there. I never expected to.

Katrina asked, "What about Mary, his wife? What did people think about her?"

"Oh, she was real popular. To be truthful, we all sort of wondered how she married such a jerk. A woman like her, you'd think she could've done much better."

Oddly enough, I'd had that very thought countless times. I asked, "So Mel, did you ever see Morrison do anything suspicious?"

"No, but hey, he was my boss, so I wasn't looking over his shoulder. But no sir, I never saw anything." He sounded rueful, like he wished he did, so he could help bury him.

We finished the car ride with Mel pointing out landmarks and offering tidbits about life in Moscow. I was struck by how ugly and depressing the place was. It was dirty; not trashy, because I didn't see any litter, but dirty, like it rained soil. The sky was an oppressive leaden color, and the buildings were mostly gray, blocklike structures that looked like they shared the same architect—a man named Stalin. Frankly, it's no wonder he hasn't been written up in *Architectural Digest* as a guy who brought glory to the profession.

Nor was the U.S. embassy any testament to palatial elegance. It was a modern, big-windowed building that looked like one of those cheaply constructed, minimally decorated high rises you see in low-rent office parks back in the States. Not that it was cheap, being the same embassy that was built with a bit of KGB skullduggery poured into its foundation. The building had been secretly wired and bugged as it was erected, and when that was discovered, to considerable embarrassment, the whole top two floors were ripped off and rebuilt, and the place ended up costing more dollars per square foot than the Trump Tower.

Inside, Mel led us to a bank of elevators and up to the office of the ambassador, who apparently wanted words with us before we spoke with anybody on his staff. We waited about five minutes before three guys came streaming out his door with their pants on fire, and his secretary signaled us to go in.

Allan D. Riser was a fairly big man, meaning tall, and heavy, with a bone-ugly, fierce face resembling a wild boar that had somehow learned how to shave. Unless it was our intention to scare the shit out of the Russians, he wasn't hired for his looks. His office was decorated with the usual assortment of power photos and trinkets. His booming voice was the first thing I noticed, however.

"Both of you sit down," he roared, the indication being that we weren't here to discuss the town's tonier nightspots.

He gave us what I'm sure he thought was his most steely-eyed look and said, "Drummond, right?"

"That's me."

"And you're Miss Mazorski?" he asked, and received a polite nod. He faced me. "And you're here to prove Morrison didn't do it, right?"

"Not exactly, sir. We're here to investigate the circumstances concerning the charges and his arrest."

He leaned back in his chair and considered my mealy-mouthed reply. I had the sense that this was a man not to screw with and made a swift mental note to behave. He said to me, "I heard on the news that he slashed his wrists."

"That's right."

"Too bad. I can't say I liked the son of a bitch, but he was good at his job. I like Mary, though, and she sure as hell doesn't deserve this shit. And to be perfectly blunt, I'm having difficulty believing he did everything they're saying."

I looked somewhat astonished, because it is not in the nature of professional diplomats to blurt out exactly what they're thinking. It makes their toes curl or something. I asked, "Why's that, Mr. Ambassador?"

He waved his long gangly arms around the air. "Oh hell, I've been doing Soviet or Russian affairs for thirty years. Always the same damn thing . . . they catch one of these guys, then blame everything from Sputnik to nuclear plants in Iran on them."

"You think they've exaggerated it?"

"No, I don't *think* that. I *know* that."

Katrina gave him a discerning look. "And how could you *know* that?"

"You two heard all the shit they're putting on his doorstep?"

"We don't expect to get the full monty until the prosecutor calls to offer a deal," I admitted.

He chuckled. "Sometimes we're worse than the damned Soviets used to be with their show trials. There's just things he couldn't possibly have done. He just couldn't."

We sat and stared at each other, us hoping he'd say something more enlightening, which he didn't. Instead, he bent forward, and that menacing expression slammed back into place. "Now, in case you haven't heard, we've got FBI and CIA people climbing all over our asses. I'm going to tell you the same thing I told them. I have an embassy to run. The mostly good people who work in this building are trying to manage the highly delicate relations between two countries that have over twenty thousand nuclear warheads. This is still the one relationship in the world that can obliterate the earth. And we need Russia's help with this counter-terrorism thing, too. Our work takes precedence over everything. Don't get in our way. Don't cause us problems. Misbehave or abuse our generosity and I'll slap your asses on an airplane so fast you'll wonder if you were ever here. Clear?"

How could it not be clear? I nodded politely while Katrina stared demurely at the floor. We made a lovely couple.

He continued: "That young captain's got an embassy car and he's been told to take you anyplace you need to go. There's a reason for my generosity. Be careful in this town. It's run by mobsters, there's Chechen bombs going off sporadically, and you can get fleeced faster than in Times Square in its heyday. Any questions?"

You know those stories you sometimes hear about those effete, limp-wristed State Department types who sip tea with a pinkie lifted and speak in polished riddles? Mr. Riser must have been sick for that day of training.

I replied, "You've made everything abundantly clear."

He chuckled at that, too. "Good. Get out of here and do what you have to do. And remember, don't abuse our hospitality."

Mel awaited us in the anteroom. He looked surprisingly cheery and said, "Hey, did you hear the latest thing the general did?"

I said, "No, I, uh, I tried to get the TV in my hotel room to work, but, uh, it was stuck on some channel."

I was of course looking at Katrina as I reported this, hoping to restore my reputation.

"They're saying that when he was on the NSC staff and reports would come in on what the Russians were up to, he would modify them and sometimes even add pure distortions to mislead the President."

I shook my head. "No kidding? That's what they're saying?"

"That's the latest," Torianski confirmed, leading us back down the hall to the elevators. "Well, what's next?" he asked, looking at Katrina instead of me, which frankly showed healthy instincts. She was much more invigorating to look at.

I told him, "We want to meet the head of that big investigating team you mentioned."

There was a choking sound, and his eyes nervously darted around. "Mr. Jackler? You're sure?"

"Would I have asked if I wasn't?"

He took us into the elevator, pushed a button, and we were off. The doors opened on the seventh floor, and just as in Eddie's building, two armed guards were standing straight in front of us. They didn't have Uzis pointed at our chests, although otherwise the place had the earmarks of an Eddie Golden extravaganza. The whole floor reeked of lethal determination and obnoxious self-importance.

The guard on the left muttered, "What do you want?"

I replied, "We're Morrison's attorneys. We want to talk to Jackler, the guy in charge of your show."

He walked off and left us in the company of the other guard, who was staring curiously at Katrina—not curiously like she was a suspect; curiously, like what was she doing that night, and, uh, maybe she'd like to see what it was like to do the salami dance with a real man. Maybe I should have told him what she does to guys she catches cheating.

The other guy returned a minute later and led us around a few corners to a small office at the back of the building. Mel, like the courageous lion of lore, let Katrina and me go in and then stopped at the doorway, like, Hey, I'm with these two, but not really *with* them.

Jackler, the man behind the desk, made no effort to get up. He looked to be about fifty, and in terrific shape for his age—or any other age, for that matter. He had a crew cut and a nose that had been broken with extreme prejudice, as they say in the trade, and looked incredibly like Sergeant Joe Friday, if you added fifty pounds of hard muscle, a misshapen snout, and made his personality even less scintillating. It was a great face for an inquisitor.

He didn't invite us to sit down in the chairs in front of his desk, but stared at them, willing us to sit. So we did.

His chilling eyes examined me. "You're Drummond, right?"

"I'm afraid so. And this is my co-counsel, Katrina Mazorski."

He did this funny thing with his face that was akin to a nod, only without moving his head. It was a gesture every aspiring badass really should master, and I tried to do something with my face, too, only it made my earlobes itch, so I don't think it created the impression I wanted.

"You asked for this meeting," he said in a severely icy tone.

"Right. No doubt we'll be interviewing the same people, and I don't want to get anything confused."

"I knew you were coming," he informed me.

"I'm sure you did. A guy like you probably knows everything."

He was looking at me quizzically. "What the fuck's that supposed to mean?"

It was probably best not to answer that, so instead I asked, "Who do you report to? The Agency or the prosecutor's office?"

"We run everything through Golden first, then he decides what goes forward. Why's that? He a buddy of yours?"

"Oh yeah. Like this," I said, twisting two fingers together. "Of course we ended up on different sides this time."

This earned a big guffaw. "Yeah, and he's really gonna kick your butt, too."

"Well, yeah," I chuckled. "Except the other guy

should take some of the heat off my client."

"What are you talkin' about?"

"What? You're kidding, right? Eddie hasn't told you what we've got?"

"He hasn't told me shit. With him it's always take, take, take."

"I know, I know," I said, shaking my head in commiseration. "I mean, I love him like a brother, but the boy's got a few kinks and flaws. You might find this hard to believe, but some JAG guys think he's a real prick."

"Do tell," he said very impatiently. "What's this shit about this other guy?"

I winked at him. "Why do you think we flew all this way? We get the name and we trade it to Eddie for a *big* sentence reduction. A few more small details to wrap up, and then, badda-bing, the big press conference."

"Aw, you're shittin' me."

Katrina suddenly bent forward with a puzzled expression. "I'm sorry, I'm a private citizen. Don't you government people . . . well, don't you share these things?"

I stared at her, because I hadn't really expected any help. He, of course, was staring even harder. He said, "You mean, you're not jackin' me off?"

I said, "Look, it's the unwritten code of the JAG Corps—never surprise each other. We're not cannibals, right? Make one or two guys look bad, and pretty soon everybody's making everybody look bad. Eddie keeps me clued in on the big stuff, and I return the favor."

He was shaking his head like this really sucked.

"That son of a bitch. He sends me all the way over here and never tells me about this other asshole."

"Well, that's shocking," I said.

He scratched his stubby butchcut. "See if I got this straight. You and Golden already know about this accomplice?"

"Right . . . here in the embassy . . . under our very noses. We don't know exactly who yet, but we have a few leads. But hell, don't worry about it. In a few days, you'll learn all about it at our press conference."

FBI and CIA people really, really hate it when outsiders discover their moles and turncoats. Guys like Jackler get early retirement. He asked, "So there's another friggin' traitor here in the embassy?"

"It would seem that way," I assured him, trying to look regretful, while Katrina tried to mimic my expression.

He pondered his desktop, his jaws bunching and unbunching, and said, "Listen, you find anything, I mean anything, you let me know right away, okay?"

"Sure." I asked, "And you'll return the favor, right?"

"Uh, yeah, sure, of course," he said, "whatever we get, you get."

Of course we would. Anyway, I replied, "Jesus, you *are* a good sport. And Eddie said you were a royal bastard. He said I should just tell him when I found the accomplice. But I don't . . . I mean, sure, I might be Morrison's attorney, but we're all on the same team, aren't we?"

"Yeah, yeah, same team," Jackler replied. His hands were fidgeting. He apparently couldn't wait till we got our tushes out of his office so he could rush out and strap down some of these embassy nerds on the rack.

"Well, listen," I said, "time to get back to work. I mean, the sooner *I* find this accomplice, the sooner we get our deal."

"Yeah, right," he said, standing up and literally shooing us out.

Katrina kept mum till Torianski dropped us off back at the hotel, although the second our elevator door closed, she said, "Am I missing something here?"

"You mean that thing with Jackler?"

"Don't give me that innocent shit. Silly of me, but I like to know what I'm getting into."

"Quite simply, we're sowing dissension in the enemy's ranks."

"And this is a smart thing to do?"

"Very smart. So far these guys have had it all their way. They've been working for months on this case, and they're going to keep us in the dark as long as possible, right?"

"So it would seem."

"But the thing with government agencies is, they're relentlessly competitive, competing for budget dollars, for better reputations, for—hell I don't know. But Eddie's got this gigantic task force made up of agencies that privately distrust one another, so we sow a few seeds of discord and Eddie's job gets a little harder."

"If the taxpayers only knew."

"And another thing. That ambassador—if I ever met a guy who meant every word, it's him. So Jackler and his goons turn up the heat on his embassy people, and pretty soon they're at each other's throats."

"How's that a good idea?"

"It might not be. It'll be fun to watch, though."

We went to my room, where she walked to the refrigerator and pulled out two beers, tossed me one, and popped the other.

"Miller time," she said, then examined the label. "Well, Moscva Piva time." She sipped and studied me in her strange way. "This is why I became a lawyer. I'm having a great time."

"You think this is fun?"

"Fun? I said I'm having a great time."

I sipped from my can, too, and it tasted awful, like dirty water. I also thought I detected a faint trace of urine. Of course, I'd never drunk urine, so surely I was mistaken.

I said, "What's behind this metamorphosis thing?"

"I'm an adaptable person. New city, new look."

She sipped again, and the thought struck me that few sights are more seductive than a woman in buttoned-down business attire swilling beer from a can. Women of contrasts can be a very powerful turn-on. Of course, a naked woman chugging suds can be fairly seductive, too—assuming it's the right kind of beer.

But then, Katrina and I were business associates. We consummate professionals don't look at each other in naughty ways. The trick, in case you're wondering, is to compartmentalize—clean thoughts go into a frontal lobe compartment; naughty thoughts get squeezed into the back.

In fact, I was preoccupied at that moment with

weighty concerns about nuclear proliferation and global warming. "Come on," I asked. "What's with the makeover?"

She leaned against the wardrobe that served for a closet in this fleabag. "I took this job because I thought it would be a lark."

"A lark?"

"Spies, espionage, the military angle—that's heady stuff . . . very intriguing."

"Okay."

"I've moved past the intrigued stage."

"Which puts you where?"

"This is a very important case. You realize that, don't you?"

"That's what everybody keeps saying."

"And I keep asking myself, what if Morrison didn't do it?"

"Yes, but probably he did. Inconvenient, I know, but that's how it looks."

She shrugged. "But what if he didn't? Wouldn't that be mind-blowing?"

"If turtles could fly, there'd be turtle crap all over your car roof. But we're losing the thread on your transformation."

"I'm getting to it."

"Slowly," I couldn't help noting.

"I've entered a paradigm shift."

"A new kind of karma?" I suggested.

"Up yours." She sipped her beer. "The way I dress works for me. Walk into the Fourteenth Street precinct after midnight dressed like a legal tightass and see where it gets you."

"Harmful for business, huh?"

"People from the street don't see thousand-dollar suits in a friendly way. Some of the best-dressed street lawyers are the hungriest."

"Uh-huh."

"But yours is a more tight-assed world. I didn't care for a while. Actually, I got a kick out of the reactions. I'm now committed, though. I don't want to be a detraction for our client."

"Well, I'm happy with your new look. It wears well on you."

"Happy my ass. You're relieved."

"A matter of semantics. Could I have another beer? Maybe the second one starts to taste better."

She put down her beer and studied me. "What if he is innocent?"

"Innocent or too hard to convict?"

"Innocent."

"You're getting too theoretical. I'll settle for making it too hard to convict him."

She polished off her can, crumpled it, then tossed it in the wastepaper basket. "I'm going to take a nap. Feel free to watch that dirty movie again. Just keep the sound down."

I was sputtering something as the door closed.

The moment she left I called Imelda back in Washington. I updated her on our progress, which was a brief report, obviously, then asked, "How's it going on your end?"

"Makin' headway," she replied in her typically

cryptic manner. Had she been the more verbal type, she would no doubt have said that all the boxes were unpacked already and she was busily digging through the files.

I asked, "Anything interesting turn up yet?"

"Nothin'. There's a bunch of things written in Russian, and since you two over there, I asked a friend in the Pentagon to get 'em translated."

"Good thinking."

"Golden's office been callin' nearly every hour. He wants a meeting. Wants it quick, too."

Obviously, the sand had run out in the hourglass. I told Imelda to stall him, promised to check in soon, and then hung up. Eddie's Chinese water torture was finally wrapping up. The game of public releases and dribbled evidence was nearly over, which was a relief, in a back-handed sort of way—unless I came back from Moscow empty-handed, in which case the relief was going to give way to sheer panic.

CHAPTER SEVENTEEN

I HAD set my alarm for 4:00 A.M. and as soon as it went off I leaped out of bed and dressed in jeans, a T-shirt, and a warm jacket. I rushed down to the lobby and outside to the Kierskaya station, the subway stop three blocks down. Unlike in American stations, there were no escalators, just long, dark, spooky stairs that carry you deep underground. The entrance to hell probably looks something like this.

In fact, Moscow's subways were once considered

among the world's greatest architectural achievements. There has to be something Freudian about how Stalin decided that of all things to compete in, it would be subways. While nearly everything the Communists constructed above ground is drably ugly, Moscow's subway stations are massive caverns filled with fabulous wall carvings and statues strewn here and about so you could swear you were in some surreal art gallery instead of an underground train station. Of course, you have to be deeply into Communist relics to really revel in it.

I strolled past two or three statues till I found one of a striking Amazon with a scarf on her head wielding a scythe, carved, I suppose, to display what a properly virtuous Soviet woman should look like. I could see immediately why the Soviet birthrate had dropped so precipitously.

I peeked around to be sure nobody was looking, then pulled out a piece of chalk and made three two-inch stripes on the marble base, right beside her left foot. I swiftly wandered back down the tunnel and upstairs. I had forty minutes to kill, and therefore wandered the streets and observed the local fauna.

What Moscow's local fauna consists of is herds of wretchedly poor and homeless people. It was cold as hell, and still they were everywhere, huddled in doorways, standing around subway entrances, stomping their feet to keep their blood flowing, and trying to peddle everything you can imagine, from scrawny-looking sausages to used combat boots to dented-up skillets and frying pans. A fair number were old women, mostly though, they were veterans, and most of those were missing arms or legs.

I couldn't imagine what it must feel like to give a limb in Afghanistan or Chechnya and come home to this kind of bitter welcome. The state can no longer afford to pay your disability, or what payments it makes can barely buy a pair of socks, and you're reduced to spending the rest of your life on freezing street corners, hoping passersby will take pity on the legless guy in the raggedy old army dress coat with his hand held out. Crashed empires leave ugly wreckage.

I meandered up to an outdoor magazine and cigarette stall two blocks down from the subway stop, where I stared at the selection of reading materials, which wasn't all that stimulating because they were all in Cyrillic letters. Finally the guy I was waiting for walked over and began perusing the rack. I recognized him from his photo.

I sidled up next to him and mumbled, "Bill says hi."

He ignored me.

"Okay, how's this? Three coins in the fountain? No, no, that's all wrong . . . abracadabra? No, crap, that's not it, either . . . April showers bring May flowers?"

He was grinning as though I was really very funny. Well, I am very funny. Sometimes. But without saying anything he wandered away, and unsure of what else to do, I followed. He walked down the street and into a small bakery, got into line, and ordered something, while I stood inside the doorway and awkwardly wondered what to do next. Well, the smart thing would be to flee back to my hotel and forget my crazy scheme, but I had already crossed the Rubicon, so to speak, and had to see this through.

He accepted two cups of coffee and two rolls, and then walked over to a table and I took the hint.

Alexi Arbatov smiled when I got to the table and asked, "How is my very good friend Bill?"

"Not a happy guy. Miserable actually."

"Yes, I hear this. I am most sorry. Bill is my good friend."

He spoke passable English, but like most Russians, mangled the verb tenses and was clueless about articles. And his "v" came out like a "w," and so on.

I accepted a coffee and said, "Yeah, well, he's accused of spying, and you know how governments are. A lousy sense of humor when it comes to those things."

He sipped from his coffee and studied me. I studied him right back and noted that, up close, his face looked strikingly different from his photos. It wasn't just a pleasant face, it was the kind Italian artists carved on angels. The features I recognized, but there was a freshness to his skin and a crystalline clarity to his eyes that made you think there couldn't possibly be anything guileful or conniving behind that façade. It was the kind of face every con man got down on his knees and prayed to God for.

He said, "You are Drummond, yes? You are lawyer for Bill, yes?"

"Why would you think that?" I asked, trying to hide my surprise.

"Please, this is my business. You are Army JAG

officer, yes?"

I recognized this as the smarmy parlor trick it was: The great spymaster showing off the mastery of his trade, letting you know he's got your condom size and brand. Notwithstanding that, I was dismayed and off-balance. I had intended to identify myself as a government investigator named Harry Smith and stupidly thought I could get away with it.

Since there was obviously no point in denying it, I nodded and said, "Bill sent me to ask a few questions."

"What I can do to help, I will. Bill is my friend."

"Actually there is something you can do. He wants to know why you set him up," I said, launching straight for the jugular.

"Certainly Bill did not send you to ask this question?"

"Well, certainly he did," I lied.

As his lawyer, I was allowed to lie on his behalf. The real reason I came to Moscow was to meet Arbatov. Pretty clever, huh? If Morrison was guilty, he didn't seem inclined to confess it, and even if he wasn't, the one guy who'd know for sure was seated across from me. I intended to smoke the truth out of him, to put Alexi Arbatov on trial.

And along that line, I said, "Don't bullshit me, Arbatov. He's facing the death sentence. The prosecutor can barely move his lips fast enough to leak all the charges they're bringing against him. Want to hear how I've got it figured?"

This was a moment when he should have been jumpy or evasive, but he calmly replied, "Yes, please to tell me how you have this figured."

"Sometime back in '88 or '89, you and your boss, Yurichenko, found out about this young American couple who were burning up the American intelligence community. One was an Army officer who, with a little outside help, could rise through the system and end up a very high-ranking officer. Given credit for recruiting you, he'd have more clout than anybody ever dreamed. He'd become the Teflon man. They'd have to keep nudging him forward because after all, he's the only conduit to you."

He sipped from his coffee and munched on his roll, not saying a word, not gesturing, not responding in any way.

I continued, "This young officer's the perfect catch— smart and handsome and competent, but also vain and unusually ambitious, and that makes him vulnerable. So he visits Georgia, and suddenly he's got these KGB goons strong-arming him and coincidentally, you show up. You save him, and he thinks he recruits you, or halfway recruits you, and then you begin helping him rise through the ranks."

He took another sip of coffee to wash down some roll, and then said, "This is what you call Manchurian Candidate operation, yes?"

"Whatever. Next, you bring Mary into it and turn them into the indispensable couple. Having you as their trophy makes them indebted to you. Morrison trusts you. He tells you things. He thinks he owns you, but you own him."

"Very good, but in what way does Mary fit into this?"

"An unwitting dupe. She meets with you when he's not available. She keeps him informed. She comes back from meeting with you, climbs into bed with her husband, and they chatter about you before they roll off to sleep. Sometimes you probably use her to pass coded instructions or signals. Right?"

He shrugged, and then asked, "And how does Bill come to get caught?"

"I haven't figured out that part yet. Maybe somebody in Moscow told on him . . . maybe you fed his name to the CIA."

"And for what reason I would do this? He was valuable to Russia, yes?"

"You tell me," I said, searching his face for involuntary clues, which, so far, were nonexistent. "Maybe he got greedy and asked for things you weren't willing to give him. Maybe you got tired of him, or maybe he realized you were exploiting him and got pissed."

He nodded as though these were all reasonable options. "And how does Bill pass all these wonderful things they are saying he gives to me?"

"I haven't figured out that piece, either."

"No?"

"Not yet. The problem is the government's blasting him with a shotgun, and probably a few of those pellets are bull's-eyes, but the rest are stray shots, things they suspect him of giving, or things somebody else gave that they're blaming on Morrison . . . I don't know. But you snookered him into giving a few things, and now he's facing the hangman's noose."

He put down his coffee cup and brushed some

crumbs off the tabletop. "Major, I am disappointed in very big way. Have you experience in espionage?"

"I seem to have missed that class at law school."

He laced his hands into a steeple and poised his forefingers against his lower lip. "We do not expose our agents this way. To turn him in would be to lose everything, yes? Your CIA will ask what could Bill possibly betray and erase all damage. This is not our way. If Bill was target for disposal, an unfortunate accident would be arranged."

It had become my turn to sip from my coffee and try to act aloof. "So why didn't you just do that?"

"Problem two," he continued, as though I hadn't said anything, as though this were his inquisition. "I have big reasons to protect Bill. How I would betray him? He would betray me back, yes? You understand—I would be dead."

Well, yes, I thought, which could very well account for why Morrison told Katrina and me about him. Maybe that's exactly what Morrison was trying to accomplish. But then I had another thought.

I said, "He was your dupe and Yurichenko knows that. If your name gets dragged into this, you're no longer a hidden hero, you're a public hero. Maybe you thought it was time for everybody to learn how very clever you are, how you turned an American general officer."

"Major, Mary was Moscow station chief, and Bill was to become two-star general. Both were becoming more important. I would choose this moment to make their house burn down . . . how would my bosses perceive this, hmm?"

I couldn't think of any good counters to that—which didn't mean there wasn't one, or even hundreds of possible reasons. Everything about this case gave me a headache. These people were all spies and counterspies and whatever, and this was their devious little game of duplicities and counter-duplicities. I, on the other hand, was a novice, with only the vaguest notion of what Morrison was accused of, and even those ideas were wildly suspect and probably exaggerated.

I took a wild stab anyway. "Maybe Morrison was dealing with somebody else in your organization, too? Or maybe somebody in your SVR learned about him, was jealous of you and your relationship with your boss, and burned him to make you look bad."

"Then I would be already dead. And why would anybody who learns of Bill burn him? They would"—he paused to search for the right word—"poach?" I nodded that I approved, and he continued, "This is not uncommon in our trade. Is known to happen. But to burn an invaluable resource for reason of jealousy? No, I think not."

I stared into my coffee and contemplated the realization that I might be over my head here. True to his CIA profile, Alexi Arbatov was frighteningly smart and persuasive.

Foolishly revealing my frustration, I said, "Okay, what do you think happened? Why did a bunch of tough guys show up at the embassy and bag Morrison? The U.S. government doesn't move on traitors without a truckload of evidence."

"I am asking myself this same question. Bill has my fate in his hands. If I am to become compromised, it is a most ugly fate."

"So you keep saying."

He half-chuckled. "Any day now, this could be proved. I see your three chalk stripes on the statue this morning and I am thinking my game is already up."

"Explain that."

"Only Bill and I share this signal. I was expecting entrapment."

I pondered this dilemma until he said, "But you are intriguing to me. You are only American person who tries to prove he is innocent. Everybody else says he is guilty."

"So you're saying what . . . you and I are allies?"

"Perhaps. But there is problem. I have most serious reservations concerning you."

"Like what?"

"You do not talk like he is innocent. But bigger problem is you are not trained in this game we play."

"I know what I'm doing."

He shook his head. "Please not to take offense. This morning, you make your three marks, then you go stand at meeting place like dumb duck in shooting gallery. What if I am discovered and instead of me was SVR counterespionage team coming to arrest you? What if I am really controller for Bill . . . maybe I would just kill you."

I rubbed my chin and tried to look smarter than I was. He made this a bit difficult as he continued his spycraft for idiots tutorial. "This is not how trained agents do these things. We act like dogs, yes? We mark trees, and then find vantage to watch. Bill and I choose that kiosk for our meetings because of big hotel next door. Bill always comes to meetings dressed as Russian citizen, not like L.L. Bean American. Bill uses false name to check into upper-level room, and watches to know I am alone. He does not come out until I walk into bakery. If I do not go into this bakery, is signal I am being observed, and we are in trap. Bill would then be on next flight to America."

"Okay, so I'm not a professional spy. What's your point?"

"You are posing quandary to me."

"Go on."

"You know about me. You are well-intended, I think, but dangerous."

Physical features aside, Alexi Arbatov had a certain earnestness of manner that made you want to agree with him. I found myself nodding, and then thinking he was right because . . . well, okay, yes, because he *was* right.

Time for a mental slap there, Drummond. For one thing, he was rejecting my qualifications before I even agreed to work with him, which poses something of a cart and horse problem. For a second thing, I didn't trust him. Okay, he had an alibi or counter for everything, but he was a boy genius in a profession that breeds the world's biggest backstabbing liars, *and* wasn't this how my client began his relationship with this guy? Buy into his line of crap and look where it gets you.

On the other hand, I had come all this way to get a firsthand look at Alexi Arbatov, and, well, what now?

Before I could answer that question, however, Arbatov took the choice out of my hands. He stood, neatly collected our coffee cups and napkins, and like a good citizen carried them over to a trash receptacle.

He next sauntered to the counter, where a chubby babushka was filling somebody else's order. He yelled something in Russian, and she looked up, chortled, and said something back. They both laughed. I didn't understand a word, but got the general gist. He was complimenting her on the coffee and roll, and she was responding like a thirteen-year-old who just got her hair stroked by the Backstreet Boys.

I was oddly impressed. One wouldn't expect a bloodthirsty, conniving spymaster to be so convivial toward the hired help. On the other hand, these guys are good. They know it's the little things that lend legitimacy to their biggest shams.

I caught up with him by the doorway and frantically whispered, "So what's next?"

He ignored me, walked out, and got about ten steps before he looked back. "Nothing is to be next. Goodbye."

He disappeared into the crowd, obviously having made up his mind. I could scrape all the chalk stripes on that statue I wanted; I would never see him again.

CHAPTER EIGHTEEN

OVER breakfast, Katrina filled me in on the latest revelation released by Eddie. He had turned up the heat again—or, perhaps torched up would be more apropos. In addition to everything else, Morrison was now accused of giving the Russians copies of the President's and Secretary of State's briefing papers and talking points in advance of every U.S.-Russian summit and meeting.

This whopping revelation had really set the Beltway back on its heels. It's one thing to give the Russians technical secrets, or to betray their betrayers, or even to pervert the American decision-making process. It's another thing altogether to provide the President's and Secretary of State's scripts to the Russians in advance of all their meetings. Consider some of the guys and gals who work in those offices, who frankly are glued to those scripts like coma patients connected to life-support systems.

Katrina said the newspapers and news channels were filled with outrage, innuendos, and theories regarding the release. Devise all the silly theories you want, the average schmo on the street had the bubble. No President or Secretary of State had talked to the Russians anytime lately where the Russians didn't know exactly what he was going to mutter in advance, exactly how far he was willing to go, how much was bluff and how much bluster. As diplomatic catastrophes go, it would be hard to imagine worse. The Russians had been inside the minds of our national leaders for years.

Eddie had to be delighted by his latest little release, and it did not escape notice that he was finding ways to get his name on the front page almost every single day. Katrina reported that the latest copy of *People* magazine was in the hotel lobby, and Eddie's gorgeous mug graced the cover. I nearly blew chunks all over my limp bacon and undercooked eggs. Clapper had to be delighted. His beloved tarantula was becoming the poster boy of the JAG Corps.

At nine o'clock, Mel arrived in a black embassy car to take us to the embassy. I climbed into the front and Katrina got in the back. Mel immediately made a few gleeful wisecracks about the latest revelations, taking sadistic joy in the continuing humiliation of his former boss. The man must've been a real bastard to work for.

Mel had just pulled off the main highway and turned down a side street, when all of a sudden a big truck careened out of an alley and blocked our way. He jammed on the brakes and nearly threw Katrina and me through the windshield—followed by a very quiet moment while we sat and stared at the truck. It wasn't moving.

I spun around just in time to see three men climbing out of a car at the end of the street we'd just come down. They were dressed in suits, which somehow looked outrageously incongruous, because they were all holding Kalashnikov rifles in their hands, sort of casually adjusting their stances, the way golfers prepare to tee off.

I shoved Katrina's head down and yelled, "On the floor!"

Mel spun around and saw what I was looking at. He froze.

I screamed, "Weapons? Do you have any weapons?"

He was just starting to reach across me when the first rounds came spraying through the rear windshield. I was splattered with glass and blood as Mel's head appeared to explode and his body flopped over and landed in my lap.

I instinctively shoved him off and dove for the floor as bullets pelted against the car. That's when I saw what Mel had lunged for—an M16 rifle strapped to the underside of the passenger seat, two metal clips holding it in place. I quickly undid them and yanked the M16 to my body, straining to pull back the charging handle and unlock the safety, ordinarily simple things to accomplish, except when your body's all scrunched up and keeps involuntarily flinching from the sounds of bullets striking around you.

Two possibilities struck me—I could stay in the car, pray no bullets hit me, and wait till the shooters walked in our direction to perform the coup de grâce. Or I could try to get out of the car and pray nobody shot me. Staying in the car posed one problem. Sometimes, bullets cause a fuel ignition and you get one of those Hollywood moments that just mess up your plans for the evening.

Option two had drawbacks also. If I threw open my passenger door and simply rushed out, the three shooters would nail me. They were maybe forty yards away. They couldn't miss. I yelled, "Katrina!" and through the sound of loud bangs I heard her say, "Yes."

"Open your door. And stay inside."

"Okay!" she yelled.

I gave her a two-second head start before I threw open my door. Her door was on the other side of the car, and the second it opened, it became a bullet magnet as the three shooters tried to hit whoever rolled out. I leaped out my side, and as soon as I hit the ground I scrambled for the front of the car. I could feel chips of concrete striking my legs, but I made it.

I got on my belly and scooted until I could peek around a tire. The shooters still stood casually out in the open, unaware I had a weapon, believing they were invulnerable. One was calmly changing magazines while the other two nonchalantly plunked away at our car.

The obvious choice was to take out the two who were firing. I pushed the semiautomatic selector on the M16, stuck it around the corner, took quick aim, and swept it across the two shooters. The first folded over like he suddenly got a bad bellyache, while the second was flung backward and landed on the concrete.

The guy reloading scurried behind his car—I fired two shots, but missed. At least I think I missed, although I saw no movement and there was no firing. I had expended about ten rounds, and the M16 had a twenty-round magazine, so I had maybe ten bullets left. Harassing fire wasn't an option.

I aimed my weapon in his direction and yelled, "Katrina, get out of the car!"

I hoped she was still alive to hear me. Five or so seconds passed and there was nothing, no sound from her, no movement.

Then I saw her land on the cement and scramble in my direction. At nearly the same instant, I saw the Russian pop over the top of his car, and I fired a quick burst. I had no idea whether I hit him. I was too fixated on the little round cylinder he'd thrown that was sailing in our direction.

I jumped up, tackled Katrina, and ended up on top of her. Then came the explosion. The thing about being in a narrow street is that sound does not escape. A loud boom sends its first shock wave into your eardrums, followed by an almost instantaneous aftershock from ricocheted waves.

My ears were ringing as I rolled off Katrina. She had her hands over her ears, and her elbows and knees were bloody from the effects of my tackle. Something in my left leg stung as I got up and dragged her to the front of the car.

I sat and tried to appraise our situation. The smell of cordite was heavy in the air, and there was a fair amount of smoke, but all I could hear was a loud ringing. I looked over at Katrina, and her lips were moving, but I couldn't hear a word.

What next? Check to see if the last shooter was dead? Wait right there and hope he didn't have another hand grenade and better aim?

After all the noise and racket, surely the Moscow police had to be on the way. Katrina was staring down at my leg and pointing at a spot below my knee. When

I pulled up my trouser leg, blood was pumping out in tiny spurts, an indication a significant vein had been punctured. She slapped a palm over the wound and tried to stem the flow.

She began tugging on her dress sleeve, trying to rip it, until I finally reached over and gave her a hand. I yanked too hard, because I nearly tore off the whole top of her blouse.

She tied the cloth around my leg. Three or four minutes had passed, and while I was still too deaf to hear any sirens, no police had shown up yet. I worked my way around the side of the car and ducked in long enough to drag out Mel's body. I tugged his corpse around to the front of the car, flipped him over, and found his cell phone. I didn't know the number to the embassy, but it was one of those fancy Motorola models where you push a few buttons on the side and pretty soon his favorite numbers pop onto the screen.

I handed it to Katrina. "Call the embassy."

Or that's what I think I said. It might've been "order a pizza" for all I know, because it's damned hard to speak when you can't hear your own voice. She studied the screen and punched in some numbers, and I could see her lips moving, so she was obviously talking to somebody.

We waited some more. I was fuming. I couldn't believe that in a major metropolitan area like Moscow, the police wouldn't be alerted to a major firefight right in the middle of the town and wouldn't respond right away. Russian inefficiency has to have its limits, right?

Perhaps another three minutes passed before the first

police car arrived. The dicey part was the moment the first two cops came around the side of the shooter's car with pistols in their hands. I could see Katrina's lips moving, and I presumed she was yelling something in Russian, like, "Hey, we're the good guys, so please don't shoot."

They didn't shoot. That, however, was the limit to their kindness. They kicked the M16 out of my hands. Katrina started to stand up, but one of the cops quickly flung her against the car, and before I could do anything, the other cop grabbed me by my shirtfront, lifted me off my feet, and threw me against the car, too. They roughly patted us down, and then had our arms trapped behind our backs as they slapped handcuffs around our wrists.

More cops arrived—lots more cops—and people streaming out of their apartments, coming to investigate the aftermath of the street battle. I watched them walking around, surveying the damage, and then Katrina was jammed into the back of one police car, as I was roughly shoehorned into another. Some three minutes later, my car screeched to a halt in front of a police station that looked like something out of any ordinary American slum.

I was shoved and dragged inside and led to a dirty room in the back, where I was literally tossed into a chair. I still couldn't hear a sound and my eardrums ached, which was really inconvenient, as I couldn't massage them. Funny, the little things that bother you in the worst nightmares.

A few minutes later, two guys wearing civilian suits

came in. They stood and studied me like I was an interesting new specimen brought to their laboratory for dissection. If this were America, I'd be doing the big lawyer war dance, threatening them with police brutality charges and just generally making a horse's ass out of myself.

I bit my tongue. It's always dangerous to put your mouth in gear when you can't even hear what you're saying, not to mention we were in a foreign land where lawyers are perhaps not as warmly loved and admired as they are in America.

One of them tried saying something, and I thought I heard a bit of noise. I shook my head to let them know I didn't understand—a doubly ambiguous signal, as they were probably speaking Russian, which I couldn't comprehend anyway, so how the hell did I expect them to realize I was deaf?

The guy kept talking, and I kept shrugging my shoulders and making silly faces. I suppose to any outside observer the whole scene looked nothing short of comical.

Then the door burst open behind them and in walked two more guys in suits. The two detectives stiffened, an indication that the new visitors were important men. They yammered back and forth very briefly, before a detective walked around behind me and unlocked my cuffs. I instantly reached up and massaged my ears, which was what you'd call a really happy moment.

The door opened again and in walked Ambassador Allan D. Riser and an aide. I guessed they'd uncuffed me before he arrived so it wouldn't look like they'd mistreated me.

Riser had an appropriately concerned look on his face, and he said something to me, to which I intelligently replied, "I'm deaf."

He nodded, then said something to the detectives. I was then led out of the room, placed in the back of another police car, and then driven straight to a Russian hospital. I was led into a cramped, messy operating room and plunked down on a steel gurney.

The hospital was filthy and run-down and lacked that antiseptic smell that lets you know that germs aren't welcome there. Soon a harried-looking doctor and two remarkably hefty nurses came roiling in. The nurses laid me out on the gurney and then the doctor began cleaning my leg, spilling a clear liquid on the wound, then roughly wiping it off with a white rag. He pulled out something that looked like calipers and began digging around inside my leg, apparently searching for the piece of shrapnel embedded inside.

Did I mention that he failed to administer any kind of painkiller whatsoever? I sure as hell mentioned it to him and the two sorry-ass nurses fighting to hold my leg steady. I begged them to stop and called them the filthiest names you could imagine. The only remotely good part about this was that I could finally hear my own voice. It made no difference, however. The doctor was ferociously pitiless. It took him nearly three minutes of digging brutishly around, another few minutes to stitch it up, and when he was done, tears were streaming down my face and I was sweating like a drafthorse.

They walked out and left me, moaning and shaking and staring at all the blood on the table. Then the door opened and Katrina came in with the two very important-looking guys I'd seen earlier. There were bandages on her knees and elbows, and somebody had given her a shawl to throw over her torn blouse.

She and the two important-looking men were jabbering in Russian, and although it sounded like people talking underwater, I distinctly heard the sounds of their voices.

I said, "Katrina, what are these two assholes doing here?"

She looked over at me. "Bad move, Sean. They speak English."

The two men were also staring at me, without what you'd call friendly expressions. I grinned. "Hi guys."

The suit on the left said, "I am Igor Strodonov, Moscow chief of detectives, and you will meet my assistant, Chief Inspector Felix Azendinski."

This explained why the two detectives back at the station had suddenly stiffened. The Moscow chief of detectives is like the second biggest wig in the whole city police hierarchy. I said, "Nice to meet you."

From his expression that was a one-way sentiment. "Miss Mazorski has informed us of what has happened at the site of the very serious accident."

"You mean ambush."

"Yes, this was so," he said, trying to sound like a master of the English language, which he clearly wasn't. "This is most unfortunate thing. Is great embarrassment for Russian people. The driver captain is dead with bullets in head and American lawyers are injured."

It was impossible to tell whether he was sincere or not. Most cops don't mind at all when defense lawyers get gunned down in the streets. They think it's a charming irony. I asked, "Do you have any idea who the shooters were?"

"All are unfortunately dead."

I personally didn't think it was the least bit unfortunate. "So you don't know?" I persevered.

"We have theory. We are checking out now. They are Chechens, which is not good thing. You understand?"

"No, I don't understand."

"Chechens very bad . . . what? Outlaws, yes? They kill Americans to make protest. Was terrorist thing."

I nodded as if this made sense—actually it made no sense. Not to me. But then I'm no expert on the Russian political scene. I glanced at Katrina, who stood perfectly still, an enigmatic expression on her face.

The chief of detectives said, "You very lucky to live. These Chechens, they kill good."

Leaving us with that thought, he and his assistant departed. Katrina came over and helped me get off the bloody gurney. Having no idea what to do next, she walked and I limped out of the ward, me swearing that if I got so much as a bellyache before I left Moscow, I'd make them fly me out on a medevac plane.

A black sedan with American diplomatic plates was outside, and the driver climbed out as we exited. We climbed in, and I noticed that this guy had his M16 within easy reach on the seat beside him. You can bet he wasn't real damned happy to have us as cargo.

CHAPTER NINETEEN

THE driver, whose name was Harry, had instructions to take us straight to the embassy, which was terrifically inconvenient since Katrina and I needed to get our stories—aka alibi—straight. I insisted he drive to our hotel to let us get cleaned up, and when that didn't work, I gave him the excruciating details about my recent surgery, and he either got sympathetic or bored with listening to me bitch, because he agreed to make one quick stop at the hotel for me to get some aspirin.

As soon as Katrina and I were headed up in the elevator, I urgently said, "Any thoughts?"

She retorted, "Chechens, my ass."

We had come to the same conclusion, although presumably for different reasons, and after a fair amount of hesitation, I said, "I, uh, I've got a confession."

"A confession?"

"I believe that's the right word." I stared straight ahead and said, "I met with Alexi Arbatov this morning."

"You *what?*"

"The last time I saw Morrison, I asked him how he contacted him. It's one of those discreet-marks-in-the-subway things those spies like to dream up and . . . well, anyway, I met with him."

Icicles could hang off the look I was receiving. "I'm sure you had a damned good reason you didn't include me in that decision."

"I, well, I had a reason. I thought it was a good one."

"Tell me that reason."

"I thought the less that went along the better."

"Well, fuck you," she said, which was an appropriate sentiment.

Anyway, we'd reached the doors to our rooms, and I said, "Grab whatever you're going to change into and come over. And be careful, these rooms could be bugged."

She emerged seconds later carrying a clean dress, untorn stockings, and a pissed-off expression. I unlocked my door and she and I went in. I flipped on the TV and again there were the sights and sounds of a girl loudly doing the big nasty. If the room was bugged, whoever was listening on the other end had to be impressed, and was probably at that moment turning to his buddy: "Hey, Igor, check this. That American stud comes back from a gunfight and immediately nails his co-counsel. What an animalinski, huh? And just listen to her moan. Christ, no wonder those bastards won the cold war."

I went to the shrunk and pulled out a fresh uniform, then hooked a finger for her to follow me into the bathroom, where I turned on the shower and got the water flowing in the sink—they do that in the movies, hopefully with good reason.

I stripped down to my underwear and said, "The point is, Arbatov says he's got no idea what happened to Morrison. He claims Morrison wasn't a traitor, and the arrest puts him at great peril."

Katrina was stepping out of her skirt. "That was it?"

"No. He said I'm an amateur and that worried him."

"Did you trust him?" she asked, yanking off her stockings and getting down to her panties and bra. Compartmentalize, I reminded myself—good thoughts to the frontal lobe, naughty thoughts to the rear. By the way, did I mention that she wore a thong?

Not quite tearing my eyes away, I said, "There's something trustworthy about him. Of course, Morrison thought so, too, and look where it got him."

She pulled the new dress over her shoulders. "You think Arbatov was behind the attack?"

"Yes. I didn't think he'd recognize me, but he did. I made a big blunder. I wanted to smoke him out, only I didn't think it through."

She sat down to pull on her stockings. "You put a scare in him? Is that it?"

"Best guess—he showed up to see who had Morrison's meeting signs, discovered it was me, that I knew about him, and he immediately rushed back to the office and arranged my assassination."

"*Our* assassination."

"Right."

She stopped rolling up her stockings and looked up at me. "And now, because of the police report, Arbatov knows about me, too."

"Well, yes, I think so," I admitted.

I mean, this was some poor Washington attorney I'd hired for one-fifty a day, and now I was telling her that as a result of my appalling impulsiveness the number two guy in Russia's notoriously deadly spy apparatus wanted her buried.

You watch all those great Hollywood spy movies and think how cool it is that the hero or heroine can outwit all those assassins and kill the bad guys, and save the world, and then end the movie in bed with the beautiful girl or dashing guy. That's Hollywood for you. Back to the real world, the closing scene would be a bunch of people weeping over a grave, and it wouldn't be the bad guys'.

She contemplated the possibilities and then asked, "You think he'll try again?"

"Probably," I admitted, standing in my underpants. "It won't be so coarse next time . . . a car accident or a plane crash, something that can be explained as simple bad fortune. Like, 'Gosh, those poor bastards; they survive a terrorist attack only to climb aboard a plane that loses an engine and plows into the ground. Talk about crappy luck.'"

"Put your pants on."

"I'm sorry."

"Yes, you are sorry. Put your pants on," she insisted.

"I really am sorry," I persisted.

She looked me dead in the eye. "If I had a gun, I'd shoot you. Put your goddamned pants on."

So I did. "Okay," she said, straightening her dress and adopting a very businesslike expression. "What are we going to tell them at the embassy?"

"We can't tell them about Arbatov."

"No, we can't, can we?" You could tell that her wheels were really starting to crank, because this was no longer just a law case, because now, she was fighting for her life. I threw some cold water on my face and washed down two aspirins. I turned off the shower and the sink, and she followed me out.

We climbed back into the sedan, and I told Harry to stick with major boulevards—no side streets, no alleyways, nothing but the most traffic-clogged arteries he could find. He nodded like, yeah, exactly what he was thinking, too.

We arrived in twenty minutes, and the receptionist at the entrance told us to go straight up to the ambassador's office. His secretary ushered us right in, and there were the ambassador, two guys I didn't know from Adam, and that bone-chilling inquisitor, Mr. Jackler. The two guys I didn't know from Adam made no effort to identify themselves, maybe because they never intended to, or maybe because Riser instantly bellowed, "You two sit right there," pointing at two chairs across from two couches.

As Katrina and I complied, Riser and the others arranged themselves on the couches and faced us like an Admiral's Mast. Riser squirmed around a moment, comfortably arranging his ass while he prepared to grill ours.

"You okay?" he finally asked, looking first at Katrina.

"I'm fine." She stiffly added, "Just a little scraped up."

He looked at me. "And you saw the doctor?"

"Yes sir," I said, "and I can't thank you enough for getting us out of that police station. I really can't. It was really very kind."

He bent forward. "Drummond, don't try sucking

up to me."

"No sir," I lied. "Furthest thing from my mind."

His face was reddening. "I have a dead officer on my hands. I have another American officer and an American citizen involved in a shootout in the capital of Russia. And the worst thing is, I haven't got a goddamn clue why. You see where that puts me in a very foul mood?"

I said, "The police told us it was a Chechen thing, a simple terrorist attack, and we were in the wrong place at the wrong time."

"Bullshit! They always blame these things on Chechens. What were you two up to?"

I bent forward to answer, but Katrina lunged forward faster. "That's the same damn thing I was going to ask you."

"What are you talking about?"

"What am I talking about?" Her voice rose with outrage, and I have to admit I was waiting breathlessly to hear her story as well. "We come here to conduct our investigation and *you* assign us a driver who nearly gets us killed."

Jackler lurched forward in his chair. "This Torianski guy?"

She replied, "That attack was directed at him. That's obvious, isn't it?"

All four men were now regarding her with inquisitive expressions. For their joint benefit, Jackler asked, "Why's it obvious?"

"Mel told us he was sorry he got us into this only a second before he was shot."

"He said he was sorry?" the ambassador asked.

"Didn't I just say that?" Katrina demanded.

All eyes turned to me, and Jackler asked, "That right, Drummond?"

"I remember he said he was sorry. And he mentioned something . . . something . . ." I scratched my head and looked up at the ceiling, trying to recall what he said—that he didn't really say. But that's beside the point.

Katrina said, "About the SVR?"

"Right, that part. Something about SVR bastards."

"He said that?" the ambassador asked.

"Bullets were flying through the window, so I couldn't hear real distinctly. But yeah, SVR bastards, or buzzards, or something. Anyway, Mr. Ambassador, I'm registering an official protest. My associate and I had our lives put at risk by your people."

Riser turned to one of the two men I didn't know from Adam. "Could that be possible?"

The man hunched his shoulders. "We, well, um, we hadn't even considered it. We'll have to comb through everything he was working on to see if it's a possibility."

Riser's face flushed. "Why didn't you already consider it? It's your damned job to consider it. Why do I have to sit in front of these poor people looking like a horse's ass?"

"Uh, sir," said the other unidentified man, "Phil meant we considered it . . . we just ruled it as . . . well, as a lower possibility."

"A lower possibility?"

The unnamed guy looked cunningly at Phil and said,

"Yes sir. Torianski was involved in a few things; we just . . . didn't think they were worth bringing to your attention yet. We wanted to hear Drummond's side first. We're narrowing the possibilities. Now we intend to look more deeply."

"Right," said the guy I didn't know from Adam, whose name turned out to be Phil. "We don't like giving you half-cocked theories. But now that we've ruled out these two," he said, indicating us, "we know exactly where to look."

"At the SVR thing, right?" the still-unidentified guy suggested to Phil, whom I took to be his boss, whose ass he was scurrying to save.

"The SVR thing, right," Phil adamantly replied, looking at the ambassador and nodding his head in our direction. "Which we obviously can't discuss in their presence."

Katrina appeared to be fascinated by the unfolding scene. They should start one of those reality TV shows where you get to watch trained bureaucrats play cover-your-ass.

With an aggrieved scowl, Riser said to us, "I'm very sorry. This is so embarrassing. As you can see, my own staff has been keeping me in the dark."

"It happens, sir," I said, ever the graceful type.

"For Godsakes, just assign us a driver who doesn't get us killed," Katrina insisted.

"Of course." He hastily ushered Jackler and us out of his office, apologizing profusely as we walked out his door.

Out in the hallway, we could hear his voice go off, as

Jackler said, "You two aren't bullshittin', are ya?"

"What? About Torianski?"

"Come on, Drummond. That boy didn't have anything to do with this Morrison thing, did he? He worked for Morrison, right? And you're here looking for an accomplice, and this guy gets whacked."

"You know, I haven't got a clue. I hadn't even thought of it, but it does look suspicious, doesn't it? Christ, I hope not. With him dead it would blow our chances for a deal with Eddie."

He walked away shaking his head, leaving little doubt that he intended to look fully into this matter. It would've been hilarious, except a young Army captain who had struck me as a very decent guy was dead.

Not to mention that Katrina and I were on somebody's hit list.

Not to mention this was Arbatov's turf.

Not to mention it was his game.

And if you add all that together, it was time to book two tickets on the next flight home.

CHAPTER TWENTY

I SWALLOWED three more aspirins and lay down to nap before I organized our flight from Moscow. As both Napoleon and Hitler learned, planning a retreat from Moscow is a tricky affair that takes a clear mind and meticulous preparation. I'd woken up early, been shot at, wounded, and operated on, and was left feeling a bit groggy and foggy. I don't know how long I slept, maybe a few minutes, maybe a few hours, but I awoke to a hand shaking me.

My eyes cracked open, and I found myself staring at the handsome features of Alexi Arbatov. Instinctively, I jerked forward and nailed him in the forehead with a flat-handed punch. He flew backward, and I leaped out of the bed and jumped on him. He put up no fight, just went limp and passive. I flipped him over on his stomach, got one arm wrapped around his jaw and the other against the back of his head. I said, "Move and I'll break your neck." Not too original a line, but suitable for the occasion and, more important, authentic.

"Please . . . let go," he replied, his words choked and strained, because I had rotated his chin nearly forty-five degrees to the right, poised for the quick jerk that would disconnect his skull from his spine.

"Of course . . . I let you go and you whack me." I did, however, let his head rotate slightly back toward its natural position before I accidentally strangled him to death.

He mumbled, "You are being fool. Why did I not kill you when you were sleeping?"

It was a reasonable point—unless he was like one of those old western gunfighters who called their victim before they shot. The common perception is they did that out of some heroic sense of fair play. Wrong—it was the sadistic code of the Old West to let the victim have a miserable moment to contemplate his impending death.

Anyway, I released him from the lock, and he rolled over and sat up and began rotating his head. I stayed coiled, ready to strike. He didn't say anything for a moment, but regarded me through sullen eyes.

He eventually said, "I have gotten report on attack an hour ago. We have big problem."

"True." I added, "But not the same problem. Mine is the number two guy in the SVR wants me dead. Yours seems to be how to murder me without causing the fingers to point back at you."

He scratched an eyebrow. "This is not true."

"No, and Stalin's not dead, either. He and Elvis are hiding out together at some luxurious resort in Mexico, partying their asses off."

He gave me a quizzical look. "Elvis?"

"It's an old . . . oh, forget it." I fell back onto the bed and wondered what this guy's game was.

He insisted, "Major, I did not order this attack, but is big problem for me. I am meeting with you in morning and then you have ambush. Who else knows we have this meeting?"

"My co-counsel. Only I didn't tell her till after the ambush."

"There are others, though, yes? This must be true."

His face *did* look exceedingly apprehensive, and whatever his angle was, I couldn't see it. It didn't mean there wasn't one—only that I couldn't see it. An important distinction, that.

I said, "If it wasn't you, who tried to kill us?"

Straightening his clothes, he replied, "Police say they are Chechens. This is why it comes to my desk. Acts of domestic espionage must be reported to Viktor and me immediately." He paused and then added, "But this is idiotic conclusion. Chechens do not kill Americans."

Truly, his response surprised me. Were he trying to deflect blame, the easiest thing would be to say, "Chechens? Most definitely."

Arbatov walked around and ruminated a bit, then finally stopped and faced me. "Did Bill talk about information I am giving to him?"

"No."

He got a distracted look. "You know *nothing* about plot?"

This was getting surreal, however, I'd seen enough bad spy movies to know exactly how I was expected to respond. So I said, "Plot? What plot?"

"He tells you nothing?" He studied my face to see if I was being truthful.

"No, Arbatov, he never told me about any plot."

He let loose a large sigh and walked over and stared at the curtain. I said, "Look, maybe you should tell me about this plot thing. If you're really at risk, and your fate hinges on my client, maybe you should tell me everything."

I could see his shoulders quake like he was chuckling, and, okay, so I did sound a bit ridiculous.

"Please."

He remained quiet, so I said, "Okay, so this plot is huge and momentous. And I'm not a professional spy, so you can't tell me."

"I am sorry. I trust Bill and Mary. You, I do not know . . . or trust."

"Well, back to square one then." I couldn't resist adding, "And for the record, I don't trust you either, pal."

I climbed off the bed and went to the chair where I'd thrown my uniform and started to get dressed, while he stared at the curtain and mulled his options. He finally spun back around and faced me, shaking his head, but desperation is the mother of all disclosures. He'd come to understand that truthfully and inevitably, he had no other options. The three guys resting in a Moscow morgue had joined us at the hip, a sort of literal version of a shotgun wedding.

Sounding tentative, he said, "The reason I first meet with Bill was to discuss with him about strange things happening in Soviet Union."

I was racing to pull on my pants, since it seemed ridiculous to be standing in my underwear as the deputy head of Russia's spy agency spilled his guts about some earthshaking plot. Surely, moments like this should be more dignified. I said, "Things like what?"

"You are knowledgeable about how the Soviet Union came to be ended?"

"Let me see . . . I think I recall something in the news about it."

He ignored my sarcasm. "You do not wonder how this happens so fast . . . how my seventy-year-old nation explodes?"

"No." I stopped dressing and stared at him. "I figured it was a big, rotten piece of garbage that had no reason to hold together. You build a house on a lousy foundation, sooner or later, it's going to crash down."

"Is too simplistic. Please do not get confused with your moral relativism. Your country expands in same way as Russia does. American armies march westward and conquer Spanish, Mexicans, Indians, Filipinos, Hawaiians. You defeat them, and you absorb them. Russia does this same thing. You have civil war and we have civil war. You have Ku Klux Klan, and negro demonstrations, and Puerto Rican terrorists, and we have separatist splinter groups. Yet, both nations out-live these things, yes?"

"Your point being?" I asked, not completely buying into his analogies, because frankly there was a world of difference. Well, maybe not a world, but enough to be significant.

He continued, "Inside one year, my country explodes into pieces. For seventy years, one government, one philosophy, one currency, then suddenly, one nation becomes fifteen. You see no oddity in this? This was not planned, was nobody thinking ahead about this. Suddenly, many, many millions of people are thrown into decades of deprivation and poverty and insta-bility."

"Had to happen sooner or later. It was a rotten system."

"Major, please, I am not bemoaning loss of Commu-nism. I am not some old apparatchik who misses old glories. I am like scientist, looking for reasons. How can this thing happen so fast? Forget your American prejudices and assumptions."

"Keep going."

"Was made to happen in this way. Impulses are there, yes, but big assistance was given. A glass statue can be frail, but somebody must knock it off table to make it shatter."

"And what? You think we were behind it? Hey, pal, you've been reading too many of the brochures the CIA writes about itself."

"Your CIA cannot do this . . . I know this. Was too vast, too knowing. This had to be an internal thing."

All very interesting; however, it was time to bring the conversation back on track. I asked, "And this has something to do with why you met Morrison?"

"Yes. Viktor Yurichenko, my boss, heard my concerns, and he agrees something is propelling our country toward this cataclysm."

I instantly found myself taking Arbatov more seriously, because Yurichenko had an incredible reputation, and if they both believed something stank to high heaven, maybe there was a turd in the punch bowl, geopolitically speaking, of course.

He continued in his earnest tone, "Then Viktor tells me to go look for plotters in trouble spots. I am doing this on pretext of assessing situations, but I am looking really for whoever is intervening in these factions, is prodding them, is organizing demonstrations and exacerbating local political anxieties."

"And did you find them?"

"Was too hidden. But I was becoming even more convinced something was there."

"Why?"

"Was too orchestrated. Someone knowing of our seams and stresses was tugging out stitches. You are knowledgeable about chaos theory, yes? Even in most frantic events there must be patterns, logical progressions, but to find these progressions, separate forces must be slowed and studied."

"Okay, so?"

He was becoming animated, and clearly agitated, but whether from passion or frustration I couldn't tell. He said, "This was our problem. Was happening too fast . . . overpowering Gorbachev and his government, avalanches of protests, and local political decisions, and criminal acts, and even revolutions. Everywhere this is happening, fires in every corner. There has to be some trigger, yes? There was too much synchronicity, too much *unapparent* coordination."

"*Unapparent* coordination?"

"Yes . . . was made to *appear* uncoordinated." Realizing he was a little over my head, he explained, "Imagine you are cancer researcher and twenty children from one small village get cancer. You search for similarities in children's habits, what foods they eat, what liquids they drink . . . nothing can be found. Still, you are knowing something must be there, some force connecting these diseases."

"Okay."

"Then there is Yeltsin."

"Right, then there was Yeltsin. What about him?"

"You never became curious how this secretary of one city was able to overturn entire political establishment of our Soviet nation? In your country, this would be like your New York City mayor seizing your government, tearing up your Constitution, burning your Bill of Rights, and inventing new government. Except under Soviet system secretaries were even less powerful, less important than your American mayors. How was this possible?"

"Because your people wanted freedom?" I suggested. "Because they were poor and wretched and wanted better lives? Because Communism sucked?"

He shook his head at my sophisticated insight and said, "You do not know Russians. We have famous reputation for suffering. What is your word? 'Stoic,' yes? Read our literature . . . is about suffering. Study our history. Consider Russia's most fabled leaders: Ivan the Terrible, Peter the Great, Catherine the Great, Lenin, Stalin. In what way all these people are alike? All are mass murderers. Does America have such homicidal icons? Your George Washington, your Abraham Lincoln, your FDR, they were famous killers?"

I guessed he had a good point. "Okay, then how did Yeltsin do it?"

"I never learned, but was connected as well. How else can Yeltsin outmaneuver everybody?"

Until this point, he'd nearly had me convinced, nodding along nicely, following his logic, and so on. I fixed him with a stony look and said, "Look, we have a problem here. According to our intelligence, your boss, Yurichenko, approached Yeltsin near the beginning and struck a deal. Our people say Yurichenko helped him rise."

"Yes, was true. When Viktor sees him breaking through, we know something is badly wrong, so Viktor cultivates this relationship with Yeltsin. He insinuates himself inside. We know Yeltsin has powerful allies, but who? Viktor was not able to discover this answer."

"And what? When Yeltsin finally came to power, he rewarded your boss by making him head of the SVR?"

"Was big irony, yes? Viktor was very trusted by Yeltsin . . . this was his reward for Viktor's help."

"And you were giving all this to Morrison?"

"Pieces, only. I was not knowing in the beginning what I was looking for."

"And why'd you go to Bill?"

"This was last resort for me. When I could not find what was happening, I wanted to discuss American interpretations of these developments. Sometimes, those looking into a house see better than those inside, yes?"

I had to take a moment to ponder all this. I had my pants on by then and that helped.

I asked, "Did Yurichenko know you were meeting with Morrison?"

He looked conflicted, as if this was something he was ashamed to admit. "No. Uh, Viktor would never permit this. We are very close, but Viktor is product of our old system and would consider it a most serious betrayal."

"Do you know who in the CIA got access to your reports, knew of your existence?"

"Bill and Mary, of course. And only deputy directors of intelligence and operations were . . . uh, in the loop? This is correct?"

"I think that's correct, although Morrison told me a CIA psychiatrist was involved as well. He said it was a standard practice to keep you from going nuts on them."

"Then you see where I am having big problem?"

I nodded, but as I mentioned before, spies are con men, and maybe the SVR had a bunch of Hollywood types who worked in the basement and cooked up these things. Actually, that was too wild-assed for even me to believe.

He glanced at his watch. "I must now go back to office. I am telling everybody I am at lunch. I have appointments."

He reached out to shake my hand. I took it, and he promptly sensed my reservations about him, because he gave me a shy, reticent smile, a gesture that conveyed that this was painfully difficult for both of us.

I recalled the description in Arbatov's dossier, "magnetically charming," and concluded that the CIA pegged him well. I was annoyed to find that I liked him, trusted him, and even wanted to believe what he told me.

But enough to stake my life on him? Well, no. Nor did I see where his revelation fit in the picture. It explained why he approached Morrison in the first place, but where was the connection to Morrison's arrest, or to ten years of treachery?

More important, was there a connection to the ambush that morning? Regardless, the wise thing to do at that point was call the airline and book tickets. I made reservations for midnight so we could sneak out in the dead of night.

CHAPTER TWENTY-ONE

WITHIN moments after Alexi left, Katrina knocked on my door and asked if I wanted to accompany her to the embassy. I recommended that we first stroll around the block so I could tell her what Arbatov and I had discussed. The new and improved Sean Drummond would hold nothing back from the freshly restyled Miss Mazorski. Never mess with a woman who'd stick a man's dick in a garbage disposal, that's my motto. I did her a favor, though, and gave her the abbreviated version.

Odd as this may sound, she didn't seem all that interested. I had the impression she was going through the motions of politely hearing me out, while she was preoccupied with something else. Multitasking is a very useful and admirable skill, but it pisses me off when it's happening to me.

I said, "Am I detecting a listening problem here? And by the way, why are we going to the embassy?"

"There's someone we need to talk to . . . Morrison's secretary." She paused for a moment, then added, "When you were in the bathroom the other day, Mel mentioned to me that we might want to have a word with her."

"About what?"

She began walking back toward the hotel. "He said she might have a few interesting insights."

"Like what?"

"I don't know, and it's obviously too late to ask him."

"Right."

She walked a few more paces, then asked, "Do you notice how I'm sharing this with you?"

"Yes, and it's very commendable."

"And you just had another meeting with Arbatov and didn't include me?"

"Recall that I didn't plan the meeting. He snuck into my room and woke me up."

"The circumstances don't concern me."

"No, I don't expect they do."

"You've put my life at risk."

"Yes, I know. I also said I'm sorry."

She rubbed her temples and was on the verge of saying something nasty, but settled for, "Don't exclude me again."

"Right." We arrived at the embassy twenty minutes later and went upstairs to the fourth floor, where the attaché's office is located. We walked into the reception area, and wouldn't you know?

Parked at a desk directly in front of the office door that read MILITARY ATTACHÉ sat one of the most perversely fetching women I ever laid eyes on. She had a face you wouldn't necessarily call attractive. Sinful, decadent, cruel—these were the words that popped into my mind. She was what we men call an "oh God girl," meaning the type who'd be digging your flesh out of her fingernails after the two of you did the big nasty. "Oh God" is what you say the second time she asks you out.

She had jet black hair that hung past her waist, dark, sultry eyes surrounded by purple makeup, and a downward pout on her cherry red lips that let you know she demanded to be spoiled. Upon close inspection, it struck me that she looked remarkably like the woman who'd been performing the virtuoso with the triumvirate on my TV, although I'd gotten only the most fleeting glimpse of that woman. Really.

Katrina awarded me a knowing look. No wonder Mel sicced us on Miss Nasty. Never underestimate a man who has a death wish on his former boss.

Katrina marched right up to the desk and announced, "I'm Katrina Mazorski, and this is Major Drummond. We're Morrison's attorneys."

The woman studied us through a pair of wicked irises that seemed to bore right through your clothes and replied, "And how can I help you?"

"You were his secretary?"

"That's right."

"We're interviewing people who worked with him We'd like to start with you."

She gave us a curiously indifferent look, like, What the hell, I'm bored, so why not?

I said, "Do you have a conference room . . . somewhere we could speak in private?"

For an answer she stood up and walked toward a door as if we should know we were expected to follow. I never took my eyes off her, since you never know where you might pick up your next vital clue; maybe hidden somewhere in her miniskirt, her dark net stockings, her high heels, or inside that top that seemed to be pasted to her skin.

For her part, Katrina was rolling her eyes as if she

couldn't believe what she was seeing. Truly, it took a stone-cold idiot to park this girl directly outside his office. Why hadn't the stupid bastard stuck with a chubby little grandmother, like any responsible philanderer would do?

We ended up inside a small, cramped office that appeared lived-in. A plaque on the wall from some Army training course drew my eye, and it was made out to Captain Melvin Torianski. Miss Nasty said, "He won't care if we use it."

It's always touching to see grief-stricken coworkers mourn the loss of a friend. Katrina slid over another chair, and the two of them eyed each other like a pair of hungry lionesses. I sat behind the desk, pulled out the tape recorder, and retrieved a yellow notepad from my briefcase, to sort of dramatize the atmosphere.

I began, "For the record, what's your name?"

"Tina Allison."

We established that she was a U.S. citizen, a GS-9 employee of the State Department, twice divorced, no children, and lived in embassy housing. I then asked, "And how long have you known General Morrison?"

"Eighteen months."

"How did you end up working for him?"

"The attaché's office was looking for a new secretary, they sent a request back to Washington, I was interviewed, and I was hired."

Katrina swiftly asked, "Who interviewed you?"

"Morrison. He was on a trip back to D.C. and the interview was arranged."

Well, no surprise there. I said, "How well did you

know him?"

"Well enough."

"Would you describe your relationship as professional, as friendly, as . . . ?" Katrina asked, allowing that thought to drift off so Tina could fill in the blank however she wanted.

Her lips curled up the tiniest bit. "He was my boss. We saw each other every day."

Katrina said, "Did you know his wife?"

"I saw her around."

"Were you friends?"

"I'm a secretary. We were in different social circles."

I asked, "Did you ever see General Morrison do anything you considered suspect?"

"No."

And Katrina jumped in with, "Did you socialize with him?"

"Define 'socialize,'" she replied, again with that taunting tilt to her lips. A Mensa invitation definitely wasn't lurking in her future, but she was obviously picking up on the thread here.

Katrina asked, "Did you go over to his quarters for dinner, go out for a movie together, any contact outside the office?"

"No. Never."

Then, very calmly, "Were you screwing him?"

I thought she'd howl, but instead she leaned back into her chair and with surprising calmness replied, "No."

"You're sure?"

This apparently struck her as hilarious. "There's some way you can *not* be sure on something like that?

Oh, don't get me wrong—I could've had him anytime I wanted."

"Really?" Katrina replied. "Why didn't you?"

"Not my type."

"Why wasn't he your type?"

"He's a horny, married jerk. I prefer my jerks horny and unmarried."

For clarity's sake, I asked, "But you never had an affair with him?"

She looked at me. "Nope."

I was just beginning to feel relieved when Katrina asked, "Did anyone else?"

She suddenly looked hesitant, so Katrina bent toward her and said, "There's a harder way to do this. We'll ask a judge to issue a subpoena and ask you this same question in an interrogation room back in the States."

Her indecision seemed to evaporate. "He had some girlfriends, yeah."

"Some? As in more than one?"

"He belonged to a Russian escort service that provided him with girls. He went out with a few Russian girls on the side, too."

A heavy silence hung for a few moments as Katrina and I exchanged glances, tried to maintain our composure, and generally sought not to appear as shitty and dismayed as we felt. The issue was motive for treason, and this sounded like *it*. A senior intelligence officer screwing his way through Moscow, of all places, was an invitation to blackmail.

Katrina asked her, "Did his wife know about them?"

"No."

"How do you know that?" I asked.

"Because I never told her."

"Why didn't you?"

"She was a nice lady. I figured, what she didn't know, didn't hurt her."

Katrina said, "How did you find out?"

"I get the phone bills for the office, and Russian phone companies charge for local calls. When I don't recognize a number, I track them down. That's how I learned about Siberian Nights Escorts, and the girls he'd call. But I never told anyone. At least not until the investigators brought it up."

The important point here being that Russia's intelligence agencies also had access to those phone records. And the shocking point being that Eddie apparently knew also.

To be clear on that last point, I asked, "They already knew?"

"Oh, they knew."

"How?"

"How would I know? Ask them."

On that note, Katrina shot me another of those knowing looks as she asked, "Did Morrison have any good friends here . . . anybody we should talk to?"

She replied, "Colonel Jack Branson, the deputy attaché. They did a lot of work together."

"And how do we get hold of him?"

"You walk into his office. It's right next to Morrison's."

Branson was Air Force, mid-forties, balding, thin-faced, very tall, and quite skinny, with a nondescript face, but intelligent eyes, and at the moment we walked into his office he was hunched over his desk, studying something with a magnifying glass. He looked up and took whatever it was off his desktop and stuffed it in a drawer. Intell guys are such a riot.

"Hi," he said, trying to look friendly. "Can I help you?"

I made the introductions, and he pointed at a pair of chairs. We chitchatted about him, wife, kids, life in Moscow, and so on.

After we exhausted the phony pleasantries, I said, "So, how long did you know General Morrison?"

"The whole two years he was here. I've been here three years, so I was in place when he arrived."

"Miss Allison said you were friends."

"Friends? Well, no, we weren't friends. We worked closely together, we were generally amicable, but we were hardly friends."

"Did you like him?" I asked.

"I respected him," he replied.

That's military doublespeak for "No, he was a miserable asshole to work for."

"Why did you respect him?" Katrina asked.

"He knew his job and worked damned hard at it. I won't say he had the best leadership style I've seen, but as an intell officer he was as good as any I've met."

Katrina bent forward. "What makes a good intell officer?"

"Good question." Branson paused and then explained, "In intell, you're always flooded with information. You're always getting lots of reports from lots of sources, and frequently those reports and sources conflict. It gets to be a morass. Most intell guys just shove it all upstream and let someone else try to figure it out. Morrison wasn't like that. He had a nose for what it all meant."

I said, "He could interpret it?"

"Exactly. He always seemed to know the story behind the story. It was uncanny sometimes. He just figured it out."

Big mystery there, right? Having the number two guy in the SVR feeding him explanations surely didn't hurt.

Katrina said, "I hate to pry into sensitive things, but how was his marriage?"

Branson sucked his lower lip into his mouth. Like any military officer, loyalty to his boss was bred into his being, but at the same time he had to be weighing his caution against how much we already knew. Being indiscreet was one thing; it was worse to be caught as a liar.

"Don't sweat it," Katrina prodded. "We know he cheated on her."

The lower lip popped back out, and he began shaking his head. "Well, you know then. That dumbass screwed everything he could get his hands on. Ordinarily I don't care what other people do . . . but, look, I like Mary, and I didn't appreciate it. I felt bad telling her he was at lunch when he was with some whore."

Katrina nodded and said, "Did you ever talk to him about it?"

"I tried. He's not a very approachable guy."

"Did he ever explain his affairs?"

"I don't think he knew why he did it. There was no good reason. You ever see his wife?" We both nodded. "What sane guy married to Mary would cheat, right?"

Katrina said, "Why didn't they get divorced? Did he ever talk about it?"

"I suggested it once."

"And . . . ?"

"He said it would harm the children. I didn't believe him, though. Do you want to know what I think?"

"Sure."

"His career. You can't believe how ambitious he was, and a divorce wouldn't have looked good. The military frowns on that."

I asked him, "Did everybody in the office know about his affairs?"

"I don't know. None of us ever talked about it. What's funny was, he and his wife worked together real well. They worked everything together."

So the prosecutors had been saying, but just to be sure I asked, "Then he was seeing everything she was working on?"

He began chuckling. "The other way around, I'd say. Look, there's a natural competition between the CIA, whom she worked for, and DIA, whom we report back to. We field hands are like little dogs. We please our masters by bringing back bigger bones and we get stroked behind the ears. Mary stole stuff from us all the time. Our sources would tell us about some crooked general over in the Russian Defense Ministry who looked like he could be blinkered into recruitment, and even before we could get a message off, Mary's people were already flogging the general. Happened all the time."

We'd heard more than we needed to hear, so Katrina thanked the colonel for his candor, told him we'd be back if we had more questions, and we departed in mutual misery.

On the drive back to the hotel, Katrina said, "You know that adultery charge?"

"I know." I added, "But let me remind you, you were the one who thought it was possible to prove him innocent."

She thought about this, then said, "You can't be sure it led to treason."

"You know the old Army saying about the three Bs?"

"No."

"'Booze, bucks, and broads will get you every time.' Usually because they lead to the fourth B—blackmail."

CHAPTER TWENTY-TWO

PUT two and two together and we had a king-size problem. Those transcripted telephone taps Imelda was slogging through no doubt proved that Bill Morrison had a dick instead of a brain. Nothing else explained how the investigators learned Morrison was a flagrant philanderer. Or why Eddie included the comparatively minor imputation of wife cheating among the litany of other charges.

Motive, motive, motive. Damned hard to prove with traitors, and Eddie now had two golden-oldie classics—the proverbial favorites lust and greed. My client had screwed his way through an opponent's capital, and there was that fat wad of inheritance passed down from his father, and through his mother, a manner of money laundering that was both cunning and tax free.

I hate to sound like a whiny complainer, but it had been an all-around crappy day: an ambush, a dead American officer, an operation performed by a doctor named Josef Mengele, and now this. I thought it couldn't get worse until I recognized the guy loitering beside the elevator—the same detective who had unlocked my cuffs back in the police station. And beside him stood a slick-haired putz in a well-cut Western suit, looking smugly self-important.

They marched up to Katrina and me; the putz impudently shoved a business card in my face and announced, "I am Boris Ashinakov of the Foreign Ministry. I must have a word with you. In private."

We stepped away from the elevator and he led us to a quiet corner of the lobby. He began, "On behalf of my ministry I extend our deepest apologies for the shooting incident this morning. Moscow is a very peaceful city and we find it very distressing. And of course embarrassing."

Moscow was anything but peaceful, his politeness was phony, and I wondered what this was about. I smiled back, however, and very nicely replied, "Thank you. It's very kind of you to stop by. And, well, we'd love to stay and chat but we have to get upstairs to pack. A late flight . . . I'm sure you understand."

"Actually, Major, there's no hurry."

"And why would that be?"

He scratched an eyebrow, pointed at his partner, and said, "Detective Turpekov and his colleagues are continuing their investigation into this terrible incident. There are procedures that must be followed before this case can be closed. You two are the only living witnesses."

"Fine. I'll give you the number back in the States where we can be reached."

He shook his oily head. "I think not. We must request you to remain here."

"No."

He was grinning, and really enjoying himself, and it struck me I was becoming tired of power-hungry little bullycrats. He said, "I insist. Our customs officials have already been instructed not to let you out of the country. As long as nothing unexpected turns up, it shouldn't take longer than forty-eight hours."

"I don't have forty-eight hours."

"You do now." He smiled and stuck a pudgy finger on my chest. "Moscow is a lovely city filled with wonderful places to visit. What is it you say in America? Stop and smell the roses."

Moscow was anything but a lovely city, and the only odors I'd smelled so far were cordite and the stench of homeless people needing showers. I said, "I intend to lodge a protest with the embassy."

"Please do." He picked a piece of lint off his jacket sleeve and added, "But I perhaps forgot to mention that this matter was already discussed with your embassy's political officer. He understood perfectly."

He awarded me another unctuous smile, tipped his

chin at Katrina, and said, "Enjoy your stay," before he and the detective walked away.

As I cursed, Katrina said, "We don't need this, Sean. We really can't afford it."

"That might not be the worst of our problems." I turned and looked her in the eye. "Have you considered that somebody might be trying to keep us in Moscow to kill us?"

"You think?"

"I don't know what I think."

And truthfully, I didn't. Police departments spell bureaucracy better than most institutions, and allowing material witnesses to flee beyond Russia's jurisdiction before the case is closed would be stupider than dirt. So there was that. Then there was this: That very morning, somebody tried to kill us and suddenly we were being ordered to stay within the spider's web.

The fretful look on her face indicated the full import had just struck home. She said, "To get the Foreign Ministry to do their dirty work, it would have to be somebody very powerful, wouldn't it?" I nodded, and she added, "Such as your new friend Arbatov?"

"He's not my friend," I clarified. "But I don't see it."

"You don't?"

"If the man wanted to kill us, why the visit to my room? Why that story about this secret plot? It doesn't fit, does it?"

"Then you trust him?"

"I don't trust anyone in his line of work. I just don't think he's trying to kill us."

"Then who?"

"Look, I don't even know if somebody is trying to kill us. Maybe the ambush really was about Mel."

She somewhat skeptically replied, "Maybe."

"But you see my point? If it wasn't Arbatov, who else had a reason to kill us?"

"With your penchant for making friends, the line of suspects is staggering."

I chuckled to let her know I thought that was very funny. She remained poker-faced, but surely she was laughing inside.

Then I thought of big, bad Eddie, and my chuckling stopped. Apropos of that, Katrina and I began batting around ideas for something productive to do. There actually was something I had wanted to do before somebody used us for target practice and getting the hell out of Russia loomed as the only sane course of action. Of course circumstances had changed once again and so perhaps . . .

But my new plan required Katrina's enthusiastic involvement. The problem was I hadn't done much to inspire her confidence, and as already noted, the ambush that morning had given her cause to doubt my credibility and competence, which meant I had to soft-shoe my way into this.

So I kept our game of verbal badminton going until Katrina finally suggested, "Why don't you meet with Arbatov again? If Morrison was reporting on this organization he told you about, maybe there's something there."

I replied, quite innocently, "Like what?"

"You tell me."

"Well, let me see. The idea is that somebody framed Morrison, right?"

"So he claims. But why?"

"That's why I wanted to speak with Arbatov in the first place. He was my number one suspect."

"How intriguing. Why would he do that?"

"Well, I don't think that anymore."

"Then why *did* you suspect that in the first place?"

"Because when it comes to spies, what you see is never what's there. Cloaks and daggers . . . their whole world is about lies, betrayals, and backstabbing."

"Okay."

"Everything is counterintuitive. You've got to pull back the curtains. Truth is never really the whole truth. It could be the opposite or anywhere on the spectrum in between."

"Sean . . . this is so educational . . . really. Could you *please* tell me why you suspected Arbatov?"

"I'm just warning that—"

"I've got it. I'm a street lawyer. All my clients lied."

"Okay, Bill Morrison said he was Arbatov's controller, right?"

She nodded and I continued, "Say it was really the other way around. Say all those years when they were meeting, it was a subterfuge so that Morrison could turn over things to Arbatov, who was actually *his* controller."

"That would be devious. But why would Arbatov turn him in?"

"What I thought was maybe they had a falling out, or that Morrison had asked for something the Russians weren't willing to provide. Or maybe somebody else in Arbatov's organization did it."

"But you don't believe that anymore?"

"Arbatov says if they wanted to get rid of Morrison, we'd never find a trace of his corpse."

"What about if it was the other way around? Maybe Arbatov wanted to stop betraying his country and thought this was a way to get Morrison out of his hair?"

"Wouldn't work. Too many other CIA people know about Arbatov."

"Of course."

"So that's what I thought before I spoke with Arbatov."

"And now you're thinking something else?"

"You mean, aside from the fact Morrison looks guilty?"

"I think we can rely on Golden to make that argument."

"Okay, here's the other possibility. Say Morrison was reporting something very important back to the CIA, something that somebody here in Moscow didn't want exposed."

"Like about this secret organization Arbatov was talking about?"

"Yeah, like that."

"Wouldn't Mary be reporting the same thing?"

I nodded. "That's the beauty of it. It's a twofer. He goes to the chair, and her career goes into the toilet. Because he was a traitor, everything either Morrison ever reported loses credibility."

"But Arbatov's still around. The secret's not safe as

long as he's alive."

"Exactly. And the next step is to take out Arbatov."

"Why didn't they do that in the first place?"

"I don't know. It's just a theory rumbling around my brain. But I think it's what Arbatov's worried about. He's next."

"Did he say that?"

"Not in so many words. But why else did he come to my room this afternoon? Why else did he talk to me in the first place? I don't think he's getting much sleep."

She paced around a moment, taking in all this. She finally said, "Then you need to talk to him again."

"Not a good idea."

"Why not?"

"Because my first meeting with him may have been compromised. Maybe I was being followed, or he was being followed. It's the only thing that explains the ambush."

"You think?"

"I told you, I don't know what I think. But meeting with him again would be too risky, for him and for us. I stick out like a sore thumb."

As I believe I already mentioned, Katrina Mazorski was a very smart girl. Subtle hints weren't lost on her. She said, "Are you suggesting *I* meet with him?"

"I'm suggesting no such thing. It could be dangerous for you as well." I went over and stared out the window, mumbling, "Of course . . . we could take steps to minimize those dangers."

"And how would we do that?"

"A terrific disguise. Different hair color, new outfit,

the works. Since you speak the language, you'd blend right in. And I would stake out your meeting and make sure you're not observed or followed."

"I see you've already thought about this."

I shrugged.

"Is it risky?"

"Very."

She examined me a moment, then said, "What are the odds this is going to help? Tell me I'm not putting my life at risk over a wild goose chase."

"I can't tell you that."

CHAPTER TWENTY-THREE

THERE were no chalk stripes beside the Commie Amazon's feet at four-thirty the next morning; apparently, Arbatov wiped them off each time he saw the signal. These spies, they think of even the little things. I made three fresh new scrapes and wandered back upstairs to the dismal streets of Moscow.

I did some furtive dodging around, sort of warming up, and ended up thirty minutes later in a position to observe Katrina enter the coffee shop. Less than a minute later she wandered back out and peeked around, perhaps trying to spot me, which she didn't. Her hair was dyed blond and she wore thick glasses. She was dressed in a long, oversize parka, too warm and bulky for the season, but it added forty pounds to her slender frame. Had I not picked the outfit myself, I wouldn't have recognized her.

Five minutes later, Alexi exited the subway stairwell,

and I tracked him with my eyes as he strolled down the street to the kiosk. Nobody emerged behind him. He, too, entered the coffee shop and emerged a moment later, pausing momentarily to read the note Katrina had left with the chubby babushka behind the counter. The note detailed the instructions for his next stop if he wanted to meet with us. If he went back into the subway, he was blowing us off.

I had broken the normal routine and could see the anxiety and indecision on his face. After a moment, he headed across the street, and I followed along behind him, dodging into alleyways and shop entrances so I wouldn't be spotted. I saw nobody. He was alone, to the best I could tell.

He ended up in the middle of a park and stopped by one of those ubiquitous statues of a man on a horse. Russians are really into statues, I was learning. A moment later, Katrina approached him. He looked surprised and tense, then his body relaxed as Katrina explained who she was and why she was there. I saw his lips moving, and I imagined he was probably telling her how much he admired the way I had set this up. Or he could be telling her I was an overcautious idiot.

Their chat lasted nearly ten minutes. I circled the park a few times and kept an eye out. Aside from a few beggars stumbling around in the morning chill, nobody or anything looked out of place and suspicious.

Finally they shook hands and then Arbatov walked away, leaving Katrina to her own devices. I followed Arbatov as he returned to the subway. Were he being tracked, it would have to be a team that was electronically connected, passing him from one agent to the next. The whole area would have to be blanketed, taking dozens of agents. It seemed fair to assume Arbatov wasn't being tracked.

I took a zigzag route back to the hotel, and a few minutes later there was a knock at my door. It was Katrina, grinning and beaming. Sweat was still running down my face, from exertion and anxiety. I knew enough to be distressed; she obviously didn't.

She stepped inside and said, "Well?"

"Nobody was following. I'm nearly certain of it. And how did your side go?"

"Fine."

"That's it? Fine?"

"He was very nice."

I tapped a finger on my knee. "Did he trust you?"

"Of course. He thought using me was brilliant. He said he's got a lot of information to pass to us, and this was much more workable than meeting with you."

"What else did he tell you?"

She smiled. "He said he had spotted a strange man following him, who was at that very moment circling the park and watching us." She pointed a finger at me. "Oh my God, you're dressed just like the guy he described."

Very, very funny. "What else?" I grumbled.

"He said he knows a great restaurant that serves genuine Russian cuisine, and that I'll love it."

"He . . . what?"

"We made a date. He's taking me to dinner."

"A date?"

"Look it up in the dictionary."

"I know what a date is. This wasn't in the plan."

"You have a problem with this?" She crossed her arms and smiled. "Is this because you didn't think of it?"

"Absolutely not."

"Perhaps you like it better when you get to skulk around, lurking behind bushes and acting like a real-life spy. Did I spoil your fun?"

She was pulling my chain, I detected. I started to say, "Look, this is—"

She was shaking her head. "Don't even try arguing against this. We can have one more rushed ten-minute session in the park or I can spend an entire evening listening to what he has to say."

She was right. And I knew that in most ways it was even a very good idea. But I had a misgiving I just couldn't shake.

Something in my expression must've communicated this, because she said, "Don't worry, I can handle him."

"I'm not worried about you. I'm worried for him."

She chuckled.

I groaned.

She left and I looked around at the walls. I have never been good at killing time, particularly when I am keyed up and trapped in a hotel room in a strange and miserable country I don't want to be in. The third time I used the phone to call Imelda with nothing new to discuss or report, she informed me that she was ridiculously busy and if I bothered her again she would climb on the next plane and come kill me. The shop in the hotel lobby had two American books, a trashy novel by Jackie Collins and a thick biography of Ronald Reagan titled *Dutch* by Edmund Morris. I chose the trash. After one hundred pages of Hollywood murders and affairs, I went numb and fled. I went outside and walked around, trying to get someone to follow me, or ambush me, or whatever. Did I mention that I was bored?

At six o'clock, Katrina knocked on my door and I opened it. She stepped inside, and I . . . well, I froze. She looked breathtaking, ravishing, and most problematically, dripped with sex appeal. Her hair was still dyed blond, and she wore it up like a diva. She had apparently slipped out and bought a dress, because she wore this very lovely black number that stopped about seven inches short of her knees and a few micrometers from her nipples. If she sneezed or even laughed hard, Arbatov was in for an eyeful. She wore stockings and high heels, and makeup tastefully applied, and a very nice perfume, and as we say in the Army, she had cleaned up right nicely.

I like eye candy as much as the next guy, but her timing and judgment was awful. Inconspicuous was the code word for the evening and she was anything but. Katrina Mazorski was going to draw plenty of stares, and she was going to be remembered everywhere she went.

I very grumpily said, "You look like you got confused. This isn't a real date."

She smiled. "But it has to look like one. Don't I look genuine?"

It struck me that she was getting into this gig a bit too

well, and I decided a firm note of caution was in order.

"Katrina, let me remind you that Alexi Arbatov is the number two in Russia's spy agency. This is the real world. He is not James Bond and you are not Moneypenny. When people get their throats slit in this studio, they don't bounce back up when the director screams 'Cut.' In short, this is not a game, and what you are doing is very, very dangerous."

She leaned against the door and patiently heard me out. In a light tone I found immensely irritating, she said, "Don't worry. I know what I'm doing."

"No, you're an amateur. Don't forget that." I gave her a fierce stare until she stopped grinning, then said, "Now, your instructions. Be back by midnight at the latest. If you're not back by then, I'm going to call the embassy and tell them you're missing. Got that?"

"Midnight at the latest."

"Listen to everything he says carefully, but skeptically. I'm not saying he's lying, but these people are weaned on treachery and duplicity, and we still don't know what his game is. I expect to be briefed on everything the second you return."

"Yes sir."

"Don't smart-ass me. I don't approve of this."

"You're worried about me?"

"Damned right."

"How sweet. Really, I'm touched."

I shook my head. "This date was his idea, right?"

"Right."

"Think about that." I gave her a hard stare and added, "And be damn sure he picks up the tab. This is Russia and these cheap bastards will stiff you every time."

She giggled and fled. I paced around my room awhile. I felt guilty that I'd gotten her into this, anxious about her safety, and angry that she seemed to consider this a lark. I went back to Jackie Collins. Another hundred pages of murder and sex later, I went downstairs to the bar. I watched a soccer game on the television, drank some genuine Russian vodka, watched a pair of slick whores move in on two flabby American businessmen, and returned to my room at eleven-thirty to await Katrina.

At one I gave serious thought to calling the embassy. But to say what? My co-counsel just happened to be going out on a date with the number two spy of this country, you know, the top foreign asset none of you are cleared to know about, and now she's missing? By two, I was frantic, pacing the floor, kicking the bed, punching a wall, and regretting that I ever bought into this stupid, risky idea. Katrina had no idea what dirty games these people played. I had visions of her strapped to a chair in a dingy, dirty room with six big goons huddled over her, truncheons gripped in their meaty fists, blood and teeth flying in all directions.

At two-thirty there was a light knock on my door and it was her. I grabbed her by the arm and flung her into the room. She landed on the bed.

At first I said nothing. I shook with rage and tried to murder her with a perfectly malevolent glare.

She peered back with the kind of expression little girls get when they know Daddy is angry and about to take away the car keys.

I pounded a forefinger on the watch on my wrist. "Midnight! I said midnight! You heard me. I even made you repeat it."

"Cool down. Take three deep breaths and cool down."

My head jerked forward. "Don't . . . just don't. I trusted you."

She stood up and went over to the minibar. She opened the door and pulled out a tiny bottle of scotch. She turned around and said, "On me. I'm sorry, okay? We lost track of time."

"Lost track of time?" I stomped around the room a few times. She watched me with that insouciant expression she sometimes got, as I fought the impulse to strangle her, and frankly it could have gone either way.

She finally said, "I have the most amazing story to tell you."

"I'm not in the mood."

"Sit down, drink your scotch, and get in the mood. My knees are still shaking."

Was she playing with me or what? I got a glass, poured in the scotch, and knocked it back in one swig. She went back to the minibar and got another. She said, "I think I see why somebody wanted Morrison taken down."

I fell into the chair by the bathroom door, she brought me the bottle, and then she went and sat on the bed. She gave me another moment to compose myself, before she very calmly asked, "Are you ready?"

"I'm . . . yes, I'm ready."

"Alexi said he already told you about this cabal that has been manipulating Russia's foreign policy, starting wars, performing assassinations, and overthrowing governments at will. This is what he has been reporting to the Morrisons since 1991, when he first met Bill."

I sipped from my scotch and considered this. Arbatov had obviously told me about this cabal, but he had mentioned nothing about it being active after '91. Katrina suddenly had my undivided attention. "He says it's still around?"

"Definitely."

"Like active today?"

"Like for the whole past twelve years. He says it's a hidden group of men with enormous power, money, and resources that has been operating like a hidden hand. His boss has had him searching for it the whole time."

"This is Viktor Yurichenko?"

She nodded and said, "He compared it to the British East India Company, which used to make its own foreign policy and led Great Britain around by the nose. Or like our American Fruit Company, which used to run the banana republics and manipulate our policies in Latin America. Only this group is completely hidden. He and Viktor have hunted it for years and never discovered who's behind it."

"What kinds of things is this group doing?"

"You wouldn't believe it."

"Try me."

"Where do I begin?"

"I don't know. But it's late, so begin."

She went to the minibar and got herself a bottle of red wine. It was a Russian vintage and probably tasted like rotten vinegar. I sipped from my scotch and hoped it gave her a splitting headache.

She sat back down on the bed, took a sip, and said, "Let's start with Georgia. How much do you know about it?"

"Let's see. Small country, south of Russia, Stalin came from there, so they don't have a lot to brag about. How's that?"

"I didn't realize you were such a man of the world."

"I once watched a three-hour PBS special on political issues in Eritrea. It completely cured me of my compulsive curiosity toward countries I don't really give a crap about."

"I see." She took another sip and no doubt considered the fact that I was a moron. I actually knew more about Georgia than I admitted, like I know the people there speak a language called Georgian, but I don't believe in showing off.

She said, "You'll recall that this was where Morrison and Alexi first met, back in 1990 or 1991?" I nodded as she added, "Alexi confessed that, yes, their first meeting was a setup."

"Why?"

"Because when the KGB and border troops were sent in by Gorbachev to control the riots, they were under strict instructions not to respond violently. If the Georgians turned violent, they were supposed to withdraw. Gorbachev didn't want them to create an explosive situation. Instead they committed two massacres that incited the rest of the Georgian people and caused the situation to fly out of hand."

"I don't understand."

"Alexi and Viktor suspected that somebody manipulated the situation. Somebody persuaded the KGB to ignore Gorbachev's order, to create the massacres, and undermine Gorbachev's position. Alexi wanted to find out what the CIA knew about it."

"We're still stuck back in 1991."

"Don't get impatient. After the Soviet split-up, the Georgian people turned to Eduard Shevardnadze and asked him to return and lead the country. Are you familiar with him?"

Indeed I was. Shevardnadze had been Gorbachev's foreign minister during the eighties, had orchestrated the peaceful end of the cold war, and was a huge international hero as a result.

I nodded and she continued, "The Georgians thought that if Shevardnadze took over, he had the international stature to reduce Georgia's dependence on Russia and open ties with the West. He knew all the world's leaders and had that fantastic reputation. So he came back, and one of his first steps was to start wooing Western companies to build pipelines across Georgia to carry trans-Caucasus oil and natural gas to the Black Sea. Russia didn't like that plan. For obvious reasons it wanted the pipelines to go through Russia."

I yawned. I mean, this was a very interesting history lesson, but it was late at night and Georgia sat right beside Eritrea on my give-a-crap meter.

She somehow detected my growing disinterest and

picked up the pace a bit. "The point is that before Shevardnadze could even get his balance, a civil war erupted in Georgia. The Abkhasians who live in the northwest corner of the country somehow got their hands on a large arsenal of tanks and artillery. There was a very short, very brutal war, but because of all these tanks and artillery, it was completely lopsided. By 1995, the Abkhasians had defeated the Georgian army and driven tens of thousands of Georgians out of the Abkhazia."

"The Abkhasians you say?" She nodded, and I said, "Well, I don't recall it."

"Stop being a jerk. When that happened, the Russians offered to broker a cease-fire, Georgia had no choice but to agree, and Russian troops have been stationed inside Georgia ever since. The effect was to castrate both Shevardnadze and his plans for the pipeline. After all, who's going to build a multibillion dollar artery through such an unstable country?"

"Okay, got that."

"What piqued Alexi's curiosity were the T-72 tanks and BMP fighting vehicles and heavy artillery. Alexi said it was top-of-the-line equipment that just mysteriously appeared."

"Couldn't they have bought it? Russia was a mess back then, its troops weren't being paid or housed, and they were selling anything to feed themselves."

"I asked him the same thing."

"And?"

"He said rifles and grenades were for sale on every street corner. But the heavy equipment, tanks and artillery, were strictly controlled and well secured."

"And there's a point to this, I presume."

"Yes, and you should pay better attention because this is where it gets very interesting."

"I'm paying so much attention my brain's about to freeze."

"Wiseass. The point is that Alexi was tasked by Viktor to find out where this equipment was coming from. It was Russian equipment. It had to be manufactured here. He sent out teams to the battlefield to collect serial numbers from destroyed tanks and artillery. They brought back the serial numbers, ran them through the Ministry of Defense's databases, and none of those serial numbers existed."

"That is strange."

"It gets stranger." Next came a very long tale about the same kinds of shenanigans in the war between Armenia and Azerbaijan. I didn't understand what the war was about, or what stake Russia had in the fight, except that somebody mysterious also gave lots of tanks and artillery to the Azerbaijanis, who used them to win. This was followed by an even longer description about how Yeltsin never wanted to fight the Chechens when they declared independence from Russia until this same cabal organized and supplied an uprising of Russian citizens inside Chechnya that failed miserably and shamed Yeltsin into sending in the Russian army. Indeed, Katrina was in the process of explaining how this cabal also scuttled each of the Chechen War cease-fires, most recently by blowing off bombs in Moscow apartment buildings and blaming it on Chechen terrorists, when I'd finally had enough.

I interrupted her spiel, saying, "Do you believe in this cabal?"

"Yes . . . I think." With some exasperation, she said, "Don't you understand what I'm telling you?"

"Sure. Russia has been meddling in the affairs of the countries it used to own and doesn't really want to let go of."

"That's how it's been made to appear, but that's not what it is. Alexi said the Russian government's policy was hands off. It was drawn into those situations but didn't cause them."

"Katrina, do I need to remind you that these guys in frumpy suits with bushy eyebrows have more experience concocting foreign revolutions and wars than anybody? It's what they do. Don't be naive."

"I'm not. And please recall that my parents fled from this region. I know something about it, and I don't look at it through rose-colored lenses."

"Point in your favor."

"Thank you."

"Are we done?"

"No, there's more. A lot more. The same kinds of mysterious things have been happening in Turkmenistan, Uzbekistan, Belarus, just about all the former Soviet republics. This secretive cabal has been treating them all like banana republics, engineering coups, murders, even wars. These were the things Alexi was reporting to Bill and Mary."

"I see. Do you mind if I get another drink?"

"Get me one, too."

As I was reaching into the minibar, I said, "What did you have for dinner?"

"What?"

"For dinner, what did you have?"

"I had venison."

"And Alexi?"

"A bowl of borscht."

"And did you drink?"

"We split a bottle of wine."

"Just one?"

"Yes, why?"

"Big bottle? Small bottle?"

"Stop it."

"Okay, I'll stop it. Did Alexi offer any proof?"

"Of course not. If he had proof, he and Viktor would've exposed and ended this cabal years ago."

"I see."

"No, you don't see. And damn it, stop condescending to me."

"I'm not. I'm treating you like a fellow attorney. You, yourself, described this as a fantastic tale. I need evidence, proof, something."

"I'll try to get it tomorrow night."

"What do you mean?"

"We made another date for tomorrow night. Alexi's taking me to a ballet, then out for drinks."

I jumped out of my chair and walked across the room toward her. A new and very disturbing thought had suddenly popped into my head. "You made another date? Without consulting me?"

"Relax. Everything went fine tonight."

"Really? Where were you all night? Don't tell me you were in the restaurant till this hour?"

"Cool it. I don't like the way you're talking to me."

"You don't . . ." I drew a heavy breath. "Answer me . . . please."

"We left the restaurant around nine. I went to Alexi's apartment, where we continued our talk."

I shook my head. "And?"

"And what?"

"And did you . . . you know?"

She stood up. She pointed a finger in my face. "Don't go there."

"He's a witness for Godsakes."

"He's not a witness. You'll never get him into a court."

"Regardless . . . did you . . . you know?"

"Unbelievable." She put down her wine and shook her head. "You can be so pathetic."

Me? Pathetic? My definition of pathetic is sleeping with a foreign agent and losing your perspective when you're supposed to be collecting evidence that can keep your client from getting thirty thousand volts jammed up his ass. But that's just me. Silly me.

I put my hands on her arms. "Katrina, listen. I know this is intoxicating. A foreign capital, espionage, handsome rogues with mysterious tales to tell, and all that crap. Don't be fooled."

She backed away. "You hypocrite. You used to sleep with our client's wife, and now you're wondering if I've stepped over the line?"

"Don't confuse the issues."

"No, I'll leave it to you to do that." We traded nasty stares until she said, "And no, I didn't sleep with Alexi."

Oops. She lifted her purse off the bed and left me, alone, stammering something incomprehensible. I gave her a minute to get back inside her room, remove her earrings, get settled, and so forth. I knocked gently on the door that connected our rooms, and said, "I'm sorry."

After the fifth time I said it, I realized it was a lost cause and went to bed.

CHAPTER TWENTY-FOUR

LATER that day was worse. Katrina was coldly and efficiently avoiding me. I knocked on her door a dozen times and called on the phone two dozen times. No answer. She was there, though. She was walking on her tiptoes, but I could hear her breathing and the toilet flushing.

I called Imelda, briefly explained what happened, and sought her advice. She was a woman and should be able to offer a solution to this mess. She said I should kill myself in some extravagantly excruciating manner and leave a note explaining I was sorry. She said it wouldn't buy forgiveness but would show that my heart was in the right place. She further informed me that the calls from Eddie's office were now incessant, and he was threatening to withdraw the offer of a meeting if I didn't get back to D.C. immediately.

I called the embassy and spoke with the same lousy

political officer who had given the green light for our extended stay. I told him to send Golden a message confirming our situation or I would call a judge back in D.C. and have the officer cited for impeding our case.

I finished the Jackie Collins novel. The heroine ended up with the sensitive, handsome guy who was hung like a horse and made love like a tireless animal—big surprise.

At five o'clock I yelled through the connecting door, "Katrina, I know you're in there. And I know you're leaving any moment. We need to talk before you go. This is business, Katrina. Be professional about this."

No answer. Not a peep of acknowledgment.

Ten minutes passed before there was a knock on the door. I opened it, and she stared up at me, deadpan expression, hair still blond and swept up, a new dress, this one passionately red in color, and although slightly less revealing, still sexy enough to have men tugging at their crotches. I, however, had learned to keep my prudish observations to myself.

I smiled very charmingly and said, "Hello."

"I have to leave. What do you want?"

Goodness. "You look . . . well, great."

"Thank you."

Didn't sound like thank you. Sounded like screw you. I said, "Can you step in a moment . . . please?"

She did, as I said, "Look, I got out of line last night. I'm sorry."

"What else?"

"About tonight . . ."

"What about it?"

"I've thought about everything you told me. Look, I'm not saying it's not true."

She appeared mildly surprised. "You're not?"

"No. I'm a typical American, and what the hell do I know about this region? Maybe it's just like Arbatov says."

"Are you humoring me?"

"I'm dead serious."

"Then you agree with me?"

"Not yet. Tonight, you need to press Arbatov for substantiation. Katrina, it's a wild story, and you and I are inclined to *want* to believe it. Golden won't be. And a jury won't be. We need to get something hard out of him."

She regarded me a moment, still rather coldly. "Have you even considered Alexi's position in this?"

"What do you mean?"

"He's been working with our government for over a decade. He has done this as a matter of conscience. Now he could be in serious trouble."

"And as the defense attorney for a man accused of treason, I'm in serious trouble. What's your point?"

"Now he's working with us to save Bill. He's risking these meetings with me and disclosing everything he knows, out of loyalty to Morrison."

"And please be sure to tell him I appreciate that."

"What I'm telling you is that he is a remarkable man."

"Yes he is. I agree."

"Courageous, principled, and noble."

"All the above."

She studied my face to see if I was serious. I was, and she said, "No curfews."

"Uh . . . okay."

"No second-guessing what I do."

"No guessing at all. Honest."

"All right, then. I'll see you at breakfast."

"Breakfast it is."

"You're buying. And fresh flowers on the table would be nice."

"Roses. A dozen of them."

"You can't get roses in Moscow in November."

"Right . . . ragweed or whatever."

She walked out, leaving me with the uncomfortable sensation that I had somehow agreed to something below the surface of our conversation. It struck me that she might be infatuated with Alexi Arbatov. It further struck me that the problem with a civilian contract employee is that you have very little leverage over them. Were she a soldier, I would have reminded her of her duty and my rank, and that would be that.

At 5:00 A.M., after a night of tossing and turning, I heard her door open and shut, her shower running, and, a few minutes afterward, the sounds of her settling heavily into bed.

Katrina looked like hell at breakfast: limp-haired, rosy-cheeked, eyes bloodshot. I bit my tongue. A deal's a deal, no matter how hard it is to stomach.

We exchanged a few banal pleasantries of that awkward kind where we avoided each other's eyes and inner feelings. That done, I shot straight to the subject. "Well?"

"He has no proof. At least nothing definitive."

"I see."

We both began playing with our spoons, the way people do who make each other uncomfortable. She said, "But he said we should look more closely at Yeltsin's reelection in 1996."

"What specifically?"

"He said that if we go back and check the news accounts, as late as three months before the election, Yeltsin's poll numbers had him down in the single digits. Three other candidates led him by huge amounts. Every prediction said Yeltsin would lose, that he didn't stand a chance."

"So he ran a good campaign."

"Alexi said that wasn't it. He said the country was a complete mess. The war in Chechnya was enormously unpopular, the Mafiya had taken over, and Yeltsin's cronies had stolen or seized every valuable asset in the country. Shootings and murders were hourly occurrences in Moscow. People were freezing and starving, and it was one public scandal after another. Even Yeltsin's daughter was accused of stealing millions of dollars. Everybody in Russia blamed Yeltsin, his alcoholism, his crookedness, his inability to govern the country. He didn't stand a chance."

"Then how did he win?"

"This cabal. Hundreds of millions of dollars suddenly flowed into Yeltsin's campaign chests, bribes were given out everywhere, even the Russian press mysteriously stopped criticizing Yeltsin. Alexi said it was extraordinary, the most massive political fraud in history."

I recalled that Yeltsin's reelection had been a huge upset, but the details escaped me. I said, "That's quite a charge. Does he have evidence, Katrina?"

"He says there is something we should check. In the fall of '96, at the height of Yeltsin's unpopularity, the American President came to Moscow and on Russian television gave a speech praising Yeltsin. The visit was deliberately timed to influence the election. The President even went so far as to justify the Chechen War, telling the Russian people it was the same as our own civil war."

I sat back and fingered my coffee cup. Katrina's voice, tone, and demeanor conveyed that she believed every word of this. Of course her actions the night before further conveyed that her objectivity got lost somewhere in Alexi's sheets.

Since I wasn't sleeping with Arbatov, I hadn't lost mine, however. A very powerful impulse wanted to believe Arbatov, because if there was such a cabal, and the Morrisons were trying to expose it, well, then, we had a defense to build on. That said, the notion that our own President was a puppet at the hands of this group had sort of drop-kicked this thing fairly far beyond the goalposts of credulity.

I very politely asked, "So he's saying this cabal arranged the President's speech?"

"I think what he was suggesting is that the cabal has tentacles into Washington, that it could actually control the White House and our actions toward Russia."

"Like . . . what the President says . . . his policies, whatever?"

"Something like that, yes. Alexi said he was always amazed that Russia could get away with what it was doing, or at least appeared to be doing, in the former republics, and Washington never took any firm stand or action."

"I see." I put down the spoon I had been playing with. "That's a very bold charge. And does he have evidence of this?"

"He said we should go find the President's speech."

"That's it?"

My skepticism was beginning to get on her nerves, and she put down her spoon, too, and said, "Stop it."

"Stop what? Evidence, Katrina. You're an attorney. Where's the evidence?"

Her eyes narrowed. "I see what you're doing."

"What am I doing?"

"You're pissed because of my relationship with Alexi."

"Ah, well, now that you've raised the issue, it's in play. In fact, you're right. It's unprofessional and per-haps damaging to our client."

"Unprofessional?"

"That's what I said."

She nodded and drew a few deep breaths. "I see."

I coldly asked, "Now, do you have anything else to report?"

She even more coldly replied, "Only one thing. I told Alexi you were having difficulty believing these things without corroboration. He said that can be very easily cleared up. He said you should speak with the Morrisons and the CIA. It turns out the CIA agrees with him completely. They've been hunting for this cabal the whole time as well."

My jaw dropped, or whatever it is people do when they are experiencing a cold shock. I said, "The CIA agrees with him?"

"That's what I said." She stood up and looked down at me. "I have to pack, and if you don't mind, I'll take my own taxi to the airport."

CHAPTER TWENTY-FIVE

KATRINA and I arrived at Dulles International Airport at 10:00 A.M. and went straight to baggage claim. The whole plane ride back to America we had sat side by side without exchanging a word. We had watched three lousy movies because it gave us an excuse to ignore each other.

Our relationship was fraying. I'm no expert on women, but the yardstick I have learned to go by is that when they frown and sneer at you more than they smile, love is not in the air. Astounding flash of the obvious you might say, but back in kindergarten those girls who sneered at me the most actually wanted to play doctor. And recall, please, that when it comes to men and women everything is complicated. And of course, generationally, culturally, and otherwise, we were wildly different, and that spilled over also.

I spent a good part of the flight, however, contemplating Alexi's assertion that the CIA agreed that this mysterious cabal existed and was ripping apart his region. I couldn't make sense of it. I mean, if the CIA knew such a thing, why hadn't it been made public? There are things you keep from the public and things you don't. True, the CIA has this weird thing about secrecy that sometimes goes to extremes, but I couldn't comprehend how this one could be kept in the bag.

In keeping with Russian efficiency, it turned out our luggage had gone to who-the-hell-knows-where, adding to my already foul mood. After forty minutes of hassling with the lost claims folks, we drove straight to the Virginia office, where Imelda was waiting. Safes were parked everywhere and having run out of wall space, Imelda had begun stuffing them in my tiny cramped office, turning it into an unusable storeroom.

Imelda looked awful—her hair was frazzled, and papers were piled in stacks and mounds everywhere.

She shoved her glasses down on her nose and said, "Hope you two had a great friggin' time while Imelda been doin' the real work."

Sensing that my mood was already crappy enough, she stopped grumbling and said, "Ain't found nothin' that's gonna help, tell you that. We gotta client with a trouser snake problem. They got it on tape, too, him talking to girlfriends and ordering up whores from some escort service."

"Right . . . we know. What else?"

"They had him under physical surveillance for a few months, so there's safes full of logs and reports. Might be twenty or so entries where he went to hotels, sometimes at lunch, sometimes in midafternoons, usually with women who did *not* resemble his wife." She rubbed her eyes, another sign of how stressed out and exhausted she was, then added, "The good shit ain't here yet, though. Golden's still sittin' on it."

I patted her shoulder, and Katrina stayed to help clean up or, more likely, avoid me, while I went into my office and called Eddie's secretary, saying I was ready to meet.

That distasteful task done, I called Homer's house to warn him I was coming. In reply, he just hung up the phone. Forty minutes later I pulled into the circular driveway in front of the big white-brick house. The Porsche had a temporary metal fence constructed around it—not wanting to seem too uninventive, I crouched down and let the air out of the rear tires.

That put me in a slightly better mood as I marched up to the front door and rang the bell. You'd think that since I had called, they'd be primed to answer, but two minutes passed before the door swung open. It was Mary, with that toe-curling smile.

I shuffled my feet. "Hey. How's things?"

She leaned against the doorjamb. "Except for these damned never-ending releases about the things my husband was supposed to have done, okay. Would you like to come in?"

"I'm not in the mood to run into *him*. Let's walk."

We studied each other's faces. One of the things about Mary was that she always could read my mind pretty well. And one of the things about me was that I always could read her face pretty well. So she knew I was troubled, and I knew she knew, if that convoluted trail of logic makes any damned sense. The point being, we were both on notice.

We strolled down the driveway without saying anything until we got to the street and were passing beneath the naked branches of the trees. The fall had been incredibly warm, but the weather was finally turning frosty, and you could smell rotting leaves and the odor of wood burning in fireplaces.

She asked, "How was Moscow?"

"You knew I was there?"

"I tried calling you at your office. Some grumpy female sergeant told me where you were."

"Crappy, disappointing, and dangerous."

"Why was that?"

"There was an ambush. Katrina and I got caught in the middle of it."

She grabbed my arm. "Oh my God, Sean. What happened?"

"We were in an embassy car when a truck blocked our way. When I turned around there were three goons holding guns."

"But you're okay?"

"I'm fine, but an Army captain named Mel Torianski isn't. Forever isn't, if you get my meaning."

Her expression turned sad. "I knew Mel. He worked for Bill. He was always very nice. God, I can't believe he's dead."

"The ambush was intended for him . . . one of those wrong-place-at-the-wrong-moment deals for Katrina and me."

Okay, yes, I was lying to her. Shame on me for that, but I was offering her plausible deniability. Given her employer and those lie detectors, she might need it.

On a more selfish note, the fewer people who knew of Katrina's and my little conspiracy to conceal the truth, the better. As I mentioned earlier, I'm a lawyer.

Anyway, she was shaking her head. "Poor Mel. I always liked him. I don't get it, though. Why would anybody want to kill him?"

"I don't know. The Russian police said it was Chechens. Some of your spook buddies were looking into it, but obviously weren't sharing their theories with us."

"Well, I'm just glad you're okay."

I drew a few breaths and wondered how to approach this next point, because frankly it was delicate, delicate, delicate. Unfortunately, there just wasn't any way to soft-shoe into it.

"Mary, I've also learned a great deal about your marriage."

She didn't say anything, so I continued, "For example, about Janet Winters, and how you played hardball to get rid of her."

"That was years ago," she replied.

"Yes, it was. And I learned that Bill subsequently screwed around on you more times than I've brushed my teeth. I learned all about the Siberian Nights Escort Service, and all the other women he was sleeping with. You knew about them, too, didn't you?"

"I do now," she admitted.

"Why didn't you warn me about this?"

She looked away and replied, "How did you learn about it?"

"Adultery is on the list of charges. Bill put us on to

his former secretary, and folks in the embassy told us about the rest."

She turned back to me with a sad, resigned smile. "I'm sorry. I know I should've told you. I thought about it a few times."

"That isn't an answer."

"No, you're right. Which reason do you want to hear? The one that will make me sound good or the truth?"

"Start with the truth. If that's too ugly, we'll take a stab at the prettier one."

She started walking. "All right, truth—Bill wasn't the man I thought I was marrying. You've never heard that one before, right? When we were dating he seemed so damned perfect—kind, solicitous, witty. He can be incredibly charming when he wants to."

"But he changed afterward?"

"Not really, no," she said, seeming perhaps confused, or maybe troubled. "He was a good husband. Parts of him were hard to take . . . his vanity, his ambition. Irritating things, certainly, but in the scheme of things, not worth wrecking a marriage over."

"And when you discovered Janet Winters?"

She looked at the ground and chuckled. "There was a bad day. I learned about her from the charge card entries. Do you believe it? I don't know what made me madder—her or the prosaic way he let me discover it."

"Her, would be my guess."

She nodded. "I confronted him, of course. We'd just had Courtney a year or two before. I was shocked . . . heartbroken . . . every stereotypical thing you expect a cuckolded wife to be. And he was everything you expect a cheat to be. He swore it was the first time, that he'd been stupid, crazy, was sorry, and the rest. He promised it wouldn't ever happen again."

"And you believed him?"

"I wanted to. I went through the next phase every wife who's been cheated on goes through. I wondered what I did wrong, how I wasn't meeting his needs, the whole list of insipid questions." She paused to chuckle again, I suspect not because she thought it was funny, but the opposite. "I went on a diet, opened an account at Victoria's Secret, took cooking lessons. You wouldn't have recognized me."

"And then Moscow?"

She nodded. "The second time around you don't get hysterical. Trust me, I've read every pop psychology book there is on the subject. The second time, you either divorce them, kill them, or become resigned to it. I obviously didn't divorce or kill him, so you know the second half of this tale."

"Did you confront him?"

"No."

"That's a little odd, isn't it?"

"Perhaps. I thought my reasons were good. In every other way, our marriage was strong. The kids were happy and I didn't want to destroy that, either. What I did was stop having sex with him."

"He didn't wonder why?"

"He knew why. He didn't want the ugly confrontation either."

"Okay, I got all that. How come you didn't warn me?"

"We're still on the truth?"

"Still there."

"I was too embarrassed. I . . . well, I couldn't tell *you.*"

"Because we used to be an item."

"Exactly. For some odd reason, I wanted you to believe we had a perfect marriage."

"Silly reason."

"I guess."

I took another deep breath. "By the way, I met Alexi Arbatov. Nice guy."

Her face turned blank. "You . . . you *what?*"

I thought if I slipped that in damned quick, we'd get past the hard part. This falls under the old mashed-potatoes-and-peas theory, where you hide the peas under the potatoes so your mother thinks you ate them. It never worked then, either.

"Mary, he's a witness. Maybe the key witness."

"Sean, what were you thinking? Oh Christ."

"It's okay. I did that little three-stripes-on-the-statue deal and we met secretly."

"Bill told you about that? Don't you know what you're doing? Alexi's the most important asset we've ever recruited. Do you have any notion what they'll do to him if he's caught? This isn't about you and your client."

"Yeah, it is. Inconvenient, I know, but I have an obligation to follow every avenue, and Alexi's an avenue."

"Wrong. Bill's using you. He's turned you into a puppet. He's manipulating you into exposing Alexi."

"You sound like you think Bill's guilty."

"No, I don't . . . or maybe . . . oh hell, I don't know what I think anymore." She rubbed her forehead, like she had a king-size migraine. She said, "Bill's angry, right?"

"Oh, I suppose you could say that."

"I know what he's like when he gets this way. He gets vengeful. He's probably mad enough to try to burn Alexi to get back at the CIA. You can't be part of that."

The only problem with her logic was that it had been my idea to meet with Alexi, not his. You could argue that Morrison left a trail of breadcrumbs that led me in that direction; I just didn't believe that he was that devious. Or that I was that gullible. I said, "Why didn't he expose him before? Say Bill was a traitor, why didn't he give him away long ago?"

"I'm afraid it doesn't prove anything. Exposing Alexi would've been suicidal. If Alexi were arrested by the Russians, there would've been an internal investigation. It's routine, and only ten living people know about Alexi. The rest of us take lie-detector exams. Bill would've hung a neon sign over his own head."

"Yeah, well, Alexi thinks Bill's innocent. In fact, he agrees with Bill that this whole thing's a frame job."

Her face turned very still and very tense. "He told you that?"

"He's convinced of it."

"And did he say who framed Bill?"

"He thinks it's some cabal in Moscow he's been trying to crack for about ten years."

She stared off at the trees. "Oh shit, Sean . . . not

Alexi's cabal."

"He told me you knew about it."

"Of course I know about it. He's been mumbling about it for twelve years. It's his fixation. For God-sakes, we even encouraged his belief. It was all part of the plan."

"What plan?"

She suddenly stopped talking. She folded her arms across her chest and stared down at the ground. She had obviously already crossed that line where Alexi's name was going to be a topic of discussion at her next lie detector session. Up to this point, though, she could blame it all on her husband's pesky lawyer and his incessant nosiness. The next explanation was the big one, the disclosure that put her on quicksand.

When she looked up, she put her hand back on my arm. "Sean, how do you think we recruited him in the first place? The first time he met Bill he began complaining about some mysterious force that was tearing apart his country. He was obviously groping to see what we knew. So we sent back Bill to tell him we suspected the same thing. It was a ruse. We used his vulnerability to establish an alliance. Like many people of extraordinarily high intelligence, Alexi is paranoid."

"How do you know that?"

"Because the Agency's top psychiatrist has been helping us manage him this whole decade. Do you know the code name of this operation? 'The Patient.' Alexi's paranoia is the hook that allowed us to make him an asset. We fed it. We constructed operations to exacerbate it. Why do you think he betrayed his country? Alexi is extremely patriotic. In his mind, he's not betraying his country, he's trying to defeat some dark hidden force that hijacked his nation. Sound familiar?"

"What about Yeltsin's election? The way he tells it, there's no plausible way Yeltsin went from zip to victory inside three months."

"Oh, please. What the hell does Alexi Arbatov know about politics? For Godsakes, he's a KGB hack. His knowledge of politics was shaped at Moscow University under the Communists. Do you know what he was taught? That democracy is a capitalist farce where rich men buy candidates and foist them upon the poor working class. To get inside his head we even got copies of the course books he was taught with. You have no idea how much work and effort went into recruiting and managing him. If you expose him, the whole world is going to crash down on your head. I'm worried for you. That's why I'm explaining this."

"You still didn't explain how Yeltsin won."

She very patiently said, "Yeltsin won because the other candidates were too unattractive and politically clumsy. He won because the big money backed him, and he was an incumbent who used the power and prestige of his office. It happens in this country all the time. Look at some of the hacks that hold high office and get reelected again and again. But when Alexi told us about his dark suspicions we said, 'Yes, yes, you're right, Alexi, there does appear to be something mysteriously sinister.' The same thing with Chechnya and Georgia and Azerbaijan. I assume he told you about those, too.

We were validating his fears, Sean. We were maintaining him as an asset."

To my credit, I had entertained the notion that Alexi's tale was suspect—that he was lying to me, or leading me down a blind path or was just plain wrong. But I'd never even suspected he was delusional. My client struck me as delusional, but Alexi?

But then I didn't have a highly paid psychiatrist guiding me through the twisted labyrinths of Alexi's head. It now seemed so obvious. The CIA torqued his paranoia in a calibrated campaign to turn him into a traitor. He was a highly moral man who worked in an immoral profession for an immoral government and constructed bogeymen to salve his troubled conscience. They'd focused on his vulnerability, exactly as folks in their profession are taught.

I stared off at a wisp of smoke trailing out of a chimney. "Wow."

She was holding both my arms and staring into my eyes, measuring something, maybe whether there was a brain somewhere inside that head. Then she smiled. "I know your intentions were good. You're out of your depth though. Just . . . please, be more careful. I talked you into taking this case, and I'd never forgive myself if you got hurt."

We began walking arm-in-arm back to the oversize barn she called home. I said, "And about your husband's cheating . . . I'm sorry it turned out that way. It must've been miserable for you. Believe me, I took no joy in discovering it."

"I warned you it wasn't a perfect marriage. I wasn't

exaggerating, was I?"

"Why didn't you just divorce the son of a bitch?"

"The same reason I married him instead of you."

"And what was that?" I asked.

"I misjudged."

We were at the front door. She turned and looked into my eyes. This was one of those earthshaking moments when a real dramatic thing has been said, and some kind of equally dramatic follow-up is needed. She was leaning slightly toward me—all I had to do was pull her into my arms.

I'm not a complete stickler on professional ethics, but I have my limits. She was married, and that's one thing. She was my client's wife, and that's another thing. She was a vision from my past who tugged at my heart and filled my dreams, and that's yet another thing.

I pondered all these clashing thoughts until the moment turned awkward, she backed away, went inside, and closed the door.

I was not having a good day with women.

CHAPTER TWENTY-SIX

I FLEW back to Kansas City the next morning. Katrina took a separate flight, I think because she was still peeved and wanted to avoid me. The frosty look she gave me at the prison entrance tended to support that theory.

Anyway, I had bigger fish to fry than her hurt feelings, like for starters, a client who insisted he was innocent when every indication and piece of evidence screamed guilty, guilty, guilty.

Morrison was already manacled to the table as we walked in. Before we could even sit, he demanded, "Well? What have you accomplished?" His tone was petulant and bossy, a general officer talking down to two inferiors, and it pissed me off.

"We went to Moscow," Katrina swiftly intervened, smart enough to ignore his lousy manners.

"Yeah, so . . . ?"

"We accomplished a great deal," I said, ticking off points with my fingers. "We discovered the prosecution will have no difficulty getting a conviction for adultery. Incidentally, your office phone was bugged and it's all on tape."

For a mere instant he appeared surprised, perhaps even shocked. Then the look melted. Given everything else he was accused of, the womanizing probably struck him as an incidental distraction. It would be embarrassing in court, but little more than a sideshow.

"Oh, and by the way," I added, "Mary knew about it, too."

This wasn't news to him, I was just confirming it, but Katrina looked surprised. "We also met with Alexi Arbatov," I continued, "and he thinks you're innocent, that you were probably framed, but he doesn't know by who, or why. Oh, and last but not least, somebody tried to kill us."

"Moscow's a dangerous place," he dryly observed.

Even Miss Hold-your-temper lost it on that one. She said, "Somebody tried to *assassinate* us. We were ambushed. Mel Torianski got his head blown off."

That dryness instantly evaporated. "By who?"

"The police claimed it was Chechen terrorists. But the ambassador said they blame everything on Chechens."

He contemplated that a moment. "He's right. It was someone else."

I asked, "Like who?"

But he wasn't listening to me. At first he seemed buried in thought, then suddenly his expression turned elated. "Don't you see? This proves I've been telling the truth. Whoever tried to murder you is worried. They know you're looking."

"Nobody knew I was looking. We met with Alexi in secret."

"You *thought* you were meeting him in secret. Obviously you were wrong."

We'd already come to that conclusion ourselves, so I conceded the point.

Then he asked, "Where was Mary? Did you check on her whereabouts?"

"At work and her father's home. Why?"

He began waving his arms around in excitement. "That proves nothing. It would've been so easy for her to arrange. Did she know you were there?"

"So what if she knew," I said, realizing with an ugly jolt what he was implying.

He kept going anyway. "And if she guessed you were meeting with Alexi, she probably . . . oh shit . . . I was the one who turned him. I was the one he trusted. But with me out of the picture, she'd own him completely. She couldn't let you expose him. She needs him for her future. Don't you see it?"

"What the hell are you talking about? If you're convicted of treason, the CIA won't let her get within a continent of Arbatov. And the closest she'll ever be allowed to get near that big building in Langley will be her father's house. Her career's over."

He gave me a sly look. "She tell you that?"

"Nearly verbatim."

"Drummond, you're such a sucker. With me out of the picture they'll be completely reliant on her to retain Alexi. Don't you understand how important he is? And if she gets credit for turning me in, she'll get a gold medal from those bastards she works for. They'll love her for it. She chose her country over her lousy traitorous husband . . . what greater love for her country and all that crap. You beginning to see it?"

"What I'm seeing is a complete asshole."

He leaned back into his seat and grinned. "I did a lot of thinking in that hospital bed. I thought, now, who would know me well enough to set me up like this? It had to be an espionage specialist. Nobody off the street has the knowledge or skills to pull this off. It would have to be somebody with a motive." He looked at me expectantly. "She had a motive, all right. You discovered it yourself."

"You're losing it."

"You stupid asshole. You have no idea how she plays. She's not the sweet little thing you think, Drummond. How the hell do you think she got so far in the Agency so fast? She cut people's nuts off before they even heard her coming."

But before I could say another word, Katrina smoothly said, "Okay, we'll look into it. I promise. In the meantime, we're also considering other possibilities."

"Like what?"

To which she replied, "Did you ever hear Alexi share any theories about some mysterious Russian cabal?"

He was distracted by other thoughts and offhandedly said, "Uh, yeah, sure. All the time."

"And what did you think?"

"It's Russia. If it sounds rotten there's probably some truth to it. But so what? You gotta understand Russians."

"And what do we have to understand about Russians?" asked Katrina, who was raised by a Russian and therefore had a few insights.

"They're the most conniving race on earth. Their whole history is a never-ending series of coups and palace manipulations. It's their national sport."

"So you think there is a cabal?" Katrina asked.

"No. But Alexi believed it, and I used his suspicion to lure him in. Probably somewhere in Moscow there's some group up to something, and Alexi has blown it out of proportion. Hell, there's probably a hundred different groups, and Alexi has jumbled them all together into some single gargoyle. If there was something as big as he suspects, we would've detected it."

"How?"

"Because our penetrations have increased a thousandfold since the Big Bang. Used to be it took work. It was a closed country with cops and soldiers and

KGB guys on every street corner. If you joined a Russian for a drink, you had a thousand prying eyes on you, and afterward the poor bastard would get a late-night knock on the door that led to broken bones and yanked teeth and all that. It doesn't happen anymore. The whole country's a big fishing pond. Cast a line and you get a hundred bites."

"So you think Arbatov's paranoid?" I prodded.

"What Russian isn't? Especially one with his background."

"And what's so special about his background?" Katrina asked.

"He was raised in a small farming village about nine hundred miles south of Moscow. His father was a pig farmer. You believe that? His mother died when he was two, and his father when he was ten, so Alexi was placed in a state orphanage. A year later he won some national math championship and got hooked up with Yurichenko."

"I don't see the connection."

"Yurichenko was the head of the Soviet Union's version of an exalted Mensa society, this group of people with extraordinary IQs. Not geniuses . . . hyper-geniuses. So Alexi was flown up from his orphanage to meet with him. The old man virtually adopted him, then got him into accelerated courses in Moscow and then Moscow University. Hell, Alexi lived with him until he graduated from college."

"So they're close?" Katrina asked.

"Closer than father and son. But Alexi can't escape his roots. Sure, he's got good manners and seems poised and polished, because Yurichenko gave him that. But he still has peasant's blood, and that makes him distrustful of everybody in Moscow, the same way farmers in Kansas feel about people in Washington. We fertilized that impression every time Alexi brought it up. It was the central motif of his treatment."

I nodded, because at least on this point, Mary and her husband seemed to be in agreement. Plus, the time had come to break the bad news.

I leaned back in my chair, knowing what was coming. I said to him, "The prosecution wants to offer a deal. We've agreed to meet with Golden tomorrow morning."

"What kind of deal?"

"We don't know the details yet. We suspect they'll offer to waive the death sentence in return for a guilty plea at the pretrial hearing."

He chuckled. "That's fuckin' crazy. I'm not going to plead guilty."

I didn't chuckle with him. "It will probably be a one-time shot. Once the offer's withdrawn we'll never get it back."

"What are you saying?"

"We've found nothing that exonerates you. To the contrary, every rock we've turned over just looks worse for you. And we believe Golden is still sitting on his most persuasive evidence."

He was shaking his head. "So what? Because you and this bitch here are incompetent, you expect me to plead guilty? Is that what you're saying?"

I bit down hard on my cheek. "What I'm saying is, it

doesn't look good at the moment, and if we turn down the deal there's no going back."

His whole demeanor suddenly changed. His face turned instantly suspicious. "You're not working this with Mary, are you? What's going on here? Have you and that bitch cooked up some kind of deal?"

I knew he was emotionally distraught and was lashing out. I also knew how much enjoyment it would give me to reach across the table and snap his neck. Of course, I'm a professional. We compartmentalize, right?

I mustered up my calmest, coldest voice, "My loyalty belongs to you. If I thought Mary had something to do with this, I'd go after her with everything I've got. I'll be back once I've heard their offer. It'll be your choice. If you don't trust me, then replace me."

I spun around and left. Katrina remained behind for a few minutes, I think to try to smooth things over. When she finally joined me out in the parking lot she looked a bit shaken. She said, "He was upset. He's convinced his wife's framing him. And he's frustrated that we haven't made any headway."

"And he's an asshole. It would serve him right if she did frame him, but the whole idea's ridiculous."

"I suppose," she said, an answer notable only for the assertion that she neither agreed nor disagreed.

Then came an awkward moment. Gentleman that I am, I decided to be graceful about this. "Listen, I'm sorry about Alexi. Remember, just because you're paranoid doesn't mean you're not a nice guy."

"Paranoid, my ass," Katrina replied, predictably, of course.

"Look, it isn't just Morrison saying so. I talked to Mary last night. She said the Agency headshrinks pinned him for a bona fide nut right from the start. She said that was the vulnerability they exploited since that first meeting, that the Agency even put together a few ruses to feed his fears."

It was that "nut" word, I think. Perhaps I should've used something more clinical.

Her whole expression changed. "Don't you *ever* use that word about Alexi. They're full of shit."

"Look, I . . . well, everybody's afraid of something. Alexi's fears are just, well, I guess, a little bigger than everybody else's."

She stuck her middle finger in my face. I stared at it for about twenty seconds, till she put it down. We walked back to the office, neither of us saying a word, neither of us liking the other very much.

One of Imelda's girls handed me a note when I came in. Lieutenant Colonel Charlie Becker's name and phone number were written on it—the same Charlie who'd gotten me the files on Arbatov and Yurichenko.

I grabbed the phone and dialed the number. Charlie answered on the third ring, and I said, "Charlie, it's your favorite JAG officer."

"I don't have any favorite JAG officers. I believe they should all be put on a big ship, floated out to the Arctic Ocean, and somebody should torpedo the boat."

"Do they at least get life vests?"

"Good idea. They'll all slowly freeze to death. We'll get it all filmed on satellite, and on dull days I'll sit around and eat popcorn and watch all the lawyers die."

"Wouldn't work, Charlie. Lawyers have ice in their veins."

"Bullshit. You're all full of hot air. Listen, you asked me about Viktor Yurichenko."

"Yeah, thanks for the packet."

"No problem. The thing is, Yurichenko's coming to America. He's supposed to meet with the new CIA director. He always likes to do that."

"When?"

"Arrives tonight. He's supposed to stay through tomorrow and fly back to Moscow tomorrow night."

"He staying in Washington?"

"This is the part I'm not supposed to tell you about, on penalty of death. He's booked at the Hay-Adams Hotel, and for security reasons, he's traveling and staying under the name A. Ames."

"No shit?"

"Viktor's got a real keen sense of humor that way. Last time he came, he used the pseudonym Rosenberg, if you can believe it."

"Buddy, I do owe you."

"You're right. You do."

I hung up, informed Katrina, and then I called Imelda, who was still back in the Virginia office, and informed her also, before I asked if it was possible to rearrange our tickets in the event we decided to come back to D.C.

Imelda immediately snapped, "Get your asses to the airport right now. I'll handle them tickets."

"Well, I haven't made up my mind yet," I said.

"He's a witness, right?"

"Well, he obviously knew all about it. He's in charge of all external intelligence operations. Morrison's material would've gone to his agency."

"So drop a subpoena on his ass."

I looked over at Katrina. "Imelda says to slap him with a subpoena."

She shrugged. "I don't think that's possible."

I said to both of them, "He's surely traveling with a diplomatic passport and thus is invulnerable to our laws. Not to mention, no judge is going to allow us to slap a subpoena on the head of Russia's intelligence agency."

To which Imelda said, "You think I didn't think of that? Serve papers on Ames. This guy Yurichenko checks in under an alias, you got the right to nail him. Besides, you ain't arrestin' him, but requestin' his presence as a witness. Draw up the papers and find the right judge."

I said, "Have the papers prepared before we get back."

It was a wild outside shot, but the game was winding down and I'd shoot from the bleachers at this point.

CHAPTER TWENTY-SEVEN

EVERY decent lawyer knows a judge or two who's willing to bend the rules a bit. Maybe they're lenient by nature, or they're sloppy and you know you can slip one past them, or they know you and feel sympathy for your plight.

I happen to be the one lawyer who doesn't know

anyone like that. What I did know was a world-class drunk named Colonel Andrew Cleaver, who by six o'clock every evening could be found at the Fort Myer officers' club bar, guppered to the gills. He was a sly devil who brought bottled-water containers filled with gin and then spent the evening ordering tonic water. He mixed his own under the table, thinking nobody knew, but everyone did know, because lawyers watch judges like hawks and trade rumors like old ladies in a knitting club.

At 7:00 P.M. I made my entrance into the bar. Imelda had done an expert job of preparing the packet, having made out the top sheets against A. Ames. Tucked six sheets down in the stack was a mealy-worded statement that vaguely implied A. Ames might be an alias for Viktor Yurichenko.

I plopped into the chair across from Cleaver and said, "Evening, Judge."

The judge—a tiny man with a tight, pinched face and a potbelly that pushed hard against the buttons of his shirt—was one of those drunks who could look at you perfectly straight-faced and clear-eyed, even though his brain was swollen up like a blowfish. He replied, "Evening Drummond. Care to join me? I'm a bottled-water man myself."

I waved for the waiter, who rushed over. I told him, "Scotch on the rocks." And he left to retrieve it. I needed Cleaver to feel chummy and hospitable.

I nonchalantly slid the packet across the table. "I, uh, I hate to bother you after hours, but I need to get this subpoena authorized this evening. Nothing serious, and

I might not even have to use the guy as a witness, I just have to go through the motions."

He was sipping from his glass and staring at the shapely derriere of a young female officer at the bar. "What case is it?"

"Morrison's, Your Honor. He's being tried in the Military District, so you can authorize it. Some guy he used to work with in Moscow just flew in, and he's expected to leave tomorrow. I wanted to serve him while he's still here."

"Morrison, huh? What's that bastard like?"

"A first-rate prick, but as they say, he's my client."

He chuckled at that. "God, we see some assholes, don't we?"

"We sure do," I admitted, taking my glass from the waiter.

He began patting his pockets looking for a pen, and I quickly reached into my breast pocket and whipped one out. He took it.

He asked, "Think this Ames guy knows something relevant?" He was going through the motions of ascertaining the legal validity of the authorization, no matter how much his heart wasn't really in it.

"I'm fishing. If he's got anything intriguing, I'll see if I can drag him back for the trial. He did work with Morrison, though."

He picked at something on the tip of his nose. "Don't know if anything you do's gonna help your client, Drummond. According to the papers, he's guilty as hell."

"Well, you know how the papers lie."

He cackled and signed, and then took another sip of his "bottled water." He said, "And you got Fast Eddie on the other side, right? You know some asshole started a betting pool on the Internet?"

"Uh, no, I hadn't heard that," I replied, quickly taking the papers and stuffing them in my briefcase.

"Well, if it's any consolation, I bet on you."

"Sir, that's very kind." I was actually touched that this old guy had thought enough of my legal abilities to wager on my behalf. I promised, "I'll try to live up to your confidence."

He cackled again. "Shit, Drummond, I was drunk. I wouldn't ever have wagered on you if I was sober." He kept cackling as he reached down to his water bottle and prepared a refill.

I walked away pondering the fact that the only folks who thought I could win this case were drunks who regretted it in the morning.

Anyway, armed with my freshly signed subpoena, I retrieved Katrina and we went straight to the 14th Street precinct, where my co-counsel used to hang out and fish for customers. She got us ushered into the back, where I shoved my papers at the precinct commander and asked him to provide a police escort to help us serve them. He walked us out to the desk sergeant, who went and located a pair of beat cops.

One was named Officer Murtry and the other was Officer Blackstone. Murtry looked like an ex-jock who knew exactly where all the donut shops were located, and Blackstone looked like a skinny, pimply-faced rookie who was still learning how to put on his uniform.

Murtry looked at Katrina and said, "Hey, Miss Mazorski, nice to see ya again. Haven't seen ya around the precinct lately."

Katrina smiled back. "I took some time off."

"Good for you. Anyway, where's this Ames guy located?"

I said, "He's staying at the Hay-Adams."

"The Hay-Adams?" he asked, looking surprised. "Funny place to serve papers."

By which he meant that the Hay-Adams is one of the swankest inns in Washington and therefore doesn't attract the kinds of customers the D.C. police would ordinarily be interested in.

"This guy's special," I said. "He's more of a character witness than a crook. But it isn't going to be easy. He's likely to have some people guarding him. He considers himself a very important man and doesn't like to be bothered by us everyday working slobs. You know the type, right?"

Murtry flexed his still-broad shoulders for Katrina's sake. "Hell yeah, I know the type. That's the curse of being a D.C. cop. Everybody in this town thinks they're important. Leave 'em to me. I'm not the kind of guy who takes no for an answer."

Officer Blackstone was energetically nodding his head, like, Yeah, me too. Let's get right over there and kick some butt. Just let me at 'em.

We went out and climbed into our cars. Katrina and I followed their patrol car, which actually worked out pretty well, because they parked in a no-parking zone directly in front of the hotel and we slid in right behind them. Then we trooped inside and Officer Murtry asked the lady at the desk where A. Ames was staying. She apparently surmised that he was part of the security arrangement for her very special guest, because she immediately provided him the room number, which happened to be at the end of the hall on the seventh floor.

We crowded into the elevator and went up. The doors opened and we walked down the hall to Yurichenko's room, which I was fairly certain was the one with the two muscle-bound goons standing beside the entrance.

Officer Murtry, with Officer Blackstone beside him, walked right up to the goon on the right and said, "Don't give us no trouble, buddy, but we're here to serve papers on the guest. Let's just keep this cordial."

The goon's expression didn't change in the least. He stared at Murtry as though he didn't understand a word.

Murtry said, "You hear what I'm tellin' ya? Open the friggin' door and let me get this over with."

The goon continued to stare at him, until Katrina, who was standing next to me, said something in Russian. This the goon understood. He began violently shaking his head and saying something rapid-fire and emphatic.

Katrina just as emphatically said something back, and we were suddenly at a loud stalemate with the goon shaking his head and yelling something in Russian.

Murtry looked at Katrina and said, "Hey, what language is that?"

Katrina said, "Russian. He says he can't let us in,

under any circumstances."

Murtry said, "Yeah? Tell him this is our fuckin' country and if he don't let us in, I'll bust his ass."

By this time, everybody was yelling, and it seemed only a matter of time before some guests got bothered enough to call the desk to ask for security to come up and check on us. This was not part of the plan. The hotel no doubt had instructions that if there were any problems for the guest named A. Ames they were supposed to immediately notify the State Department, or the CIA, or whoever.

Fortunately, the door to the suite suddenly flew open and, lo and behold, Alexi Arbatov poked his head out. He looked at me and at Katrina and displayed absolutely no surprise or recognition. He said something to the goon on the right that I assumed to be the Russian version of "What the hell's going on here?"

The goon started to answer, but I quickly said, "Excuse me, buddy, but do you speak English?"

Alexi nodded. "Yes. And you are who?"

"Sean Drummond, William Morrison's attorney, and we've got a subpoena to serve on the man who checked into this room under the name A. Ames. Would you happen to be him?"

"No. My name is Arbatov, but Mr. Ames cannot be disturbed under any conditions."

I waved the paper through the air. "Wrong. I've got a legal document to serve, and I'm not leaving until I've spoken with him."

Alexi was studying me curiously, halfway amused and halfway not. "Are you aware of Mr. Ames's, uh, indifference to your American laws?"

Which was a very sly way of asking if I had any idea who Mr. Ames really was.

"I don't care if he's Boris Yeltsin or Viktor Yurichenko himself, I intend to talk with him. This is America and I advise you to let us in."

Alexi pondered that a moment, then very politely said, "I can allow you and this enchanting young woman inside, but would be impolitic if your police were to come also. Mr. Ames would be most upset about this, yes?"

Katrina swiftly put a hand on Murtry's arm. "It's okay. Can you just wait here for us?"

Murtry squared his big shoulders, put on a stern expression, and said, "You need me, holler, and I'll bust through this door. Got that?"

Young Officer Blackstone also worked up his version of a menacing expression. "Right. We'll bust right in."

It was a good thing this wasn't going to be necessary, because the two goons by the door probably knew ways to kill these two using only their eyelashes.

Anyway, Alexi threw open the door and waved us inside. A long hallway led to a living room. Seated at a dining table was Viktor Yurichenko. He wasn't exactly what I expected, since he was only a little over five feet tall, a tiny, sprightly-looking man who glanced up from a chessboard the moment we entered and asked, "Alexi, who are our guests?"

"Viktor, this is Major Sean Drummond, who is saying he is attorney for General William Morrison. I am afraid I am not knowing the name of his assistant."

"Katrina Mazorski," I said, walking toward Yurichenko, who had stood up and had his hand stuck out to shake. "Forgive us for bothering you, but I have a subpoena for you to appear as a witness at General Morrison's trial on treason charges."

Yurichenko grinned and chuckled and slapped a hand against the side of his trousers. "A subpoena? Surely you're aware I'm immune to your laws."

I grinned, too. I couldn't help it. There was something infectious about Yurichenko, like talking with a beloved grandfather who just seems infinitely wise and captivating.

"I'm aware of it," I admitted, sensing this was not a man to try lying to. "I pulled a little ruse on a drunken judge. It's vital that I talk with you."

He looked over at Alexi, who raised his arms like, What can you do? These Americans are such ballsy, unpredictable people.

Back at me, Yurichenko smoothly said, "Major, do you play chess?"

"Yes, actually I do."

"Do you play well?"

"Not too bad," I said, which was true. I actually was a damned good chess player.

Yurichenko sat back down and began gingerly arranging both sides of the board. He looked positively delighted to have a fresh opponent. "Please," he said, pointing at the chair across from him. "I am afraid I can't give you much time, because I am an old man and require more sleep than I used to. I have very important meetings tomorrow. I hope you'll forgive me."

I sat across from him, as Alexi and Katrina positioned themselves to watch. I said, "Two out of three?"

He chuckled. "One to learn each other's technique, is that it, Major?"

Well, yes, exactly it, I thought with some surprise. You don't like to think you're that easily read.

I started with pawn to d5, a classic opener. I said, "There's no need to dance around, Mr. Yurichenko. I'm here because I've got a client accused of treason and murder, and you're the one person in the world who can say whether it's true or not."

Without hesitation he moved a pawn to e6 to block mine. He sounded even more amused. "You are actually here to ask me whether Morrison was reporting to my people?"

"That's why I'm here," I admitted, moving another pawn to clear a space for my castle.

"Simply extraordinary." He swiftly moved a pawn to make space for either his queen or a bishop. "Of course you know I can't reply."

"No, I don't know that," I said, shifting the pawn to make room for the castle. "What's the harm? If he's innocent, he gets to go free. If he's guilty, you're just confirming it."

"If I confirmed it, what good would that do you?" he asked, moving out his bishop to b4.

"It would tell me how to run my defense. I wouldn't waste time trying to prove he's innocent. I'd concentrate on punching holes in the prosecutor's case. Or, if the prosecutor offers a deal, I'd be better informed about how to respond." I moved another pawn, opening a path for my bishop and queen.

He looked up from the board and studied my face. "Do you wish to start over?"

"What?"

"The game, Major. Do you wish to start over? You've already lost. We could waste time on the next five moves in your strategy, but it would end in defeat."

I looked down at the board. There was no way he could predict what I'd do on the next move, much less the next five.

He grinned and reached down and moved my queen to g4, which was exactly what I'd intended. He moved his queen, then moved my castle to a position to threaten his queen.

"This is how we were maneuvering, correct?"

I nodded.

"And you can see now where three more moves would end in your defeat. You can see that, can't you?"

I looked at his face to see if he was serious—he was grinning—and then I studied the board. Well, no, I couldn't see it.

Yurichenko pointed at his queen and said, "I would sacrifice my queen to your rook. In the process I would move my bishop here. See your problem now?"

I saw my problem very clearly. I was one move away from checkmate. It was inevitable.

He began reorganizing the pieces for a second game. I figured the first one had taken just shy of two minutes, although that might be a charitable estimate.

While he set up the pieces he said, "Concerning Morrison, I don't wish to be obstinate or coldhearted, but I have no incentive to clarify his loyalty. If he was spying for me and I admitted this, I would be betraying a precious trust. In our business, if word got out, I would be finished. Who would ever again sell us your secrets? It is the golden rule of the profession."

He made the first move, shifting the pawn in front of his queen.

"Say he *wasn't* spying for you. Why can't you confirm that?"

"Who would ever believe me?" He chuckled. "But even if your government did, you must understand how we play our game. Right now your intelligence agencies are scrambling furiously to discover what he betrayed and to set it right. The more they suspect, the better for our side."

"Why so?" I asked, shifting a pawn to d3 so I could move my queen.

He shook his head, and I couldn't tell what he disapproved of, my move, the naiveté of my question, or both.

"Your people are in the process of collapsing vital programs they believe Morrison betrayed. They are calling in cells and pulling out agents and traitors they think he might have compromised. It is a windfall for my side. Believing Morrison disclosed our traitors, they now doubt everything they were given. They are confused, dismayed, defensive, and will take years to recover. If I stood up and said, 'No, Morrison never told us a thing,' I would be cashiered. In our business, Major, it's nearly as profitable to have a valuable traitor discovered as it is to have him in place. And if he never actually spied for us, well, that's a double windfall, isn't it? I know that sounds immoral, but it is how we play."

We moved a few more pieces, then he moved his queen two spaces to f6. I moved another pawn that opened up space to move my right bishop from g1.

I said, "Then perhaps you can recommend a solution to this quandary. If Bill Morrison's innocent, it would be a travesty for him to be found guilty. He has a wife and two children. He'd be facing death or at a minimum life in prison."

He moved another pawn that opened a space for a bishop to move.

"I wish I could help. I truly do. I'm obviously familiar with Mary, and frankly I admire her. She was superb competition when she ran your Moscow station. She's very clever, very skilled. But I must think of the needs of my country first. General Morrison knew the risks when he entered the intelligence profession. It's tragic, but the die is cast."

I moved my bishop six spaces to f5, where it could threaten one of his pawns.

He looked up at Arbatov. "Alexi, would you be so kind as to fix us some aperitifs? I assume you drink, Major? And you, Miss Mazorski?"

We both nodded. "Good," he said, bringing out his bishop five spaces.

I studied the board while he leaned back and stretched. I moved another pawn to a position that blocked his bishop from attacking my queen.

He chuckled. "A better position, but you will not last six more moves."

"Really?"

He reached down and moved another pawn to d6, to open his right bishop. I moved my queen six spaces to the left. He smiled and moved his bishop to a position where I either had to take it with my queen or shift my queen to a nonthreatened spot. Either would expose a pawn whose loss would threaten my king. I counted. Depending on how I moved he would either beat me in three or five moves. There was no way to prevent it.

He gave me a knowing look. "Some things are inevitable. You should play Alexi someday. We've competed for years. A few times he has even beaten me."

Alexi was smiling down at him. "Very few, Papa."

I said, "Then Morrison's fate is inevitable?"

"I'm afraid so. Please believe I wish it was different, but life is not like chess. The playing board is not always fair or just. I'll tell you this, for whatever help it might be. Bill created this situation himself. He made mistakes that undid him. He is an arrogant and selfish man who overestimated his own talents and the loyalty of those around him."

What was he trying to tell me? I mean, there's a lot you can learn about somebody from the way they play chess, and after getting my butt kicked twice in less than five minutes I'd learned this. Viktor Yurichenko was probably the smartest man I'd ever met, if not the slyest. He'd never hesitated a single second to make his next move, just nonchalantly watched me unfold my strategies, then brushed them aside like he was swatting flies. His own moves had been surefooted and deceitful. You can move three ways on a chessboard: forward, sideways, or diagonally. Both times he'd beaten me using only his diagonal pieces, his queen and his bishops.

He was still coming at me from the diagonal. Was he saying Morrison had been a sloppy, overconfident traitor who brought this on himself? Or was there some other implication and I just couldn't see it?

I nursed my drink, hoping to drag this out a little longer. Yurichenko struck me as one of the last of that dying breed called old world gentleman, who'd never throw out a guest without letting him finish his drink.

He suddenly smiled and said, "So how do you like law, Major?"

"I like it well enough."

"But you started your career in the infantry, if I'm not mistaken. You saw combat in Panama and the Gulf. Don't you miss the excitement?"

I tried not to let my jaw drop open, but I couldn't completely disguise my surprise. He obviously knew all about me. I said, "Law can sometimes be pretty exciting, too."

He sipped from his drink. "Had I been born in America, I would have chosen law. You Americans make it a delightful game of wits. Unfortunately, we Russians have never relied on our courts. Under the Communists they were façades. Under democracy, nothing has changed. We settle our disputes in the streets with guns."

I said, "I had a little experience with that when I was in Moscow."

"I saw the report," he said, then looked up at Alexi. "Did you ever receive an update from our friends at the detective bureau?"

Alexi looked at him, then at me. "They are still saying the Chechens were behind it. The two officers of the patrol that failed to respond in a timely fashion have been removed from the police."

Yurichenko was shaking his head. "You see what we must contend with? And to think we were once the second most powerful nation on earth. How the once-mighty have fallen, eh?"

I looked down, and his hand was caressing the queen he'd twice used to thrash me. I said, "If it wasn't the Chechens, who could it have been?"

"Who can know these things? I'm unfamiliar with you, Major." Then he suppressed a yawn, which really was a very elegant signal that I'd overstayed my welcome.

Alexi gracefully intervened. "Viktor, the long flight . . . you are becoming tired. You should be going to bed while I cater to the needs of our guests. Is important for you to be fresh for our meetings."

The old man glanced up at him, and the look on his face was one of huge affection for the younger man. "You young pup, it used to be me who put you to bed." He turned and looked at me with an abashed expression. "Life is pitiless to the elderly."

Alexi led the old man to his bedroom, Viktor grasping his arm like a crutch, and I noticed that Yurichenko walked hunched over like a very old man. Only a moment before he had seemed so sprightly and energized. Now he looked feeble and depleted.

Katrina and I raised eyebrows at each other, undoubtedly thinking the same thing. Yurichenko was a piece of work. Norman Rockwell would drool at the sight of him. It wasn't hard to see why he'd succeeded in the KGB and then been picked by Yeltsin to head the SVR. He was lovably crafty.

Alexi walked out of the bedroom a moment later, shaking his head. "Have you gotten what you wanted, Sean?"

"Yes and no. I obviously didn't help my client, but I just met a most remarkable man."

He looked suddenly embarrassed. "Viktor is a, uh, he is very special to me, yes? Like father . . . you understand?"

"I can see why. I'm sorry for disturbing you . . . I had to try."

"Of course."

Then Alexi walked us both to the door. He looked at Katrina. "Were you liking Viktor?"

"Who couldn't like him? I was enchanted."

He smiled like a little schoolboy. "Then I am bigly delighted you two have met."

Bigly delighted? Well, here we were again, me trying to save my client as these two treat this like an opportunity to meet the prospective in-laws. Alexi swiftly bent forward and gave Katrina a kiss. A simple handshake was fine with me.

Then we were out the door, collecting the two police officers and heading back to the lobby. I'd given it my best try, and I'd failed. I drove home in a severe funk.

CHAPTER TWENTY-EIGHT

WHEN I entered the office at 7:00 A.M., another of those ubiquitous vans was parked outside, and a man was hefting more boxes inside. At the entry stood destiny in the form of Fast Eddie himself, leaned up against the doorjamb, emitting a smug, ever-confident glow. The fiddler had come to collect his bill.

I walked up. "Here to see how the other half lives?"

"Something like that. You got a coffeemaker in this slum?"

"Yeah," I said, and we walked inside. Katrina was already there and had brewed up a fresh pot. I saw no more than six or seven boxes.

I poured two cups and handed one to Eddie, who was gazing with great amusement at the wall safes. It no longer looked like an office; it looked like a refrigerator store stuffed with ferociously ugly appliances.

"I filled all these?" he asked, proud of his handiwork.

"And two warehouses on the other side of the post. You outdid yourself."

"I wanted to be sure you had everything," he said, smiling wickedly. "The government can't afford to be accused of withholding key evidence in such an important trial, can it?"

I gave him a frosty sneer. "We have yet to see a single thing that's even remotely damning on the charges of treason or murder."

"Oh well then, let's see if we can rectify that," he

said, moving immediately toward a box marked with the number 6. "Let me tell you what's inside this box," he announced, mimicking one of those hyper-obnoxious game show hosts. "In here are copies of highly classified documents that were turned over to us by what our CIA calls a Russian asset. A court order seals that asset's name. However, the source's identity and employment have been confirmed by the director of the CIA and a military judge."

Not liking the sound of this one bit, I asked, "And what's so special about those documents?"

"As you'll see when you go through them, some are briefing papers and talking points provided to the President and Secretary of State for their discussions with the Russians. Some are NSC internal policy papers. There's more . . . but I won't spoil the suspense. Just say it's my favorite box."

I frankly didn't see how anything he told me was going to spoil the suspense. After all, everything he'd just said had already been given to the press.

"Okay, so there's a bunch of important papers in the box."

Eddie tried to look serious, but he just couldn't pull it off. He broke into a big, jubilant smile and announced, "Each of the originals has Morrison's fingerprints on them. The papers were acquired from a special vault in Moscow where Russian intelligence stored them for historical purposes. Some go back as far as 1992. You'll note at the top of each page there's a stamp in Russian Cyrillic. Those are the log-in dates when they were received in Moscow. Do I need to spell this out for you?"

"Sure, Eddie, spell it out for me," I said, trying to look unruffled as I swallowed the bile coming up in my throat.

"Over the years, your client turned these documents over to his Russian contact. They create a trail of espionage that dates back a decade. There are no other fingerprints on these pages, only Morrison's, and that's confirmed by the FBI crime lab."

I tried to look unimpressed, because that's how we crafty defense attorneys are supposed to appear in moments such as this. I couldn't. I stared at the box like it contained the plague, too dumbstruck to speak.

Finally I said, "And you expect me to accept the fact you won't give me the name of the man who provided them?"

"Did I say it was a man?"

"I'll submit a challenge the minute the trial opens."

"Go ahead. Waste your time. It's sealed by court order. This kind of thing gets challenged in espionage and mob trials all the time and goes nowhere. Besides, our source isn't a witness. Our source was just a courier."

He was right, of course, and I asked, "And what's in the other boxes?"

"Open them and see for yourself."

I began cracking open more boxes. He leaned against a wall, sipped his coffee, and observed with all too evident glee, like a little boy watching a porno flick. The first couple boxes contained hundreds of memorandums written by Morrison from his days at State and the NSC. I only had time to glance at the headings, but they were largely policy positions or recommended responses to Russian actions. I assumed these were papers meant to prove how Morrison perverted the American decision-making process in favor of his Moscow overlords.

The fifth box contained technical drawings and blueprints, apparently the designs pilfered from the export control office. I lifted a few out of the box as Eddie said, "There's no fingerprints on those, but they came from the same Russian storage facility as the fingerprinted ones and were filed under the same source title. Oh, and don't overlook the receiving stamps in the upper corners. Compare them with the fingerprinted documents—most of the dates correspond. Call it circumstantial if you want, but any reasonable board is going to conclude they were handed over at the same time."

The next box contained statements from people Morrison had worked with over the years. While I only had time to glance at them, the words "brutally ambitious" and "amorally selfish," or variations of the same, appeared again and again.

The last box was long and rectangular. I opened it. Inside was an autographed baseball bat.

Katrina observed all this from a distance, her eyes shifting from Eddie to me. Eddie shoved himself off the wall and walked to a position about two feet from me. "So it's time to talk a deal."

I was staring at the baseball bat. I dreamed of swinging it at his face. Eddie had played it perfectly.

He'd withheld the most damning evidence until this meeting, knowing that whatever optimism I walked in with would be eviscerated by the materials in these boxes.

I took a few deep breaths. "Okay, what's your deal, Eddie?"

In a clinically chilling tone he said, "Very simple. Plead to everything and Morrison gets life. In return we get as much time with Morrison as we need to get the full details of his treachery. We reserve the right to employ lie detectors during the interrogations. If we don't trust him, or we think he's holding back, the deal's off. If we don't like his attitude, the deal's off. You have forty-eight hours to get a response from your client." He looked at his watch. "That gives you till 7:31 A.M., day after tomorrow."

As smug as he was trying to act, this was his first offer. No sensible attorney takes the first offer. It just isn't done. Even Eddie would be disappointed if I didn't try to up the ante.

"Not good enough," I staunchly insisted. "We both know our government doesn't want this going to trial. What with our warming relations with Russia, and this joint effort in counterterrorism, and the nuclear reduction pact, a down-and-dirty trial's the last thing anyone wants. And I assure you, Eddie, I intend to drag the trial through the scummiest sewers you can imagine. I'll turn everybody's dirty underwear inside out. Besides which, the sum of Morrison's knowledge is worth more than just a death sentence you probably won't get anyway."

Eddie stood there chewing on his lip. I was bluffing, but it looked like it was working. He must've just realized that he'd underestimated me. The overconfident bastard must've thought I'd just lie down and take whatever he had to offer.

He shuffled his feet, and I knew I had him. He said, "You're sure?"

"I'm sure. Thirty years with a chance of parole for good behavior is the minimum. Morrison was a great soldier, and that has to count for something. And who knows how much of this evidence I'll be able to get thrown out, or to explain. Come on, Eddie, I need something I can take to my client. Give me something I can work with here."

He looked at the bat, and then stared at the ceiling as though searching the heavens for guidance. Finally he dug a hand into a pocket and withdrew two black-and-white photos that he tossed onto the table.

I studied them—both were pictures of men, who were about early-middle-aged, fit-looking, and smiling pleasantly into the camera.

Eddie said, "One is Sergei Romanov; the other is Mikhail Sorbontzny. Sergei was married with three children, and Mikhail had two young kids. Both were recalled to Moscow. Mikhail was tortured for weeks and then shot. Sergei was just shot. Morrison's wife was their controller. She's been tested with lie detectors and didn't turn them in. That narrows it down to her husband."

I stared at the photos as he disclosed this.

He continued, his voice deadly frosty, "Don't take the

deal. For one thing, I'll enjoy kicking your ass just because I don't like you. For a second thing, your client deserves the death sentence and I want credit for the kill. Ask one more time for better terms and the deal's off. Now be a good boy and go talk to your client. You have forty-seven hours and fifty-five minutes."

With that, Eddie spun around and left, trailing the reek of vanity in his wake. As deal discussions go, I'd never seen it done better. He'd set it up to watch me gape and stutter, because that's the way Eddie is. And he'd withheld the two photos till the end to add to my humiliation.

Usually in espionage trials, the best the government can do is posit a circumstantial case. Traitors tend to be crafty fellows who work in shadows and isolation, leaving little evidence and few witnesses. Almost always when the government suspects espionage they therefore attempt an entrapment, hoping their target will walk into the setup and offer them enough evidence to persuade a jury they had the intent to betray.

If Eddie was telling the truth about what was in box number 6—and he better be or he'd face disbarment— he had the murder weapon with the fingerprints on it.

I looked over at Katrina, who sipped coffee and observed our exchange. "What do you think?"

She pointed at box number 6. "In a word, we're screwed."

"Looks that way, doesn't it?" I said, still reeling and trying to come to grips with all the nasty ramifications.

She took another sip of coffee and seemed to be thinking hard. "He doesn't care what we plead, because he believes he has an airtight case. We can't attack his key evidence because we're foreclosed from knowing how he got his hands on it. And——"

The phone interrupted, and I went over to answer. It was Alexi, saying, "I am only having a minute, Sean. Viktor is upstairs preparing for his meetings and I have fabricated an excuse to come down to the lobby."

"Well, guess what? The prosecutor just left. He came by to drop off a bunch of Top Secret documents that were stolen out of a vault in Moscow by some unnamed CIA asset. These documents verify every wild claim the prosecutor's been making. And guess what else? The documents have Morrison's finger-prints all over them."

There was a long pause. He finally said, "This is impossible. Please believe me, if Bill was being con-trolled by us, I would be knowing."

"Then either you're a liar or wrong. Maybe someone else in your SVR was running him, and you weren't in the right compartment."

"That cannot explain this," he said, sounding edgy and anxious. "The prosecutor is being certain these papers came from Moscow?"

"He assures me the director of the CIA and a military judge have verified the source."

"It had to be this cabal."

"Well, that's another thing," I replied, knowing I was probably making a big mistake by bringing this up, but the compulsion was simply irresistible. "Both Mary and Bill said this cabal thing of yours is hog-wash. They said they were feeding your paranoia to keep you on the line."

There was suddenly another long pause, and I said, "You still there?"

"Th— they are wrong," he assured me, sounding both hurt and puzzled. "How are they explaining all the things this cabal has accomplished?"

"Well, I asked Mary about Yeltsin's election. She said it was just politics."

"And what about Azerbaijan and Armenia? Or Georgia? Or Chechnya?"

"All hogwash."

"They are wrong," he said, sounding suddenly bitter. "Arms thefts . . . wars . . . assassinations, I have been warning Bill and Mary for a decade. I have told them where to look . . . what to look for. I do not make this up."

I suddenly felt sorry for Alexi. I liked him. He seemed to be a genuinely decent guy, but who knows what devils and visions lurk in some folks' brains? He was frustrated and angry and hurt, but I had my own problems.

"Look, Alexi, all I know is I've got a client I've got to defend and I—"

"Sean, please," he interrupted. "You must be keeping open mind about this. Bill is no traitor. I would be dead if he was traitor. My name would have been handed over, and I would be dead. You see this, yes?"

"No, I don't. Mary said he never turned you in because it would've pointed a finger straight at himself. Plus, you were his ticket to bigger and bigger jobs."

I could hear him sigh. Then I heard another voice in

the background and Alexi suddenly hung up. I turned and looked at Katrina's face, and a happy face it was not.

Her hands were balled into fists as she said, "You bastard. You didn't need to say that to him."

"Yeah, I did. In case you're not paying attention, the prosecutor just dropped off enough evidence to hang our client. We don't have time to waste with Alexi and his nightmares anymore."

"You're wrong. If Alexi's right, it explains why somebody went to the trouble to frame Morrison. You know that. It's—"

I held up a hand to cut her off. "I'm busy. I've got work to do. Forget about it."

Her eyes narrowed to pinpoints, and she spun around and walked out.

CHAPTER TWENTY-NINE

I WAS actually glad she was gone, because I needed privacy to consider my options. Having all of Eddie's evidence gave me the chance to piece together how he'd approach this case. And I badly needed to get my arms around it before I flew out to see Morrison about the deal, to tell him whether he was signing his own death sentence or not. More likely the former, from what I'd heard, but I needed to be clear about the odds.

Here's how I figured it. Eddie would start by painting a scandalous picture of my client and trying to establish motive. The Dorian Gray attack seemed most likely.

He'd point at Morrison seated at the defense table in his brigadier general's uniform, handsome, impressive, a man blessed by nature, genes, and birthright to succeed. He'd make a big thing about how he was born into a wealthy, successful family, attended the most elite private schools, entered the very best army, been treated to every opportunity America has to offer. He'd been diligent, hardworking, and thoroughly disliked by any and all who served under him. He'd clawed his way up, but to him *up* was never high enough, because Bill Morrison was vain, arrogant, and endlessly ambitious. No accomplishment or title or measure of success was ever enough.

He had money—a great deal of money—but not *enough*. He wanted more, and if the price was betrayal, so be it. He was married to a ravishingly beautiful woman who gave him wonderful children, a stable home, social prestige, and stature. It wasn't enough. Morrison needed more women the way rich people need newer, bigger, more expensive cars. He needed the never-ending sexual conquests to assure himself, no matter how fleetingly, of his own eminence and physical attractiveness. The Army gave him awards and rank—still this wasn't enough. Bill Morrison needed even more professional approval than the Army with all its medals and pins could provide, and he'd sought it secretly in the arms of Russia's spymasters.

This, Eddie would claim, was Morrison's motive. He had betrayed his country for no other reason than his gluttonous ego. Eddie would promise a long line of witnesses who'd testify to that endless hunger, the trite selfishness, the succession of sexual trysts, the relentless and pitiless ambition. Nor would there be a dearth of those witnesses, because their statements filled two whole wall safes, an oral travelogue to a man whose need for approval—professionally, personally, and romantically—was bottomless.

Then Eddie would promise a long procession of evidence, from the phone and house taps to the fingerprinted documents taken from a Moscow vault.

But the more I thought about it, the more I realized Eddie was missing something. There was a hole—not a big hole, maybe only a tiny one, but a hole's a hole. The case was compelling, but circumstantial. I couldn't defend Morrison's character, because, frankly, he was a selfishly philandering jerk and too many people knew it, would swear to it, and would explain why in endless detail. And the phone taps would wash away whatever doubts remained.

But the only tangible evidence to the act of betrayal was those documents stolen out of Moscow by the CIA's mysterious source. And you had to ask yourself this: How does anybody know how those documents got there in the first place? Maybe some enterprising Russian agent stole them off Morrison's desk. At least, that's what I could claim. They weren't willingly handed over; they were pilfered.

I rifled through the documents and realized how weak that argument sounded, since the range of dates on their upper corners went back over a period of eight years, including the time Morrison worked in State, and the time he worked in the White House. Any sane person would ask themself, Hey, how could some Russian have infiltrated both State and the White House—two of the most closely guarded places on earth—day after day, year after year, and stolen those papers off his desk?

But the beauty of America's legal system is that the burden of proof rests on the prosecutor's shoulders. Eddie could prove the Russians had reams of Top Secret documents with Morrison's fingerprints on them, but he couldn't prove *how* they got them.

At 3:00 P.M., Katrina walked coldly back into my office and threw a sheaf of papers on my desk. She leaned against a wall, crossed her arms, and stared at me like I was a pathetic cad.

I looked down at the papers. The cover sheet said it was a speech given by the President of the United States in the country of Russia in the fall of 1996. I saw the official document center stamp—evidently Katrina had gone through the archives to find it.

It began with all the normal opening drivel you see in any speech about how happy the President was to be there, the great honor and privilege, what great friends Americans and Russians were, blah, blah, blah. Then the meat: Neatly underlined in red pen was the section Alexi described, the President of the United States saying Chechnya was an understandable thing, much like America's Civil War, a struggle to hold the nation together. He added a few admonishments about how the Russians should be civilized and try to hold down civilian casualties and all that . . . still, he was justifying, in fact sympathizing with, their monstrous war.

I finished the key sections and looked up. Katrina said, "Well?"

"Well what?"

"Do you believe Alexi now?"

I rolled my eyes. "No. The President giving a particularly insipid speech doesn't prove any damned thing."

She waved an angry finger around at the wall safes in my office. "What other chance do you have of getting Morrison off?"

"I'm designing the defense right now. Golden's case isn't as foolproof as we thought. There's no actual proof Morrison gave those documents to the Russians. And if he can't prove the treachery, he can't prove the murder charges. They're linked."

"You're kidding, right?"

"No, I'm not kidding."

"Have you seen his witness list?"

"Of course I haven't."

"No concerns about that, huh?"

"What are you implying?" I mean, the absence of a witness list while we were still preparing for the plea hearing was self-evident. Eddie and I wouldn't have to exchange witness lists till we were staring at a full-blown trial.

"What if his wife testifies? What if Mary says, 'Yes, my husband was a traitor. I lived with him, watched him, saw his disaffection, his suspicious activities, his unexplained absences when he met with his contacts'?"

"Wouldn't happen."

"You're sure?"

"Of course I'm sure. She's protected from testifying

against her own husband. I know her. She'd never participate in her own husband's lynching. Her kids would never forgive her."

"These are the same kids who don't know their father's in jail? Hello . . . anybody home?"

I was beginning to lose patience with this woman.

"Mary won't testify," I insisted again.

"Are you an expert on women now?"

"Perhaps not, but I know Mary."

She continued. "You said she knew about his trysts in Moscow. Pull your head out of your ass. Any woman would want vengeance."

"We discussed it last night. She accepted it. She was resigned to it."

"Don't be a fool. You're ignoring your last chance to prove Morrison's innocent."

"Look, Katrina, the CIA's been watching the region like a hawk and doesn't even believe the cabal's there. If I bring it up in court, Eddie will cut my nuts off. I've got one day before the deal expires. What exactly do you want me to do?"

Her face tightened even more. "Give Alexi the benefit of the doubt. Talk to the CIA and FBI. And stop putting Mary on a pedestal. Her husband cheated on her."

My head was shaking long before she was done. She stared at me and I saw in her eyes what was coming. I had the merest fraction of an instant to divert it . . . but I decided not to.

"Then find yourself a new associate," she said, her voice tentative, as though this was a bluff she didn't want called.

"Accepted," I replied.

Her head snapped back and she looked surprised, then confused and, ultimately, resigned. Without another word she spun around and left, closing the door quietly behind her, which wasn't the way I would've done it, but then I have my flaws.

I didn't like the way this ended, but I'd lost my appetite for arguing with her. In cases like this you run into all kinds of dead ends, and you need to recognize when the street doesn't go anywhere or you'll spend days lost in cul-de-sacs. And, for the record, I didn't have days.

Anyway, I put that behind me and started going through the stacks of papers Eddie had left, searching for clues. I kept trying to focus on those papers, only it wasn't working, and at five o'clock I called Mary and left.

The black Porsche wasn't there when I pulled up twenty minutes later. I walked to the entrance and rang the bell. Mary opened it immediately, as though she'd been waiting by the entrance. She was dressed to the nines in a short skirt and a low-cut bodice. She stepped out and gave me a tight hug and a kiss.

"I'm glad you came," she said. "I'm all alone. I could use some good company."

"What, no kids?"

"I shipped them off this morning for a month at an outdoor ranch in Wyoming. They were going crazy being cooped up in this house. Nor was their grandpa handling it well, particularly after Jamie threw a football that broke a Ming vase."

"A Ming vase? A real one?"

"Sixty thousand dollars' worth of genuine Chinese porcelain."

I chuckled. "I knew that boy had greatness in him. I wish I could've witnessed that."

She chuckled and said, "No, you really don't . . . I mean, you really don't."

I peeked around her. "And Homer? He's not hiding behind the door with a knife, is he?"

"He's at some Kennedy Center shindig and won't be home until late. I'm sorry. I know how much you two enjoy each other."

"My night is ruined."

She grabbed my arm and tugged me inside. "Come on. I need a stiff drink and you look like you need one, too."

I pulled backward and said, "I'm not sure that's a good idea."

"My father has a special bottle of 1948 Glenfiddich. He's had it for thirty years and refuses to open it, like it's liquid gold."

Well, how could I possibly refuse?

She led me back to the living room, where a fire was roaring in a truck-size fireplace. No lights were on inside the room; the only illumination came from the evocatively flickering flames. She made herself a vodka gimlet and me a tall glass of scotch, and then we sat on a brown leather couch that faced the big fire. I savored that first sip and guessed it was probably worth about two hundred dollars. It wouldn't bankrupt old

Homer, but it would give him a little something to remember me by.

After a long while staring at the fire, Mary said, "Sean, I need to tell you something. No matter how this turns out, I'm going to divorce Bill. I don't know why I didn't do it earlier. What a miserable marriage we had."

I nodded, because we both knew I wasn't expected to offer any comment or condolence. He was my client. She was my former girlfriend. My prescribed role was to stoically absorb this news.

She lifted her glass and took another sip. She said, "Bill and I haven't had sex in over two years."

"Gee, two years. That's a long time," I replied awkwardly, because if you had to pick the most hazardous topic in the world for us to be discussing as we sat all alone in this big house, well, here it was. I added, "If it's any consolation, he isn't having any sex these days, either."

She stared into her glass and said, "I know about him. What about you?"

"What?"

She stopped staring at the glass and looked at me. "Are you involved . . . with Katrina, maybe?"

"Uh, no. Our relationship's professional . . . or it was . . . she quit today."

"That's too bad. She seemed very nice."

Which part was too bad? That I wasn't involved with her or that she was no longer on the team?

She leaned against the arm of the couch and put her feet up on the seat, stretching those tantalizing legs toward me. She chuckled. "Do you remember that week my father was gone and we stayed here?"

"In this old mausoleum? We did that?"

She gave me a light kick in the ribs. "Don't play the fool with me."

"I remember."

"And I hid your clothes and made you walk around naked for two whole days?"

"I wasn't naked. I wore a towel."

"A facecloth as I recall."

"Same principle."

"Not when you're wearing it on your head."

"Well, I'm modest."

"And on the second morning we were sitting in this very same room, on this very same couch, and Consuela the maid walked in?"

Like I could forget that, either.

Mary's foot landed in my lap and she started giggling. "You were racing around this room looking for a pillow to hide your private parts."

"Your father should keep bigger pillows around."

She laughed and then we sat and stared at the fire some more. Mary was obviously using this opportunity to convey a message. Or maybe two messages, one subtle and one not. That divorce thing was clearly the unsubtle news. The more opaque message was that she might need the services of a rebounder when it happened, and I'd already pushed the ball through the net a few times, so to speak, so I stood in good stead. I pondered all this for a while.

My dear friend Mr. Pudley pondered it as well. He

shifted into position, feet in the sprinter's blocks, and waited for my other brain to catch up.

I finally asked, "Have you been interviewed yet?"

"What?"

"Have you been interviewed, Mary? Has the CIA asked you to sit down with an interrogator to go over your story?"

"No," she said, sounding off-balance, like, Hey, dope, you're spoiling the moment here.

"Have you found a lawyer?"

"I haven't settled on one yet."

I tore my eyes from the fire. "Mary? Why haven't they interviewed you yet?"

"I don't know. I suppose they've been busy cleaning up everything else."

"Uh-huh. Why hasn't your name hit the news yet? I mean, it's irresistible. You'd think somebody would leak it."

She stared at my face. In the firelight she was as beautiful as I'd ever seen her, the light from the flames playing across her sculpted features, occasionally sparking a glint in her blue eyes. Mr. Pudley was getting very upset with me.

She replied, "I've been expecting it. I pick up a paper on my way into the office, dreading the headlines. I guess I've been lucky."

"Bullshit," I said. Softly, but I said it.

"What?"

"You helped snare him."

She didn't even flinch. "What makes you think that?"

The important thing to note from her response was

that she didn't say, "No, that's not true." I put my glass on the table. "Have you been asked to testify?"

It was her turn to look away and stare at the fire.

"Have you?" I asked, more harshly. "I'll eventually get a witness list from Golden. I'll know . . . eventually. Tell me now."

"Yes . . . I'm going to testify."

"Are you one of Eddie's witnesses?"

"Yes."

My lips popped open and shut a few times, like a grounded fish, but no sound came out. She finally stopped staring at the fire and faced me. Her voice turned pleading. "I had no choice. Sean, please, you have to believe me. Imagine how you'd feel if you learned your husband was a traitor. I put up with his affairs, but treason? That bastard used me. He soaked up everything I knew, undermined me, made me part of his treachery."

My lips were still popping open and shut as I tried to think of something to say, only nothing remotely intelligent was working its way to the surface.

She stood and walked to the mantel. She stared at the flames and began speaking to herself, or the burning logs, or posterity. "I didn't cause this. He did. And it's not revenge, it's self-defense. If I didn't work with them, I would've been ruined. When they were tipped off by their source, they approached me and said it was my choice. I was his wife, for Godsakes. I'd shared everything with him. I would've faced professional ruin, disgrace, maybe even prison. I've got children, Sean. They didn't threaten me, but we all knew the stakes."

That last comment showed she'd been professionally coached. I could picture Eddie saying, "Okay Mary, now listen closely. Since you're his wife, you're going to be asked if you're testifying under duress, if you're doing this because you were threatened. Wink, wink . . . you weren't, right? You're just doing your patriotic duty. You're responding like a loyal American to your husband's infidelity to his country, your country."

My voice grew cold. "Did you help catch him?"

She paused for a moment, then said, "Sean, I didn't want it to be true. I thought at first I might be able to prove they were wrong, that their source was lying." She spun around and faced me. "Think about what this feels like. They're showing you reports on your husband's movements, his phone calls, his trips to hotels with strange women. His watchers were standing in my office, shuffling their feet, avoiding my eyes, giving me the names of the women he was screwing, showing me pictures of his latest affair. He was sealing his own fate."

Her face looked stricken, her body tense, coiled. She was too emotionally immersed to realize how they'd strung her along, how she'd been played. Of course they'd showed her those pictures and let her overhear her husband's voice making dates with his floozies. If I had to guess, that was Eddie's idea also. It was definitely his style.

I abruptly stood up. "I have to go."

She came over and took my arm. "Sean, please, I didn't have a choice."

"I don't either. Now that I know you're a prosecution witness, I'm required to avoid you. It's one of those odd little quirks us lawyers are required to live with. I can be accused of witness tampering."

I left her by the fire and I slammed the front door on my way out, because, like I said earlier, I'm not like Katrina. When somebody pisses me off, I share my anger.

If Homer's Porsche had been parked in the drive, I would've firebombed the frigging thing.

CHAPTER THIRTY

MY apartment building in South Arlington is called the Coat of Arms and was built sometime in the late fifties, a big red-brick monstrosity filled with tiny one-bedroom apartments with your proverbial cramped porches off the living rooms, and broom closets for kitchens and bathrooms. When the Coat of Arms was built, kitchens were considered utility rooms instead of stadiums, and bathrooms were where you went to deposit your waste, not luxuriate in expansive, candlelit elegance.

The Coat of Arms has three things going for it: It's cheap, it's cheap, and it's only five minutes from my office. The neighborhood ain't great, but neither is it a crime-infested ghetto. It is a semisuburban place, halfway on life's journey between a slum and a modest home with a lawn that has to be cut and a basketball hoop your kids never use in the driveway.

I slept in till seven, then made my way to the outdoor

parking lot and my car. I was preoccupied, and I don't mean by Mary's confession the night before, or even by regrets about letting Katrina go. Those were niggling issues compared to something Mary had blurted out in her confession. She'd mentioned she'd been recruited to entrap her husband after a source tipped off the Agency about his treachery. A moment later, she'd admitted that she only joined the investigation to prove the tipster was wrong.

I had a new threat to consider, a fresh and unexpected turn, as they say in thriller novels. There was a tipster out there somewhere.

Somehow, in all of Eddie's materials, there'd been nothing about any source tipping off the CIA and the molehunters about Morrison—no small oversight, if you think about it. In other words, Morrison hadn't been caught by the brilliant detective work of the mole-hunters, or even by Mary turning him in. He'd been betrayed by someone, presumably somebody with direct knowledge. And if Mary was telling the truth, Eddie had the kind of witness I most dreaded—a guy who came over from the other side to testify firsthand to Morrison's acts.

I was pondering this as I opened my car door and two guys appeared behind me. I'm normally fairly observant—recent evidence to the contrary—and they appeared out of nowhere. No noise, no chatter, no footsteps; I actually smelled them before I saw them—personal hygiene wasn't their shtick. One was Latino, the other black, and they were dressed identically: baggy jeans with crotches that drooped to their knees, muscle

332

shirts, and doo-rags on their heads. Both were also big and muscular, with that street look that told you they weren't collecting for UNICEF. Particularly impressive was the .38 street special in the Latino's hand, which looked considerably more threatening than the six-inch blade the other hood was holding.

"Hey Patrón," said the Latino, his tone familiar and coaxing like we knew each other, "just relax, and this'll go down easy. You gotta wallet, right, man? Keep this low-maintenance, huh? You hand over that wallet, we let you drive off to work, we all part amigos."

He'd stopped moving toward me, while his partner kept coming, his knife held low, his grip tight. The police, who study these things, say the wisest thing in situations like this is to simply hand over your wallet. Something like 95 percent of the time, the crooks intend you no harm, so long as you pacify them by handing over whatever they ask for. Don't challenge them. Don't taunt them. Don't try to fight. Play the odds and the worst you'll get out of it's the inconvenience of having to cancel your charge cards and replace your driver's license. Even in those 5 percent of cases where the victims get hurt, fairly often the victim precipitates it, by choosing the wrong moment to act courageous, or failing to act respectful and subservient to the thugs.

On any ordinary day, I'd do exactly as the police advise. I mean, it's not like I have a lot of money in my wallet. I'm an Army guy, right?

Something, however, didn't look ordinary about this. Why did one have a gun and the other a knife? Why did the guy with the gun stand back, while the one with the knife kept moving toward me, his arm tense?

I studied their faces, and they only made one mistake. I immediately stepped to the right, putting the guy with the knife between me and the shooter. At the same instant I swung my briefcase up into his face while my right foot lashed out for his groin. It's the oldest trick in the book: Threaten the target with two simultaneous chances of bodily injury. It was a fifty-fifty shot, and he took the 50 percent most advantageous to me. Instead of a broken nose, he got his testicles driven into his stomach.

Before he could even lurch over, I rushed him, ramming his body with all my strength, shoving him toward the shooter, using him as a screen. Which turned out to be a damned good idea, because the shooter let loose two shots at my human shield before we came into him full force.

The shooter sprawled on his ass, the pistol still in his right hand, his partner's dying body still on top of him. I reached for his pistol hand and pinned it to the pavement. With my other hand, I tried to chop him across the nose but knowing the instant I struck that I'd hit something too hard, like his forehead.

I could feel his gun hand moving up, trying to redirect the pistol at my head. I let loose of his wrist and grabbed the gun barrel, trying to keep it pointed away from me. We stayed like this for a few seconds, me lying on the dying knifer's body, the gunman trapped underneath it, both of us grunting and cursing.

He was a strong man, though. I could feel the gun

barrel slipping from my grip, when the strangest damned thing happened. The dying man trapped between us screamed, "Bastard!" and furiously bashed his forehead into his partner's face. That act of dying fury saved me. I felt his grip loosen and I turned the barrel toward his own head. In the process I must've cramped his trigger finger, because there was a sharp bang and blood and brain matter sprayed all over my face.

I lay still a moment to be sure he was dead. I couldn't actually open my eyes to chcck, because my face was covered with goo. When he didn't move, I finally rolled off, dragging the pistol out of his hand, just in the event I was wrong and there was a little life-juice left in him.

I stood up and wiped my face. Then I bent over and began searching their pockets, looking for identification. The black guy's pockets contained nothing but a few reefers. The Latino had more reefers and a thick wad of money. I pulled it out and counted; five thousand dollars in used hundred-dollar bills.

A moment later I heard a siren and I nearly stuffed the bills back in his pocket, realizing as I started to do so that if the police fingerprinted the money, I'd have some explaining to do. Instead, I opened my car door and put the money under the front seat.

Then I sat on the seat and tried to look like I was shaken, which, frankly, required very little acting. The police car screeched to a halt and two officers rushed out, gripping their guns and screaming for me to put my hands where they could see them and stay perfectly still. It's an old, overused line, but I didn't argue. I always try to be good-mannered in situations like this. They looked down at the two bodies, saw they were street hoods, saw my Army uniform, and the younger of the two officers told me to sit back down and relax.

He was still taking my statement when a meat wagon followed by an unmarked car arrived and unloaded some emergency technicians, who inspected the corpses, while an older, somewhat overbearing detective named Sergeant Burrows took over the interrogation from the uniformed cop.

After ten minutes of semi-antagonistic questioning and the uniformed officer confirming my identity, Sergeant Burrows said, "Seems pretty open and shut, Major. Coupla punks make their way over from the city to score a quick hit. Probably they only wanted enough cash to buy some dope. They were hiding between some cars when you walked out. Wrong place, wrong time, shitty situation."

"Very shitty," I said.

"We'll get their prints and know who they are by noon. Both had big-house tattoos, so they got records. Won't be hard to identify."

"No, I guess not," I said.

"You know, you fucked up."

"Actually, I think they fucked up."

"What we advise in situations like this is to just give them what they want. Don't play tough-guy hero. The gun and knife were only to threaten you. They probably meant you no harm, but you pushed the situation, so now we got two dead guys."

"I feel so damned ashamed," I said.

In a very tired voice, he said, "Don't give me no lip, Major. I could just as easily run your ass to the station and book you for manslaughter. Then you gotta go through the bitch of hiring a lawyer and defending yourself."

"Actually, I am a lawyer," I told him. "I'd raise hell, you'd look stupid, and we'd both waste our time. I overreacted, okay? I saw that knife . . . I saw that gun, and I responded before I could think. I wish now I'd just handed over my wallet and took my chances. Believe me, I wish I hadn't killed those two guys."

He studied my face to see if I was sincere, and I awarded him with my most appropriately pained grimace. Either he believed it, or he decided it wasn't worth his time to catfight with a lawyer.

He said, "Okay, here's the way we'll work this. We'll find out who these two are. We'll canvass the area and see if there were any other witnesses and if they'll confirm it went down the way you said. We'll then run this through the DA's office and they'll decide what to do with you."

"Fair enough," I replied.

He stared at me another moment, then walked back to his car. I couldn't blame him for being grumpy, especially since I'd left a few things out of my answers during his interrogation. The biggest thing being why I was so damned sure they weren't there to rob me; why I was damned certain they came to murder me.

What I'd seen in the black guy's eyes was the same look I'd seen young soldiers get their first time in combat, trying to work up enough nerve or rage to kill someone. Nor did I inform him this was the second attempt on my life in two weeks, that the Latino corpse had five thousand bucks in his pocket, that somebody obviously hired them to kill me, that they'd approached me thinking I'd do exactly what the police recommend and just reach into my pocket and hand over my wallet. I didn't tell him what a great setup it was, how my body would've been discovered by the next poor slob who walked out to the parking lot, a long, fatal gash from my pelvis to my chest, how the police would've filed it under those 5 percent of cases where the normal odds just didn't work out.

Why didn't I tell him these things? Because I would've been removed immediately as Morrison's attorney. Because it would've opened a line of inquiry I didn't want opened—about my meetings with Arbatov; about how I'd managed to turn a simple legal defense into some kind of murderous vendetta against me. And mostly, because I was wildly confused and needed time to think.

And because I realized something else—my client was probably innocent, and somebody was trying to keep me from proving it. There was simply no other explanation for two attempts on my life. And if you go one step past that logic, you realize that I'd somehow stumbled onto something that scared the hell out of whoever was behind this.

Which falls under the heading of good and bad news. The good news being that if I retraced my steps, I might discover something I'd done, somebody I'd talked to, some question I'd raised that marked me for death. The bad news being that I might be attending my own funeral before I found out what it was.

CHAPTER THIRTY-ONE

I T took four knocks on Katrina's door before she answered, and you can't believe how relieved I was to see her standing in her bathrobe, her hair wet and bedraggled, a disbelieving and vividly unwelcoming look on her face.

As soon as the cops had released me, I was struck by the thought that if I was a target, well maybe she was, too. Ergo, I was standing on her doorstep, trying to look like we were still the best of chums.

"What do you want?" she asked, in a most unflattering way.

I gave her my most winsome grin. "Can I come in? Please?"

She sighed and stepped aside. As apartments go, there was nothing to brag about here, a Lilliputian efficiency filled with third-hand furniture and a few plants to give it some life. It was neat as a pin, though, the bed made, the plates put away, everything spick-and-span. And who would've guessed she was a neat freak?

I said, "We've got problems. There was another attempt on my life this morning."

Her face raced from disappointed to see me to instantly concerned. "What happened?"

"Two thugs bushwhacked me in the parking lot when I left my apartment. One had five grand in his pocket.

They were hired guns."

"And . . . ?"

"And I, uh, I killed them."

She took a second to absorb this. "And why did you come here?"

"Because you could be next."

"I'm fine. Nobody's bothered me."

"That doesn't mean nobody intends to bother you."

Her expression went flat. She looked at her watch. "I've got an appointment in thirty minutes. I really have to hurry."

Were we having a problem here or what? I could see she was still very peeved and was trying to give me the heave-ho, only her timing was awful.

I flapped my arms up and down in frustration. "Are you listening to me, Katrina? Somebody tried to kill me. They might try to kill you, too."

"Why would they? I'm off the case . . . I'm no threat."

I shook my head. "Maybe they don't know that. Or maybe they're worried you know what I know."

She was shaking her head. "This is a very important appointment. It's for a job. Odd as this may sound, you need money to eat in this country. I . . . I have to get dressed."

"You might not live to eat. Please listen to—"

Like lightning, she whipped something out of her pocket, and before you could say "ouch" a switchblade was pointed at my stomach.

She said, "I can take care of myself."

Wow. She held open her door and gave me the distinct impression I was supposed to use it. It's amazing how grumpy some people can get. But then women are different than men. They have memories connected to emotions—a poisonous mix.

I stepped out and the door closed behind me. I took the elevator downstairs and left, but didn't go far. I moved to a position across the street where I could hide behind an illegally parked truck and watch the front entrance of her apartment building.

I took a moment to study the environment. Katrina didn't live in the best of neighborhoods. Winos were stumbling around, and a few homeless people were camped out on street benches, or huddled inside doorways, hoping to scrounge a little heat. There were some teenagers hanging out by a local bodega, swilling beer even though it was only nine in the morning. They were trashtalking, and just generally trying to impress one another the way young aspiring hoodlums do. If you were looking for likely suspects, you saw plenty of them.

About twenty minutes later, I watched Katrina rush out of her apartment building with her purse tucked under her arm, the way street-smart women carry their valuables in neighborhoods like this, tightly, so nobody can tug it away and run off with it.

I gave her a head start, then dashed across the street and followed. I guessed her apartment building didn't have underground parking, or even a parking lot, so, like most Washingtonians, she had to scrounge around adjoining neighborhoods for a space. It's that kind of city, and at the end of her street she hooked a left. My eyes searched to see if anybody was following her, or taking an undue interest. I didn't see anybody, so I ran forward to keep her in sight.

As I rounded the corner, a street bum on a park bench got up and followed her. He was about twenty steps behind her and he truly did look like a bum, dirty and grungy, with clothes that were tattered and weathered. What was odd was that he didn't move like a guy who was down on his luck, surviving on handouts, pickled on dope or booze or whatever he could afford. He moved like a sprightly killer stalking his prey, right down to the butcher knife he yanked out of his pocket and lugged in his right hand.

I screamed, "Run, Katrina!" and tried to calculate the distance, wondering if I could get there before he raised it over his head and slammed it into her skull.

He turned around and looked at me, even as she turned around and looked at him, and she saw his blade, even as he spun back around and faced her. He was only ten feet from her. I was at least twenty yards away.

Cool as ice, she reached into her purse, yanked out a small canister, held it up like a pistol, and unleashed a spray in his face. The butcher knife was over his head and ready to slash down into her face when he got the full brunt of it. He reeled back for the merest instant, then swung the blade through the air, only Katrina had smartly stepped aside, so he slashed at thin air.

That's when I got there. I punched him in the back of his head, more to attract attention than to hurt him. He immediately spun around, coughing and rubbing his eyes with one hand, brandishing the butcher knife with the other.

He had no idea who I was, except that I was an enemy. He began swinging the knife wildly through the air, while he used his other hand to wipe his eyes. It was only a matter of time before the pepper spray wore off and his accuracy improved. A butcher knife is a terrific weapon. In the hands of a trained murderer, it only takes one good whack and it's over. I had no weapon. Or actually, maybe I did. I reached into my pocket and withdrew a pen. I launched a kick at one of his shins and dove at him, hoping he couldn't get the blade up in time.

We went tumbling onto the cement, him trying to bury the knife in my head, while I brought my right hand up, then swung it down, my pen gouging directly into his right eye socket. I guess I had an adrenaline pump, because I drove it about four inches into his brain. I felt his body tighten and lurch, and he let out a loud scream that sounded perfectly awful, but thankfully didn't last long.

I rolled off him and Katrina stared down in horror at the Bic pen sticking out of his eye socket. While I hate to be cold about these things, I yanked it out and stuffed it in my pocket, because my fingerprints were on it, and I didn't want the police to know I'd been there. I'd already killed two men that morning, and it would stretch credulity if they found me with another corpse, like I just happened to be involved in another homicide, and, gee, what a terrifically funny coincidence, huh?

I got up and grabbed Katrina's arm, then tugged her

down the street. Some of the kids I'd seen drinking at the bodega had come around the corner, attracted by the dead man's scream, and they got a good look at the two of us scurrying away. There was nothing I could do about that, unless I wanted to race back there and threaten them with a bloody Bic pen. From the looks of them, that would be a very stupid idea. This was one of those neighborhoods where seven-year-olds get Uzis for their birthdays. Anyway, with any luck they'd be the kind of kids who'd never tell the police anything, one of those code-of-the-hood things. Even if they did talk, what could they say? They saw a man and woman running away from the crime scene?

Katrina and I intermittently walked and ran, block after block, until I was sure we'd put enough distance between us and the corpse that even a local sweep wouldn't catch us. I finally dragged her into a pizza shop and we dodged into a booth near the back.

She reached into her purse and withdrew a Handi Wipe, passed it to me, and said, "Wipe your hair. You got splattered by that man's blood."

I did as I was told, saying, "Thanks."

She nodded. "You always show girls such a good time?"

"Not always."

"No wonder you're thirty-nine and single."

"Yeah, no wonder."

The good news here was that her sense of humor seemed to be coming back. What does that tell you about her? Line her up to get murdered and suddenly she's all bubbles. Interesting.

"What did we do?" she asked.

"Damned if I know," I admitted. "But it's got to be the same people who tried to kill us in Moscow."

"Not necessarily."

She was right, of course. There could be two different groups after us. There could be a dozen. But being right, and being *right*, are two different things. These were the same bastards; I was sure of it. So was she.

I got up and went to the counter and ordered a pizza, partly because I was hungry and partly because I didn't want to arouse attention from the shop's proprietors, who were under the perverse impression that their booths were reserved for paying customers.

When I got back to the table, Katrina was playing with a napkin and staring at the tabletop. She looked perfectly calm. It was impossible to tell she was contemplating the fact she'd just nearly gotten her head cleaved in by a murderer wielding a butcher knife.

I said, "You did good back there. It took nerve to pull out that spray while he came after you."

"Practice, practice, practice. Grow up in TriBeCa back in the good years and life was always exciting." Her eyes wandered around the shop, then she said, "What are we going to do?"

"We're not going back to our apartments. We're not going back to our cars. We better assume they're very well connected and getting more desperate."

"The police? The FBI?"

"Eventually. But not until we figure out what to tell them."

She nodded at that, because we were both lawyers,

and the first thing every attorney thinks of is how much *not* to disclose to the police. Not that either of us would consider lying, but there's always the tricky question of how high you want to stick your ass in the air. We'd introduced ourselves to the CIA's most closely held secret asset, hid the truth when somebody tried to kill us in Moscow, fled from a crime scene, and possibly committed a few other misdemeanors—littering even—the sum of which could get us in very ugly trouble with the law. I had not the slightest doubt what General Clapper was going to do to me when this story came out. If I didn't have so many other things on my mind, I would've been contemplating what I wanted to do after I left the Army.

However, we were obviously long past the point where our legal careers were our overriding concerns. I said, "Do we agree we've stumbled onto something important enough to cause our deaths?"

She automatically said, "Agreed," which, considering the circumstances, wasn't any stretch.

"Do we agree Morrison's probably innocent, that somebody's trying to keep us from proving that?"

She hesitated, and in a very lawyerly tone said, "Explain that."

"The evidence suggests Morrison's been framed. By whom is debatable, but whoever did it wants to keep it that way. You and I have somewhere, somehow, touched something that puts us at risk."

"Okay," she admitted, very practically.

"What is it we touched?"

"You're the one with the theories. Tell me."

"Try this," I said, and she bent forward, her eyes searching my face. "What's this whole thing about? What was Mary working on all those years? What did Morrison's arrest solve?"

"The mole hunt."

"Right. The CIA and FBI knew somebody was giving the Russians things . . . important things . . . sensitive things. They caught lots of small fish, and even some big fish—Ames and Hanssen—but that didn't tie all the knots. The molehunters were still stubbornly plugging away, still following clues, still tracking their prey. Eventually, they'd catch him—or her. It was just a matter of time and circumstance. So the Russians fed them Morrison. They framed him with enough things and in such a way that almost any open questions would be answered."

"So the mole is still operating?"

"And somehow, we've touched something that puts him or her at risk."

The girl behind the counter called out my number, so I went up and got our pizza. We sat and munched for a while. What I'd said made sense. It wasn't necessarily correct, but it made sense. There were other explanations, but if I was right about Morrison being innocent then you had to seriously consider this possibility.

And if you agreed with that, you'd agreed with this, too: Whoever did the job on Morrison had gone to a lot of time and trouble. They had had somebody tip off the CIA in the first place. They had planted documents covered with his fingerprints in that vault in Moscow, then released them to the CIA.

All of which added up to this: Whoever did this was an intelligence professional with extraordinary resources, somebody in the CIA or the SVR who knows espionage intimately. Possibly, maybe even definitely, somebody with tentacles in both intelligence services.

Katrina finally said, "The FBI won't believe a word of it. They'll think we're a couple of sleazy attorneys trying to get our client off."

"Yes, they probably will," I agreed, digging into a particularly greasy slice of pepperoni with sausage, struggling to ignore its resemblance to the gruesome stuff that had splattered out of the killer's eye an hour before.

She asked, "Any ideas how to handle that?"

Instead of answering that, I said, "How much do you know about lie detectors?"

"What I learned in law school. They're considered fairly valid. Some study was done that gave them something like a ninety-eight percent accuracy rate."

"Do you remember what accounts for the other two percent or so?"

"Remind me."

"Lie detectors work by sensing changes in your body temperature and normal body rhythms. There are chemicals that fool the machine. Supposedly, you can even train yourself to defeat them, like Buddhist meditation techniques, where you disenfranchise your mind from your body."

"Your point being?"

I swallowed hard once or twice. "Let's talk about

Mary." My face turned dark as I added, "I went over and had a chat with her last night. It wasn't pretty."

"How ugly was it?"

"She admitted she helped take down her husband. They approached her months ago. I don't know how big her involvement was, but it had to be substantial because they were reporting back to her on what they were finding." I squirmed around uncomfortably, then added, "She, uh, well, she also admitted she's one of Eddie's witnesses."

Katrina was toying with a slice of pizza and generously avoiding my eyes. "Do you think there was more to it?"

"I don't know. She said the Agency had a source that tipped off his treason. I don't know if she was telling the truth or not, and I'm having a little problem trusting her right now."

Left unsaid was a great deal, but Katrina was a smart girl and could fill in the blanks. For instance, why did Mary beg me to take this case in the first place? Perhaps because she knew she had an emotional grip on me. Perhaps because I was the kind of sucker every schemer dreams of, the lovelorn loser who was so easily manipulated that he refused to see the forest for the trees.

Katrina was wisely not saying anything, so I finally broke the ice. "So, let's consider Mary."

"All right, let's. One, nobody was in a better position to frame her husband. Yes, she was telling him everything she was doing, but he was telling her everything he was doing, too. Two, she could pass in and out of his office every day, steal documents, take whatever she wanted, and never have to worry about a security check. Three, Morrison's deputy attaché said she was involved in everything in the office. She had all kinds of weapons to use against him."

"When I confronted Mary last night, as I mentioned, she admitted the phone tappers and the trackers were reporting everything back to her. She had her finger on every pulse. She knew exactly what buttons to push, exactly how to make it work."

Katrina broke eye contact with me and began staring at the tabletop, like she was suddenly distracted.

I said, "What?"

"You met with her last night, right?"

"Right."

"And she knew we were in Moscow, right?"

"Yeah. So?"

Katrina didn't say anything. She didn't have to say anything. She'd given me the hints and knew better than to draw the painful conclusions for me. They were, after all, inescapable, unavoidable, and emotionally crushing. Mary had arranged the hits against us. She certainly had the reach and resources. As the former station chief in Moscow she no doubt knew enough hoodlums she could hire to take us out. And as a resident of the D.C. area all her life, she wouldn't have any trouble locating some street scum to kill us. Money sure as hell wasn't a problem.

But why? What had I done that would cause her to want me dead? Was she worried I might expose Alexi? Or perhaps she sensed that Katrina and I were closing in on her? Or both?

Katrina was studying a paper napkin. "Well, what do you want to do next?"

"We're in way over our heads. We have to tell the FBI."

She nodded, and I added, "I know a guy. He used to be a JAG officer, got out, tried a big firm, never got picked up for partner, so he signed up with the Feds. Jimmy Belafonte . . . I haven't seen him in seven years, but last I heard he's working in the headquarters here. He's not the sharpest tool in the shed, but he'll do."

I went to the pay phone and asked the operator for the number to FBI headquarters, then asked the Bureau's operator to put me through to Belafonte. A secretary answered, "Money-laundering Division."

"Sean Drummond for Jimmy Belafonte, please."

I was immediately switched. "Special Agent Belafonte," a voice answered.

"Jimmy, Sean Drummond. I don't know if you remember me?"

"Sure. JAG School, right? And according to the news, you're doing the Morrison case."

"Same Drummond. I need to meet you—privately."

"Catch up on old times, huh? Love to, buddy, only I'm busy the rest of this week. How about next Thursday?"

"How about in forty-five minutes somewhere outside your building? I killed three guys this morning and I need to talk about it."

"Some reason we can't meet here?" he asked, sounding suddenly alarmed.

"Yeah, I don't want to get shot by a sniper walking in the front door of your building. I know that sounds paranoid, but believe me, I've got good reasons. I'm calling because I trust you, Jimmy."

"There's, uh, uh, there's a Barnes & Noble with a coffee shop on M Street in Georgetown. How about there?" he asked, sounding tentative.

"Forty-five minutes. I'll be there," I said before he could back out on me.

Until this moment, I'd been stupid beyond words. I'd been playing in other people's sandboxes, and I was the only guy too blind to recognize I was out of my depth. Everybody had warned me: my client, Mary, Alexi. My libido was too puffed up to hear them. I'd nearly gotten myself killed, and Katrina also.

Somebody was making a point of showing me my own limitations.

CHAPTER THIRTY-TWO

JIMMY was not an impressive-looking guy. Soft brown skin, average height, average build, average face, all of which added up to pretty honest advertising, since on Jimmy's best day, he was just an average guy.

He was sipping from a big Starbucks coffee as he noodled through the history section when Katrina and I walked up behind him.

I tapped him on the shoulder. "Hi, Jimmy. This is my co-counsel, Katrina Mazorski."

He spun around, nodded, and his face looked

alarmed. He immediately whispered, "What's this about three killings this morning? Tell me about that?"

"Between eight and ten this morning, somebody tried to arrange two murders. I was attacked by two thugs in the parking lot of my apartment, and some ersatz homeless guy tried to whack Katrina with a butcher knife while she was walking to her car."

He studied my face to see if I was kidding and came to the obvious conclusion I wasn't. "This isn't my baili-wick, Sean. I'm a financial guy. I do money-laundering and bank fraud, not murder, or espionage."

"Yeah, but I know you, so I trust you."

"Any reason you don't trust the rest of the Bureau?" he asked, appropriately suspicious.

"Working on my client's defense, I've discovered there is probably a mole somewhere in our govern-ment. Somewhere very high up, a mole with extraordi-nary resources. I'm not saying Morrison wasn't a traitor—I don't know about that. I'm saying there's another mole, and that's why somebody tried to kill us."

Jimmy was nodding his head. "And this mole is working for the Russians?"

"Right."

"The attempt on your lives? What happened?"

"Mine was set up like a robbery that went wrong. Only the killers screwed up and gave themselves away, so I, uh, well, I killed them. The guy who tried to take out Katrina, he didn't expect me to show up."

"And you killed him, too?"

"I had to. He was swinging a butcher knife."

He nodded, as suddenly six men and women came running at us from other nearby stacks. Before Katrina or I could do a thing, Jimmy was holding a pistol in his hand, and Katrina and I were getting our hands cuffed behind our backs, our rights read, our dignity trashed.

I was swearing at Jimmy, who was obviously wearing a wire, and he held up a hand. "Drummond, take it easy. I'm a federal agent. When you said you killed three guys this morning, I had to tell my boss. You gave me no choice."

It obviously wasn't supposed to work this way. In the movies, you see guys in desperate positions like mine, they call some old buddy and the old buddy cherishes the sacred bonds, protects their confidentiality, and takes care of everything. Either those movies are horsecrap or I'd overestimated my popularity.

Katrina and I responded like lawyers naturally do, keeping our mouths shut, although I'd already crossed the Rubicon, because Jimmy had me admitting on tape to killing three guys, and all hell was going to break loose.

Katrina and I were next led outside to two shiny Crown Victorias waiting beside the curb, as a crowd of gawkers and gapers gathered to watch a real-life arrest go down. This was a fresh and incredibly unwelcome experience for me, parading in front of folks like a common felon. Katrina was guided into the back of one car, and I was shoved into the other one.

On the ride to the garage under the FBI building, I contemplated the charges they could throw at me: conspiracy, manslaughter, fleeing a crime, hiding evidence. And those were merely the charges I could think of. The FBI and Justice Department have all those highly imaginative guys with Ivy League degrees who are geniuses at thinking up charges. No doubt they could do better than me.

We parked in an underground garage and then took the elevator to an upper-floor interrogation room. Jimmy hung around while a new guy entered the room. He had that weaselly look of the professional interrogator: long, skinny face, deadpan, droopy eyes, and a mouth with no wrinkles around the edges, like he never smiled or frowned or had orgasms. He walked hunched over, with his chin protruding out and a big, beaklike nose that poked suspiciously through the air.

He sat in front of me and said, "I'm Special Agent Michaels. Do I need to read you your rights?" Belafonte, the traitorous prick, leaned against the wall. It didn't take a genius to figure out why Belafonte remained in the room. I'd made my confession to him, and his presence was to remind me I'd already spilled the big beans, so let's not niggle over the gravy.

I shook my head. "Already done."

He leaned toward me like this was some kind of melodramatic moment. "We have you on tape admitting you killed a man in Washington and two men in your apartment parking lot earlier this morning."

"All that's true," I admitted, since it seemed damned silly to deny what I'd already admitted.

He leaned back and stroked his chin. "However, we have a bit of a problem here."

Technically, *we* didn't have a bit of problem. *I* did,

and not a bit of a problem, a mountain of a problem. I said, "I know."

He continued in a perfectly dry tone. "The problem, Drummond, is nobody reported any deaths. Unless you want to count a lady who got shoved off the subway platform at the Fourteenth Street station this morning. Only the D.C. police caught the guy who did that. Or would you like to confess to that killing, too?"

"What are you talking about?"

"What I just told you, Drummond. No dead guys showed up near your apartment building. And no dead guys showed up near Miss Mazorski's apartment, either. So what the hell's going on here?"

"That's impossible. This morning, at my apartment, the police came. I was interviewed by a detective. He took my statement."

He was nodding, like, Yeah, sure, tell me more, convince me.

I said, "I'm not jerking you around. I walked out to my car and two guys approached me with a knife and gun. It was meant to look like a robbery, only it wasn't. It was a hit."

He was still nodding, only now he was biting his cheek. "And what happened to the bodies?" he asked, scratching the side of his nose, like, Gee, no shit, throw in a few Nazi spies and quit boring me?

"A meat wagon got them. It was an Arlington County Hospital ambulance. I watched them load the bodies."

"What time?"

"Shortly before eight."

He nodded at Belafonte, who nodded back and left.

"And tell me about that second attack," he ordered.

"It happened right around the corner from Miss Mazorski's apartment. Around nine-thirty . . . maybe ten. She was walking to her car and a guy who was made up to look homeless went after her with a butcher knife."

"And you stopped him?"

"Only barely. Actually, she nailed him with some pepper spray and that blinded him."

"And you what? You shot him?"

"No. I stabbed him."

He was doing that head-nodding routine and scratching that big goddamn nose again, and I wanted to reach across the table and jackslap him. He was trying to be grating, and even though I knew that, and knew I should rise above his provocation, I was emotionally entangled.

I took three long breaths, then grinned. "Okay, asshole, I've got a surprise for you."

"I love surprises. What do you have?"

I reached into my pocket and whipped out the trusty Bic pen that was crusted with dried blood and specks of gray matter around the tip.

I tossed it on the table between us and announced, "This is the pen I killed him with. I stuck it in his eyehole."

It was one of those moments when you wished you had a Polaroid camera. He stared down at the pen but refused to touch it, partly because he knew better than to get his fingerprints on it, and partly because it grossed him out.

I couldn't resist. "I believe it's your turn, Special Agent Michaels."

The door opened and Jimmy Belafonte, the big skunk, walked in. He looked at Michaels and shook his head.

I said, "What is this bullshit, Belafonte? You're not allowed to talk to me? You checked with the Arlington police and they confirmed they didn't investigate the double killing? Is that what you were signaling him?"

"That's what it meant," he admitted, avoiding my eyes, which was a good thing because they would've caused his whole body to explode in flames. He added, "And there's no bodies in the Arlington County morgue."

"So this is really weird," I said, as much to myself as them. "Look at the blood on that pen," I ordered Michaels. "If I'm lying, whose blood and brain matter is that?"

He stared at the pen. "You tell me."

It was my turn to shake my head. Interrogators are taught to never, ever lose control of the interrogation, no matter what. That "you tell me" was his half-assed attempt to regain the upper hand. I was now asking the questions and his procedures said he couldn't allow that.

"It belonged to a guy who was hired to murder my co-counsel."

"And where's his body?"

"How the hell do I know? We ran off before anybody came. But the cops came to the killing in my parking lot. I talked with them and I saw a meat wagon, and

I've dealt with enough cops to know they were the real thing. The detective was named . . . uh, Christ, I can't remember his name. But I can describe him."

Michaels's nose was sticking in my face. "No need. We already know what he looks like. A middle-aged detective in a suit who asked a lot of questions, right?"

I rubbed my forehead. I fought the temptation to tell him what a stupid ass he was. This wasn't easy. "Somebody tried to murder me and Miss Mazorski because they want to keep the lid on something we discovered."

"And what would that be?" he asked, and from his tone I knew there was no way in hell he was going to believe a word I said, much less the exorbitant tale I actually had to tell.

I pushed aside my reservations and said, "We discovered that my client, Bill Morrison, is probably being framed for treason. We talked to a lot of people and left a lot of impressions in our wake, and somebody wants to erase some of those impressions."

"Uh-huh," he said dismissively. "Let's get back to these guys you killed. Who were they?"

"I don't know."

"You didn't check their wallets? Didn't get their names?"

"I said I don't know."

"But you told Special Agent Belafonte you knew things."

"Have you been listening to me?"

His expression did not alter the slightest bit. "You mean about the three dead guys that don't exist?"

I gripped the edge of the table. I gave him my screw-you look. "Michaels, let's rearrange the bidding here. They were professional hits."

"And their bodies disappeared? Come on, Major, you've got to do better than this. Help me out here. Convince me you killed these three guys."

Michaels and Belafonte exchanged quick glances, and while I wasn't sure what they meant, it was so characteristic of these things, and so condescending, it pissed me off even more.

"Are you going to charge me?"

"We're exploring that option right now," Michaels said, very cavalierly, like, Why don't you give me a hand here, because I'm having a tough time putting my finger on what crime you did.

I stood up.

"Sit down," he ordered.

"No. Unless you've got a warrant, I'm out of here."

Michaels looked at Belafonte, and Belafonte looked at me. In a very convivial tone he said, "Sean, maybe you should tell us more about the attempts on you and Miss Mazorski? What do you think happened to their bodies?"

I walked for the door, and Belafonte stepped in front of me.

I said, "Belafonte, move before I send your gonads into your ears and you spend the rest of your life with your earlobes getting hard every time you see a pretty girl."

He studied my eyes to see if I was kidding. I wasn't. I most definitely wasn't. He almost jumped aside.

I walked into the hallway and began swinging open

every door I could find. Two or three rooms were filled with suspects and interrogators and lawyers, and they all looked up in astonished shock when I stuck my enraged face in.

I finally hit the one with Katrina and her interrogator, a woman with a big ass who looked like Michaels's twin sister, vulture nose, droopy eyes and all. She started yelling at me.

I walked in, grabbed Katrina's arm, and dragged her out of the room, while her interrogator howled. We walked down the hall to the elevator, took it down five floors, then walked out of the building.

The telling thing was that nobody tried to stop us. No guys in blue or gray suits came running after us, waving guns and shields and frantically screaming at us to halt or else.

I said, "That was bullshit."

She said, "Don't you have any real friends?"

"I barely knew him. We went through the JAG course together. He always was a conformist jerk. What the hell was I thinking? So how far did you get with your story?"

She was shaking her head. "The bitch didn't believe a word. She said there were no bodies."

"Yeah," I said, waving my arm for a taxi. "It was damned strange. Too strange."

"Speaking of strange, what happened to the bodies?"

"You've got two options. One, the police have them and there's some kind of monumental paperwork screwup. If it was just the D.C. police, what with their record on homicides, okay, maybe. But not at

Arlington, too."

"And option two?"

"We're being played. Somebody in the U.S. government is hiding those bodies and suppressing the truth. Somebody in the FBI told those two interrogators to jerk us around and stonewall us. We're being set up, Katrina."

"Option two."

"Right. They were watching us this morning. When the hit on me went wrong, they policed it up and made it look like it never happened."

"Why didn't they just kill you then?"

"I'd already attracted attention. We were in the parking lot of a big apartment building, and when the gunman's piece went off, the noise probably drew a hundred gawkers to their windows. So the cops pull up and what are they going to do? Shoot me with all those witnesses? No, they're going to go through all the normal rigmarole, take away the bodies, take my statements, and then drive off and act like it never happened."

"Obviously a repeat performance at my place."

"Right. Had we stuck around, some D.C. detective would've run us through the drill and then told us to go on our way."

She watched the passing traffic. "I think our mole knows we're coming and has more grease than we do. I'd say our mole is probably in the CIA and has been working with the FBI on the mole hunt, and she somehow wrapped the Fibbies around her little finger."

CHAPTER THIRTY-THREE

I FINALLY flagged down a taxi and had the hack drive us to the heart of the Virginia suburbs and drop us at the Tysons Corner mall, which came to an astonishing total of sixty dollars. And do you believe the taxi driver had the balls to look at me expectantly, like, Hey, where's my tip?

Tysons happens to be one of the biggest malls in the world, a huge, sprawling complex with multiple escalators and over a hundred stores that are always crammed with jostling crowds. It being late November, with Christmas around the corner, the crowds were twice as thick. We rushed through several shops, buying enough clothes and shoes to last for several days, several wigs, some hair dye—your basic disguise paraphernalia—and a big goddamn hunting knife for those unexpected eventualities that seemed to be falling our way.

I used my charge card, because I wasn't the least bit worried about giving away our location. Why should I be when we were already being followed? I didn't see them, but they were there. They'd been there this morning to see me almost get killed, and near Katrina's apartment to see her almost get killed.

Who were they? I had no idea, but they were pros. I assumed they were Fibbies, though that wasn't necessarily correct. They might be CIA people, although that would be odd, because the United States has all these quirky laws about how the CIA isn't supposed to do domestic operations. Not that the CIA always respects those laws. And I assumed it was Mary moving the chess pieces around on the board.

In my former life as a member of the outfit, we'd had pretty good instruction on how to elude followers. Since we were sometimes forced to operate incognito in places we weren't supposed to be, it was expert training. Of course, it always helps when the trailers aren't aware that you have these skills, because that lets you exploit their underestimations.

I explained to Katrina how we were going to do this, and then we promenaded into Lord & Taylor. She yanked a dress off the rack and went into the women's dressing room as I stood by the entrance like your typically bored suburban husband. About ten minutes went by with women passing in and out, while a flock of other bored husbands gathered around me, each of us avoiding one another's eyes, the way guys do when their wives are spending them into bankruptcy.

I finally walked away. I moved swiftly, knowing that if the followers were serious, there'd be plenty of them in the mall, each with those little earphone and hidden microphone thingies, squabbling back and forth as they handed us off to one another. And at that very instant, some of those watchers would be wondering what the hell had happened to Katrina, which was the heart of the plan: to get the watchers screaming at one another, frantically trying to hunt down Katrina, while I did my thing.

I dodged into the ground floor of Nordstrom, then trotted up the escalator to the second floor. I ducked down low, hiding in the clothes racks as I raced swiftly through the women's section and dove into the women's dressing room, where I immediately dodged into a stall.

A minute later I waddled out between two other women, looking not the least bit bewitching in my paisley muumuu dress with bags of clothing tied around my waist, a red wig on my head, and a large pair of women's glasses, grasping two other bags of clothes to hide the whiskers on my jaw. I wobbled ungracefully toward the entrance, praying this worked. I had this nightmare of a bunch of Fibbies converging on me, drawing a big crowd, and there'd I be, exposed as a transvestite with pitiful tastes.

I went straight for the hot dog store in the middle of the mall, where a svelte blonde dressed in tight jeans and a black butch T-shirt and motorcycle boots sat munching a king-size dog, watching for a supremely ugly redhead in a muumuu. The muumuu was Katrina's idea. I'd never forgive her. I looked like a cow. I mean, if you're going to do this cross-dressing thing, it hardly seems fair to have to look like an elephant in a tent.

I went for the exit; she waited a minute, then followed. On my way out, I saw a guy dressed like an overage surfer looking frantically around. A thingie was stuffed in his ear and he was talking into his chest. He watched me waddle past doing my act, grimaced, and looked elsewhere.

I went into the covered parking garage, and a minute later Katrina sneaked up behind me. How did I know this? She had the nerve to pinch my fanny and say, "Hey, doll, looking for a good time?"

I flinched and grumbled, "Yeah, ain't I the friggin' hottie?"

She chuckled.

"Wheels next," I said, and we walked across the street and down to Route 7, where the local suburbanites make all the car dealers congregate along one long road, each within sight of one another, trying to filch one another's customers. Liar's Alley, the locals call it. I dodged into the restroom at the Chevy dealership and changed into jeans and a button-down dress shirt, with Top-Siders, and then emerged looking like your typical suburban yuppie.

Katrina and I walked over and ogled a 1996 BMW four-seater convertible parked in the lot. Out of thin air a guy dressed like a *Miami Vice* cop appeared.

"Hey folks, like it?" he asked, with the prototypical smile and unctuous manner of his breed.

"Depends how it drives," I said, stroking the paint job. "Even brought the wife along, 'cause we're serious. I'm not looking, I'm buying, and if you convince me, you'll get a fat check as I'm driving off in this thing."

He beamed. He caressed me with his eyes. He then eyed Katrina, because I was already bagged, and all he had to do was to charm the little woman into wanting it too.

"Hal Burton," he said. "Just a sec and I'll run in and get the keys. It's an incredible car. You sure you can handle it?"

"Born to it," I said, one overtestosteroned jerk to another.

He winked and then ran in to get the keys.

Katrina said, "Is there a point to this?"

"You like it?"

She stared at the car. "Not my style."

Hal came trotting out with the key. He winked again as he tossed the key across the hood, like we were a couple of real swell pals, weren't we now?

He got in the back while Katrina and I climbed in the front. It started up with a throaty roar. We pulled out into traffic and headed straight for the Beltway, Hal babbling about what a titsy car it was, how frequently and expertly serviced, how beloved and pampered by its previous owner, how much the car was . . . well, us.

I hit the GW Parkway exit and began heading toward D.C. Hal in the back said, "Smooth, ain't it? Like the way it drives?"

"Oh yeah," I said, nodding enthusiastically.

He said, "Hey, sorry to mention this, pal, but the dealership's gotta rule about staying within a five-mile limit. Not that I don't trust you, 'cause you look like swell folks, but rules are rules."

I said, "Gee, Hal, I'll try to get off at the next exit."

Hal grinned. That grin died when I zipped right past the next exit.

"Hey, uh," he said, bending forward and tapping my shoulder. "You missed that exit."

"Sorry. The way this thing drives, you get caught up in it. How much did you say it cost?"

He leaned back. He grinned. He imagined where he'd

spend his commission. "List at eighteen five, but you're obviously a man of the world, so you know that's negotiable."

While he droned on about everything he was willing to do to fit us into this car, I took the Key Bridge exit. He grinned and was still prattling about what a swell car it was, and what a swell couple we were, when we came to the stop sign at the end of the exit. I put the car in park and looked over at Katrina.

"Don't you just *love* this car?"

"I told you earlier, it's not my type."

I looked back at Hal. "Sorry, pal. The little woman doesn't care for it." I tossed a twenty in his flabbergasted lap as we got out. "For gas. Incidentally, the car's got one broken shock, and it needs a valve job."

We left him fuming and cursing as we began walking across Key Bridge toward the Georgetown section of D.C.

Katrina said, "I'm sure you have a really good reason why we did this the hard way?"

"We arrived in a cab, so the watchers were expecting us to leave in one. If they're CIA or FBI they'd know five minutes after we called the cab company, and they would've been waiting for us at the other end."

She grinned. "Aren't you the clever one?"

"The trick in modern society is avoid anything electronic. The police are spoiled. Between charge cards, ATMs, e-mail, telephones, car rentals with computers, hotels with computers, airlines with computers, the feds have these software programs that sweep through all that clutter, and they find you. If you're electronically invisible, they're bewildered."

"And I suppose you know what to do next?"

"No, actually, I don't. From here on in, we're on the fly."

She scratched her head and said nothing for a minute. Then, "Do you trust Alexi?"

I had to think about that. I guess I did, within limits. Yes, he had an extra bat in the belfry, but as I mentioned, that didn't mean he wasn't a decent guy. There was no question how she felt about him. After all, she'd done the big swami dance with him.

"What exactly do you have in mind?" I asked, sort of a delicate way of not answering her question.

"Let's call him."

"Why?"

"So he can hide us."

Oddly enough, the idea of calling a Russian intelligence officer to hide us from the American government had a certain ironic charm. Added to our lack of other workable options, I thought why not.

"Okay," I said, "but let me do the talking."

We walked into a grungy-looking record store filled with teenage kids combing through the stacks, hunting for the latest hip-hop hit. I approached the girl at the counter.

"Hey," I said, "we've got an emergency and I don't have a cell phone. How about if I pay you to use your phone to make a call?"

She snarled, rolled her eyes, and started to say, "Store policy is—"

I whipped out of my pocket the thick wad of money

that I took off the thug that morning. "Two hundred bucks."

Her lips froze. She handed me the phone. I handed it to Katrina. "You got his number?"

Her hand went into her purse, digging for it. I said, "Just talk to his secretary. Tell her we lost a briefcase and we're wondering if Alexi had any idea where it is. Give her the number for this store and ask for him to call us."

Katrina dialed the number and in Russian gave Alexi's secretary our message. When she was finished, I handed the girl the two hundred bucks, then told her we'd be getting a return call any minute. She smiled and licked her lips, and I saw two of those little silver beads sticking through her tongue. We stood by the counter for twenty minutes watching a procession of young kids dressed almost identically in baggy jeans and oversize sweat shirts, nearly all of whom had dyed hair, tattoos, and earrings or small silver beads punched all over their faces. Katrina fit right in. I looked like a guy who mistook this place for a tofu bar.

It sucked being young in this era. In my day we only had to look like fancified dorks in disco drag. At least we didn't have to get stabbed and tattooed. I mean, those old disco clothes, you send them to Goodwill and glide gracefully into becoming a fat, balding, middle-aged guy. Just throw out all your old pictures and your kids will never know what a jumbo jerk you used to be. All those holes and tattoos—they'll know.

The phone finally rang, the clerk picked it up, said, "Just a minute," then handed it to me.

Alexi's voice said, "Sean?"

"Yeah, Alexi," I said, then unloaded the whole story, including the fact that my government was somehow mysteriously implicated.

He listened patiently, then said, "This is something very big happening here, Sean. I would offer to put you in safe house, but this could be compromising. It would be better to be using Four Seasons Hotel in Georgetown. My people will book you a room and charge it to our expense. It will be under Mr. and Mrs. Harrington. I will be calling you later."

I hung up, and then Katrina and I walked down the main drag to the Four Seasons. If you have to go on the lam, this is the kind of place to do it. As soon as we were ensconced in the room, I had room service send up two filet mignons and a bottle of wine. It was on the Russians. Why not?

Alexi called twenty minutes after we finished eating.

He said, "Is everything all right?"

"Katrina and I just polished off a sixty-dollar bottle of wine. Hey, you know what, Alexi? Put some booze in that girl and look out. She's been climbing all over me, licking my ears, making all kinds of lewd suggestions. You'd hardly recognize her."

Katrina flung her big purse at me.

"Heh-heh," I said, but neither of them laughed. I thought it was hilarious.

"Anyway," I said, "we think we've got this thing figured out. What we believe is there's a real mole in our government that Morrison was framed to protect. You guys do those kinds of things, don't you?"

He didn't answer for a moment. Then he said, "To protect one that is most important, this could be possible. Is very difficult operation to construct, Sean. Is most difficult to match moles with acceptable surrogates. You understand? We have saying about this. 'The shadow must match the body.'"

Now, here's the thing. I was in an absolutely desperate position. Somebody was trying to snuff me, for some reason my own government seemed to be accommodating that effort, and Katrina and I were alone, without resources or allies, a raft floating in the middle of a murderous ocean. My only hope was Alexi. So let's see—maintain my pristine personal integrity, or live a few years longer? Exactly.

I said, "Well, here's what I think, Alexi. I think Mary's working for this cabal of yours. I think she's been on their payroll this whole time, convincing the CIA your accusations were wild ravings and protecting the cabal's existence. I think she's been filching her husband's papers. I think whoever provided those papers to the CIA gave only the documents she pilfered from Bill, while the stuff that would've pointed at her is still locked away in Moscow."

"What?" he asked, clearly surprised. "You accept the cabal's existence?"

"Yeah."

"And you think Mary is with these people?"

"Nothing else makes sense. I mean, it was Mary who told me it was baloney, right? She was trying to mislead me. And if she's not working for the SVR, it means she's working for somebody else in Moscow, right?"

"This would make sense, Sean. This cabal has extraordinary resources and reach. It could be that Mary is somehow connected. I have never considered this. The shadow certainly fits the body, yes?"

The poor guy was so smitten by his phantoms, he was leaping at any thread that substantiated, fed, and justified his paranoia. I felt sorry for him. But not so sorry that I wasn't willing to exploit it, as the CIA had done for the past decade.

"There's a way to find out," I said. "I'm going to have one of my assistants question Bill. He should be able to confirm whether it fits or not."

The idea intrigued him, and he said he'd call me in six hours to see what turned up. I immediately placed a call to Imelda. I explained our predicament and why I couldn't set foot on a flight to Kansas City without alerting the authorities. She could, though; so I told her to.

I explained what I wanted her to do and asked her to smuggle a cell phone into her interrogation, and then gave her the number to our hotel room. Then Katrina and I sat and did our best to kill the hours as we waited. We watched an Oliver Stone movie, and we both laughed hilariously, because he was the only guy in the world more paranoiac than us. Katrina asked me about my childhood and I asked her about hers, we talked about politics and sports and college days, and when we ended up discussing our favorite ice-cream flavors we both knew we were in serious trouble.

The phone rang at 11:40 P.M. and I dove across the bed to answer it.

After some opening banter, Imelda said, "Went over the dates with him. Mostly they match, sometimes they don't."

What she was referring to specifically were the dates on the documents from the Moscow vault Eddie had provided us. She was showing them to Morrison and asking him where Mary was at those times, how she might've gotten her paws on them.

I said, "Okay."

She said, "Wanta talk to him?"

He came on with his typical blast of selfish, overbearing horsecrap. "Where the hell are you, Drummond? How come you haven't visited? I don't like dealing with sergeants. God damn it, I'm a general officer and I'm owed some respect. You're—"

"Shut the hell up and answer my questions. How do you think Mary framed you?"

"Don't tell me to shut—"

"Shut your mouth!" I yelled. "I've killed three men this morning, and at the moment I'm having visions of flying out there and killing you. This was all because of you. Frankly, you're not worth it, so if you don't shut up and answer my questions, I'll be on the next flight." Katrina was giving me the evil eye, so I took two deep breaths and tried to calmly ask, "Now, how do you think Mary framed you?"

"I don't know," he petulantly replied.

"Yeah, but you've now looked at the prosecutor's key evidence. How could Mary have gotten all those papers out of your office?"

He fell quiet a moment. "She could've gotten some

of them easily."

"Not *some,* damn it . . . *all* of them. The President's and Secretary of State's talking papers? The blueprints for the technologies denied for export approval? The North Korean talking points? How could she have gotten her hands on those papers?"

"Shit, Drummond, I already told you I never saw the tech stuff, or the North Korean stuff. As for the rest of it, no, she couldn't have gotten all of it from me. It wasn't like I was bringing those papers home. She hardly ever visited my office at State or the White House. But I wasn't the only one handling those papers. Maybe Mary pilfered them from someone else, too. Did you ever think of that?"

Of course I had thought of that. Just as I had thought of the fact that all the White House and State documents had Morrison's fingerprints on them.

I said, "Let's be clear on this. Just the talking points and policy papers. The ones with your fingerprints on them . . . could she have gotten *all* those through you?"

"Some, maybe, but others, no way. No."

I had this sudden sense of depression because Mary was my only suspect. I didn't want her to be my suspect, but I needed her to be the one, if that makes sense. And this was no longer just a legal case; it had become a fight for Katrina's life, and mine, and that was no small consideration, either. I couldn't move on Mary with a flimsy case. I needed granite proof.

In frustration, I said, "Damn it, you've seen the evidence. You tell me how that stuff ended up in Moscow."

"I have no idea. That's what I hired you to find out, you asshole. Those papers are the most closely guarded secrets in our government. Do you have any idea, Drummond, how few people lay their eyes on the President's talking points before he meets with the Russians?"

"How few?"

"A handful. And those papers came from State and the White House over an eight-year period. Except for the National Security Advisor and the Secretary of State, there might be three other people who could possibly have gotten their hands on all of them. Except we changed National Security Advisors once, and had two different Secretaries of State during that period."

I thought about that a moment. I asked, "And who would those other people be?"

"Actually, I can't think of anybody. Nearly everybody changed jobs or left the administration and was replaced. Eight years is a couple of lifetimes in Washington."

"And you fed those papers up your chain?"

"At State, I gave them to my boss and Milt forwarded them. At the NSC, I passed them through the NSC Advisor and he usually carried them directly to the President."

"Were you staffing them with anybody?"

"Sometimes. But there's some documents here"—he paused for a moment, "like this one, dated June 14, 1999, that I carried to the President himself. A former American naval officer had been arrested for spying in Moscow, it hit the news, and I gave the President a talking paper to use to call Yeltsin. Even the National Security Advisor didn't see that one. He was on a trip to Germany and it was three in the morning, his time. It wasn't that big of a deal that I wanted to wake him and make him approve the paper before I gave it to the President. I carried it in myself."

I was scratching my head. "So nobody saw that paper but you and the President."

He thought for a moment. "Well, Milt saw it."

"Martin?"

"Yeah, I always sent everything to Milt."

"Even when you were working at the NSC?"

He suddenly sounded defensive, like, why was I questioning his bureaucratic virility? "Look, Drummond, Milt was the king when it came to Russia and the former republics. Nobody did anything that concerned those regions without running it through him first. Milt played for keeps. If he found out you were undercutting his prerogatives, or giving the President recommendations behind his back, he took you down. More than a few Assistant Secretaries from Defense and State got sent packing for screwing with Milt."

"So you sent him all your papers so you wouldn't piss him off? That it?"

"I sent him my papers because he knows the region inside out. He was the architect of our policies there. Besides, Milt and I had a special relationship. He looked out for my backside and I looked out for his."

I was staring at the white wall in the hotel room with a truly awful scowl. "And how did Martin get your papers when you were in the NSC?"

"I ran them off the computer, put them in a pouch, and had a courier hand-carry them over. They were too sensitive to be sent electronically."

"So he got all these papers with your fingerprints on them?"

The import of what we were discussing suddenly began to hit him.

I said, "Did Martin have access to the technology export requests?"

His voice sounded suddenly parched. "He, uh, yeah. He was on the oversight council. He wouldn't ordinarily have looked at the individual requests, but he'd have access if he wanted. I didn't participate in any of that. A few times a month he'd go to the council meetings alone."

There was another momentary lull; then the full consequences hit him like a Mack truck. "That bastard! That traitorous prick! He used me. He set me up. I . . . shit, I trusted him."

"Yeah, well," I said, "he trusted you, too. He trusted you to take the fall for him."

And suddenly it all became crystal clear. It was brilliant. Morrison had been his fall guy, his buffer, his screen. He'd used Morrison for eight long years, even elevated him higher in Washington's bureaucracy to cover the trail of his own treachery. Of course Morrison never suspected him. Morrison wasn't the type to look a gift horse in the mouth. Morrison was too vain to believe anybody could use him as a stooge.

I could hear the sounds of more cursing on the other end, and I called Morrison's name a few times and could hear him venting. I could just imagine the fit he was throwing. Then Imelda came back on the line. I thanked her profusely and hung up.

Katrina had overheard only my part of the conversation, so I gave her the abbreviated version of Morrison's responses. We sat and stared at each other in stunned silence. Then we began hypothesizing and knocking pieces into place. No wonder the FBI was helping out Martin. God only knows what story he'd told them, but it must've been a whopper; like maybe he was being harassed by his former employee's defense counsels, and we were threatening him, and as a former high level official, he needed protection.

She finally said, "This actually *is* mind-blowing. The President's asshole buddy."

"At least I never voted for him."

"Right," she acknowledged. Notice how she didn't say she hadn't voted for him?

"Next issue . . . ," I said. "Alexi."

"What about him?"

"You and he are a . . . what? Fill in the blank any way you choose."

She studied me a moment and quite possibly considered saying, "Screw you and none of your damned business." Truthfully, it wasn't, but also it was. She finally said, "We're tight."

"Tight? I'm generationally handicapped. Take it back ten years or so."

"You mean, like, are we in love?"

"Yes. Exactly."

"We're a work in progress. Give us a bit more time

and we'll probably rendezvous there."

"Okay, me. What's my status?"

"You mean, am I still pissed at you?"

"Exactly again."

"Consider yourself on probation."

"Do I owe you an apology?"

She smiled. "More than one. I'll compose a list and get it to you."

"That would be kind."

"You did save my life. Always a good place to start."

"But I'm still in the minus column?"

"Oh yeah."

I thought about that.

I finally said, "You realize what that guy probably got away with? He literally shaped our policies for eight years. Christ, the Russians were actually running our policies toward them. It's staggering."

"Indeed. Now think about this . . . no evidence," she said, the trained lawyer going right to the heart of the matter.

"Or time," I said, because after all, trained killers were out there hunting us down, and that wasn't a trifling detail.

"Well, you're the government man. What do we do?" she asked.

We then wasted thirty minutes or so discussing alternatives and knocking holes in each other's suggestions. Calling the FBI or CIA was out of the question: They wouldn't believe us; the watchers would end up on our tails again; the killers would be mobilized, and the next time they'd leave no room for failure. As for the Army, what could it do? It's the most conformist institution in the world and it would no doubt refer the whole matter to the FBI and CIA, and we'd be right back where we started—setting the conditions for our own funerals.

I thought about calling the press and giving them the story, but any reporter in his right mind would say, "Yeah, no kidding? And you're Morrison's defense counsels, right? Boy, you guys are really creative."

The phone rang and it was Alexi.

After assuring him we were fine, I said, "Milt Martin? You know him?"

"I have met Milt at some conferences. He was most powerful man in your last administration, yes?"

"Yeah, well, what would you say if I told you he's our man?"

Alexi chuckled. "And you are making accusations about me fabricating nightmares. Sean, this is not possible. Martin was your President's best friend. All policies toward my country were being made by him. And I would most certainly have known."

That's when I remembered something. When Morrison had first told me about Alexi, he'd said that Arbatov was always selective in what he provided. If he thought it had to do with his mystical cabal, the information flowed like a river; otherwise, he was a loyal Russian intelligence officer. He'd never given the Morrisons the names of our traitors; he'd picked his disclosures with great care.

So maybe Alexi knew all about Milt Martin. Maybe he knew Martin was the jewel in the SVR's crown and simply wasn't going to admit it, even to me and

Katrina. And if that was true, his alarm bells would be going off right now, because here he was protecting us, and if we were about to launch off to prove Martin was Moscow's most valuable spy, well, that would surely compromise Alexi's standing and future job prospects—and health.

I looked over at Katrina; there was no way in hell I could share that suspicion with her. Like I said earlier, the thing about this world of espionage is you can't trust anybody. Everybody's got conflicting loyalties. Even those folks you trust, you can only halfway trust—conditionally.

I said, "Uh, yeah. Listen, why don't Katrina and I do a little more checking, and I'll call tomorrow if we find anything."

That was fine with him, and we hung up. I turned to Katrina and said we needed to go to the hotel's business center. She gave me a curious look but followed me downstairs. We bought two cups of coffee in the snack bar, then filed inside the business center, found an idle computer, and made ourselves comfortable.

The thing about the Internet is that you can find out a few things about almost anybody, but famous international figures like Milton Martin are open books. I typed his name into Google.com and got 12,753 hits. The only tough thing was deciding which listings were worth reading, because otherwise Katrina and I would be at that computer for two weeks reading entries, most of which were repetitive, and many of which were just silly.

After two hours, here's what we had: Milton Martin

was born on March 7, 1949, in Amherst, Massachusetts, the only child of Mark and Beth. His father had been managing partner of a private equity firm and was worth millions. Milt had been sent to Groton School at the age of thirteen. He'd done Yale undergrad, where he majored in Russian studies and, as already noted, roomed with a future President. He looked like a long-haired egghead in a picture from that period, his nose the only thing that poked out from a mop that actually covered his eyes. He was a good student, except for getting arrested twice for involvement in antiwar protests that turned violent. He ended up doing graduate studies in England, and then went back to Yale for a Master's, also in Russian studies.

The articles weren't clear on exactly what he did in the years right after he finished his grad work, but it seemed he was trying to make it as a writer. Apparently it took him seven or eight years to find his voice, because that's when he published his first best-seller, a book on the origins of the cold war that exposed all kinds of underhanded dealings by the CIA and American military in various places around the world. What was striking about that book, most critics agreed, were the shocking revelations of dirty operations that were supposed to have been among the government's most closely held secrets. It was widely agreed that he had extraordinary sources. No kidding.

That book led to a series of hearings on the Hill and caused an American President to authorize a bunch of wiretaps to try to find Martin's sources. When questioned by the FBI, Morrison stood behind his First

Amendment rights.

His second book was an exposé of America's secret war in Vietnam and Cambodia, again noted by critics for its inside look at operations that were never supposed to see the light of day. This time the inevitable congressional hearings led to a large number of firings in the CIA, mostly of operatives whose names were included in the book, making them useless as clandestine operators in any regard.

Martin's last best-seller concerned arms control, and in it the author exposed the deep fractures in America's scientific community, as well as its arms control community, making the hawks sound like Stone Age, bellicose morons who played dirty against the humanitarian altruists who were trying to rein in the madness, and how Russia's doves were marginalized by the policies of America's hard-liners, preventing the world from achieving sanity.

He'd never married. His mother died in 1989, and his father in 1995, leaving him a pile of money. He'd taught at five or six universities and was an accepted member of ten or fifteen prestigious institutes and organizations, making him a bona fide member of the Establishment.

All of which begged the big question: Why would Milt Martin betray his country? He was rich. He was wildly successful. He was respected and accepted. I'd met him and he seemed like a decent enough guy, with none of the rough edges or overweening ambition you smell from some folks—like my own client, for instance. So why?

I called the concierge and had them order me a rental car to be charged to the room. Katrina and I picked up our bags and went downstairs to wait. It was five hours to New York City and we needed to be in midtown Manhattan by eight. If we drove fast, we'd just make it.

CHAPTER THIRTY-FOUR

WE needn't have rushed. Martin's black limo didn't pull up to the front entrance of the Society for International Affairs building until 10:00 A.M. Martin, it seemed, worked banker's hours.

He stepped out of the limo carrying a five-hundred-dollar leather briefcase, wearing his Burberry raincoat, that prominent nose of his the first thing to emerge. He turned around and stuck his face back into the car, told the driver what time to pick him up, then spun around to head confidently up the short stairs and into the building: Mr. Establishment arriving for another day at the money mill.

At that moment, the guy who'd been casually leaning against the building's wall shoved off and began to walk past him. Martin looked vaguely at the guy but took no particular notice, and in any case wouldn't have recognized me with my dyed blond hair and glasses, wearing jeans and a bulky parka.

The trick to kidnapping is speed. Shock value counts for everything: You have to dumbfound your victims, traumatize them, make them too senseless to react, too passive to resist.

At the instant we passed, the fingers of my right hand drove directly into his throat. He wasn't expecting it, but it came too fast for him to put up a defense anyway. One second he was walking upright to the entrance, and the next his throat felt like it was on fire and he couldn't breathe.

He lurched over and, like a Good Samaritan, I swiftly bent down and slipped an arm around his shoulder to help him. It was New York so a few pedestrians were passing by, barely paying attention. Katrina had been parked down the street in our rental; she came screeching up to the unloading zone in front of the building.

She wore a blond wig, and a fake mustache, and big black-rimmed glasses, and looked goofy as hell, but it was a great disguise. I'd also taken the precaution of stealing a license plate from a parked car, in case anyone saw us and was inclined to report the kidnapping to the police.

Martin was desperately trying to struggle away from me, and I was loudly saying, "There, there, buddy, you're going to be okay. You probably just got a piece of gum stuck in there. Here, I'll give you a ride to the hospital," as I maneuvered him toward the car. Katrina leaned back and flung open the rear door. I shoved Martin inside, banging his head against the door frame, which sent his glasses spilling into the gutter and made him howl.

I piled in, and Katrina pulled out into the street. While Martin was fighting to force some air down his bruised windpipe, I pulled some rope from my pocket and tried to grab his hands. He tried shoving me away, slapping at my face like a little girl, so I popped him hard on the nose, an easy target because the damned thing was so huge.

His hands flew up to his schnozz and he was whimpering and trying to keep the flow of blood from spilling all over his Burberry, while I began using the rope to tie his hands together. He tried protesting, and I screamed, "Shut up or I'll kill you!"

Once I got his hands tied, I pulled out the hunting knife I'd bought at Tysons Corner, held it to his throat, and threatened, "One wrong move and I'll cut you, asshole."

I yanked a ski mask over my head, while he stared at my face, trying to place me, trying to fight his fear, trying to figure out how he got into this nightmare.

He started to talk, and I told him to shut up or I'd slice open his throat. This also was part of the treatment. I wanted him so scared he'd pee in his pants. Katrina headed uptown for the George Washington Bridge, which would compound our crime by taking us across state lines. But hey, once you've just assaulted and kidnapped the most powerful former Assistant Secretary of State in history, why sweat the small stuff?

About every five minutes I reached over and slapped or punched Martin, sometimes in the face, sometimes in the stomach, not because I'm a cruel bastard but to keep him terrified. He needed to know I was pitiless. He needed to feel pain. The more helpless he felt, the quicker and easier we'd get this done.

I could see Katrina wince every time I hit him, and

she no doubt was regretting she'd ever agreed to my plan. But her role during this stage was to be perfectly silent, to be the mysterious lump in the front seat. I just kept reminding myself of Mel Torianski's exploding head and the three guys who tried to murder Katrina and me, and my qualms abated.

We took the Palisades Parkway exit and headed toward Bear Mountain State Park. The drive took about forty minutes, with me smacking Martin every few minutes, Katrina shaking her head, and Martin mewling like a lamb dancing with the big bad wolf.

We crossed the Bear Mountain Bridge and took a left, heading toward Garrison. After about two miles I told Katrina to pull over at the next dirt road leading into the woods, which she did. I reached across Martin, swung open the car door, and shoved him out into the mud. He flew out face first and yelped. I came out right behind him, grabbed him by the scruff of his fancy Burberry raincoat, and dragged him into the woods. Katrina followed.

She asked, "Where you are taking him?" using a fabricated Russian accent.

"Where nobody can see me cut his throat," I yelled. The shock of that registered instantly on Martin's face.

Then we were into the bushes. I dragged and shoved Martin through the thick underbrush and every time he tried to stop, I slapped him across the head, the loud whacks echoing through the forest. We moved like this for half a mile, him occasionally slipping and falling onto the ground, and me kicking him in the ass every time he did, because Martin was a guy who'd never been humiliated in his life, never been subjected to such indignities, a guy who'd led a perfectly spoiled existence—Groton, Yale, a comfortable writer's life.

I finally grabbed his collar from behind and threw him stomach first onto the ground. He let out a loud "whoomph," then looked up, his expression hurt and terrified. "W-what do you want? Money? I'll pay you. I'll never tell anybody, I swear."

This is the standard plea of all kidnap victims, trying to regain some sense of power, some control over their destiny. It's a natural response to try to negotiate, to find your tormentor's motive, to assert any kind of grip you can get on the situation.

I kicked him in the chest so hard that he went somersaulting backward and onto his stomach. I reached down and lifted him by his collar and the back of his pants, then hurled him through the air. He came down on his stomach with a loud scream.

He had to know I was much stronger than him, that he was powerless, that negotiation was out of the question. He had to know he had no control. He had to feel the sheer terror of being in the hands of a wildman.

I bent down on my haunches and put my face squarely in front of his. I flashed the hunting knife.

His eyelids stretched open, while Katrina said, "Oh, God, I cannot watch this. I must return back to car. I will be getting sick."

Martin's eyes darted from me to her. You knew exactly what he was thinking, because the thoughts scampering through his addled head were exactly what he was meant to think. What was with this woman's accent? And she was obviously his only chance against the pitiless bastard with the knife. If she left, he was dead.

He yelled something in Russian, his voice trembling with fear.

Katrina said something back, and I yelled, "You two stop it! Speak goddamn English."

Katrina coldly said, "He begs us not to kill him. He says he can make it worth our while."

I let loose a nasty chuckle. "And your government would find us and kill us. Let's get this over with."

The shock of that registered very clearly on Martin's face. "The Russian government?" he asked, sounding dismayed. "Please, there has to be a mistake. W-what are you talking about?"

I inched closer like I had no intention of discussing this with a man I intended to butcher.

"Please," Martin begged, looking imploringly into the eye-slots of my ski mask. "You're making a mistake. The Russians don't want me dead."

I was shaking my head, while Katrina swiftly said, "The order I have been given is most clear. You are to be disposed of. Is no mistake."

"No, no, it's wrong. I work for the Russians," he squealed, literally howling as I positioned the knife against his throat.

Katrina barked, "Stop! Not yet." Then to him, "What are you talking about?"

As scared as he was, he was no fool. In that instant he realized that Katrina was the boss of this operation, and that I was most likely a local hire under her employ.

His eyeballs shifted in her direction. "Please," he sniveled. "Please listen to me. This is a mistake. I work for the Russians. I swear I do. Your people don't want me dead."

I snorted with disdain, while Katrina looked puzzled. "You are being ridiculous. You do not work for us."

"No, no. I swear I do," he said, completely confused, because he did work for the Russians, and if she did, too, then what was the deal here?

I moved the knife a centimeter to the left, enough to draw a little blood, enough to make his whole body shudder.

"Don't listen to his bullshit," I growled. "Let me cut his throat and collect my damn money."

"You will be doing what you are told," said Katrina in a most commanding and imperious tone. She took a few steps to get closer to us.

She put her hands on her hips and bent over Martin. "I am SVR agent. I have been ordered by Alexi Arbatov to dispose of you. Nobody has been making mistake here."

"No, you . . . you're wrong," he assured her, struggling to cringe away from the knife. "P-please, I swear it. Arbatov's a traitor. He works for the Americans."

Katrina reached down and pulled my knife hand away from his throat. Still bent over, she stared down at him curiously and let loose a most convincing snort. "Alexi Arbatov is deputy head of SVR. He is Viktor Yurichenko's protégé. And you are saying he is traitor?" She let go of my hand. "Go ahead and kill him."

"No, I swear!" he yelled, speaking rapid-fire. "Arbatov's been giving the Americans information for ten years. Yurichenko knows that. I'm Viktor's man. I've been working for him for twenty years. I swear. Please, don't kill me. Just ask him. He'll vouch for me. You'll see."

And in that instant, Katrina and I both froze. Martin was working for Yurichenko? And Viktor knew about Alexi? This wasn't what we had expected to hear. I had figured Martin was working for Russian military intelligence or one of Russia's other intelligence agencies, but for Viktor? For that sweet little old man who had adopted Alexi? Were it not for that ski mask, Martin would've seen an expression of shock and horror on my face. I glanced at Katrina. She had spun away from Martin, as though she were thinking this through, a very facile feint to hide her face.

As it was, Martin detected something in our physical responses to his confession. Fortunately, he mistook it for progress.

"Don't you see?" he nearly screamed, feeling his chance coming into reach. "Why did Arbatov tell you he wanted me dead? What did he say I did?"

Katrina faced him, and I had to give her credit, she gave no hint of her horror. "Reason is simple. You helped expose the American general Morrison, who was most valuable SVR asset, and you are critical to American case to convict him. Unless you disappear. We owe Morrison this for his brave service, yes?"

"No, no," he insisted, shaking his head. "Morrison was never a Russian spy. Morrison was set up. He was my cut-out. Viktor and I picked him ten . . . twelve years ago. That's why I hired him to work for me. That was our plan from the start. The whole idea was to make him my bureaucratic twin so we could use him to cover me. Don't you see?"

I edged the knife back closer to his throat. "This is bullshit, lady. You're not going to let this worm lie his way out of this, are you? For Chrissakes, I want my money."

Katrina held up her hand, slapping a leash on her overeager killer. She appeared to be pondering this matter, like she wasn't sure what in the hell was happening here.

"Listen," Martin said, his voice now cajoling, "if you kill me, when Viktor finds out, he'll hunt you to the ends of the earth. Believe me. He's like a father to me."

"Convince me this is true," Katrina ordered.

"I've known Viktor thirty years, ever since I was in college. I wrote three books," Martin said, still speaking rapidly, his brain and mouth in overdrive, trying desperately to convince her. "He told me to write the books, for Godsakes. He gave me the names of American CIA agents to put in them. He told me about CIA operations so I could expose them to the American people. He let me listen to wiretaps of American officials debating arms control policies. I swear to God it's true. You can check. For Godsakes, all three books were best-sellers."

"I do not have time to check this," Katrina said.

A fresh idea struck him. "Then check the newspapers for everything they're saying Morrison gave them. I can tell you the story behind every document I sent to Viktor. I was the President's best friend, for Godsakes. Do you really believe it was Morrison who was manipulating American policy? He was a lowly lieutenant colonel . . . I was the Assistant Secretary of State. It was me. Get the newspapers and I'll prove it."

Katrina was suddenly sounding much more amenable. "And how were you, an American big shot, getting these documents to Viktor?"

"That's the beauty of it. Nobody suspected me. You're not going to believe how we did it."

"You had better make me believe how you were doing this," she said, sounding ominous.

"The mailbox. We created a false mailbox in my apartment building in Washington. Whenever I wanted to send something to Viktor, I just dropped it in that mailbox and a courier dressed as a mailman checked it three times a day. Please, ask Viktor. You'll be saving yourself. Arbatov's a traitor and Viktor knows it."

This seemed to jar Katrina's suspicion, so she said, "Now I am having big credibility problem with you, Martin. If Viktor is knowing Arbatov is traitor, why is he having him work as number two in my bureau?"

"I don't know," Martin said, "but I'm not making it up. I swear. I think Viktor's running him as a double agent or something. I've thought that for a long time. Look, I was the one who warned him about Arbatov."

She let loose a cynical chuckle. "And how were you knowing about Arbatov?"

"Because Morrison told me. In his opening interview with me ten years ago. He wanted the job so bad, he was trying to impress me, so he bragged about how he was the guy who recruited Arbatov, how he was still his controller. I swear it's true. Later he even told me about other traitors his wife was controlling. I gave all their names to Viktor. I exposed those traitors to the SVR, not Morrison."

I looked up at Katrina and she looked down at me. Frankly, we'd learned everything we needed to learn. In fact, we'd learned more than we ever wanted to know.

I yanked the ski mask off my head, and Katrina pulled off her mustache and glasses and wig. Martin's eyes searched both our faces. Then came the moment when clarity set in. There was this instant when he realized who we were and that he'd just told us enough to get him the electric chair.

In shock, he said, "You're that lawyer. Drummond?"

I pulled the tape recorder out of my pocket. I clicked the off button. I smiled. Not a happy smile, but I smiled.

Katrina, good New York girl that she was, said, "You're a scumbag, Martin. And now you're screwed."

And I added, "I don't give a crap how good your lawyer is, you're going down."

A silly threat, I know, but what do you expect from a lawyer? Then the two of us left him there, on the muddy ground, a shocked expression still pasted on his face. His scream shot through the forest as we walked away.

Katrina drove while I replayed the tape over and over, considering the full ramifications of everything he'd confessed. We were just getting on 95 South when Katrina said, "We have to get Alexi out."

I nodded and didn't say anything. I don't think she expected me to say anything. Getting Alexi out was impossible. We both knew that.

CHAPTER THIRTY-FIVE

A T 7:00 P.M., I called Mary from our hotel room in the Four Seasons.

"The Steele residence," Homer answered, pronounced like, What the hell do you want?

"Hey, Homer, Drummond here. How's the Porsche looking?"

"You son of a bitch. I knew it was you. You touch my car again, I'll have you arrested."

"Speaking of things of yours I've touched," I interrupted, "is Mary there?"

I heard a bang that I assumed was the phone hitting the floor, and almost two minutes later Mary said, "Sean, where you are? Are you okay?"

Her tone was real warm and deferential, like she was genuinely concerned for my health. Of course if you read between the lines, it sounded more like, I'm having you followed and you somehow slipped away, so please fall for my act and tell me where the hell you are.

I said, "In thirty minutes I want you and Harold Johnson to be huddled in his office. I have a tape you both need to listen to, and if you're not there in thirty minutes, you'll read the contents of that tape on the front page of the *New York Times*. It won't be a good day for you, Mary. Thirty minutes."

Then I hung up. There's nothing like bossing around the deputy director for intelligence of the whole CIA. It's a good feeling knowing you've got a tape recording in your pocket that will blow the sides off his building. Thirty minutes later, I went down to the lobby and spied around till I saw a tired-looking businessman with a cell phone hooked to his belt.

I approached him with that overused spiel: "Have I got a deal for you."

He gave me a wary, distrustful expression.

I pulled the wad of money out of my pocket. "Here's the way this works," I said, peeling off bills. "You get five hundred dollars to let me make one call on your cell phone. It's local. It won't cost much. I'll be right across the lobby, so you can keep your eyes on me."

I can be mighty generous with the money somebody was paid to murder me. He stared at the wad in my hand. "What's the catch?"

"No catch. I'm in a very generous mood. I learned I just won the lottery and I need to call my broker to tell him to take a big breath and get ready for a windfall."

Which, as metaphors go, was actually pretty good. He looked at me like he couldn't believe it. "You're bullshittin' me, right?"

I waved the five hundred dollars. "Two more seconds and I move on to the next lucky guy."

Before you could say "take it," I had his cell phone and he had my money. I wandered over to the corner of the lobby. I went through this little charade because I figured the CIA had some sort of tracing service and I couldn't afford to let Johnson and Mary know where I was. I didn't want some goon squad showing up and spoiling my day.

I dialed the number for the CIA and told the switchboard lady to put me through to Harold Johnson's office.

"Hello, Major, Mary's here. What's this about?" he asked, his tone sounding edgy, like he just knew this wasn't going to be a happy moment, because he'd already had one sour experience with me and the bad taste lingered. As I mentioned before, it's always nice to know you're remembered.

"Put me on the speakerphone. You both need to hear this."

As soon as he assured me I was on, I played the whole tape. You could hear the occasional slaps and howls, but the voices came through very clearly.

Johnson's voice sounded alarmed and disapproving at the same time. "Whose voice was that?" he barked.

"Milton Martin's," I replied, then said nothing, knowing both their faces were going pale with anguish.

Johnson put me on hold so I couldn't hear their conversation. I didn't need to. I knew damn well what he and Mary were jabbering about, and while I would've enjoyed overhearing the panic attack that I'd just paid five hundred dollars for the listening rights to, I patiently waited for two minutes while they tried to figure out how to handle me and an audiotape that would shoot to the top of the charts on anybody's list.

The speakerphone finally came back on. Johnson

said, "Drummond, that confession sounded coerced."

"Well, Mr. Johnson, it was coerced. So what? I did your dirty work for you; I found the mole you couldn't find."

"Where's Martin? Did you kill him?"

"No. I left him in the woods across the river from West Point. I thought you'd appreciate the irony, West Point being the fort Benedict Arnold tried to betray. He was a little distraught and wasn't very good company anymore."

Mary said, "Oh my God, you didn't."

"Oh my God, I did," I said. "And one way or another, it's your fault."

"How do you get that?" Johnson asked.

"Because you people set me up."

"We weren't setting you up," Johnson insisted.

"Bullshit. You were following and watching me. When somebody tried to murder me and my co-counsel yesterday, your people came along and cleaned up afterward. Did Martin put you up to that?"

"You don't know what you're talking about, Drummond."

"I don't, huh? What happened to the bodies of those guys who tried to kill me and my co-counsel? Where'd they disappear to? What about the runaround I got from the FBI when I tried to get help?"

I heard a murmuring sound as Mary and Johnson clued each other about how to handle me. Then Mary, the woman I used to do the hokey with, said, "Sean, you've got it confused."

"Confused, huh?" I yelled into the phone. "I saw

your guys in Tysons mall when I gave you the slip. Don't lie to me, Mary. If I lose trust in you, I'll call the *Post* and *Times* and play this tape for them."

Which was an overstatement, because I'd already lost trust in Mary, and in Johnson's case, I'd never trusted the bastard in the first place.

Johnson said, "Don't do that, Drummond. For Godsakes, don't even make that threat. You'll set back our relations with Russia by a dozen years. You're a soldier. A scandal like this will seriously harm this country."

My voice grew louder. "I'm that classic rat driven into the corner. You put me here. I don't think about consequences any longer, I just lash out. Guys like me are really, really scary."

I heard more murmuring, and if I had to guess what was being said, it was Mary telling Johnson it was true. I was really, really scary.

"Okay, okay," Johnson came back on, trying to sound placating, the professional hostage negotiator who knew how to calm the nerves of an overwrought subject. "We'll get through this, Sean. Calm down and we'll get through this."

By this time, my anger was reverberating over their speakerphone. "I've survived two attempts on my life. A fellow officer was brutally murdered. You got the number for the Senate Intelligence Oversight Committee? Those right-wing politicos on the committee love this kind of shit. They think we're suckers for getting closer to Russia, anyway. Ah, hell, don't trouble yourself. I'll get the number from the operator. Listen,

I've got a lot of calls to make, so I've got to run."

Mary, sounding desperate, said, "Sean, don't. Please. Just talk this out."

I yelled, "Talk it out with the newspapers! I don't want to hear your lies and—"

"You're right," she interrupted.

"About what?"

"We were having you followed and watched."

"Why?"

"Ever since Moscow. Ever since that first attempt. Mort Jackler's our man. He's not stupid, Sean. When you tried blaming that attempt on Mel Torianski, he knew you were lying. We saw you meeting with Alexi. You've been watched ever since. We had to know why someone was trying to kill Bill's defense team. And we had to protect Alexi."

"If you were watching, how come Katrina and I almost got killed?"

"We were caught flat-footed. I swear it's true. We couldn't protect you. It all went down too fast. And when you told me Katrina wasn't on the team, I pulled off her security."

"But you could hide the attempts afterward? And you could have the FBI cold-shoulder us? You could do that because you wanted us to stay out in the cold as bait. You used us. Jesus, Mary, you are one cold-blooded bitch."

"You brought it on yourself, Sean. You got overinvolved. I warned you. You were talking with Alexi. I warned you not to do that."

"And what? When somebody tried to kill me, you

thought you'd use me to figure out who? Was it that cold?"

"I didn't like doing it, Sean. I swear I didn't."

"No, of course you didn't, Mary."

Johnson, knowing this thing was going south, quickly interjected, "It's true, Sean. She argued against it. I overruled her."

I shook my head. Sure she did. They thought they were so clever. That's the problem with people who rise up to the heights of their bureaucracies and get big fancy titles. They actually begin to think they really are smarter than everybody else.

I said, "And what about Bill Morrison, my client, Mary's husband, the man accused of treason?"

Johnson said, "Um, well, until this conversation we were convinced he was our man. God damn . . . Milt Martin. I'm still having trouble believing it. Of course, Morrison's still guilty of some serious crimes. According to your tape, he gave Martin the names of our assets. That was a serious security violation that led directly to their deaths."

"Uh-huh," I commented. "And what are you going to do about Arbatov?"

"What about him?" Johnson asked.

" 'What about him?' " I sarcastically mimicked. "He's been exposed. Victor knows about him. He's at risk."

Johnson's tone sounded deeply sympathetic. "Yes, it's a shame, isn't it? That's always the risk in our profession. Alexi knew this, of course. He knew it from the moment he first made contact with Bill Morrison."

"I asked you what you're going to do about it."

There was another quiet moment and I could almost visualize them exchanging signals of some sort.

Mary finally said, "There's nothing we can do about it, Sean. Ordinarily in these kinds of operations we have a prearranged signal we give our asset that warns him to flee. We don't have an arrangement like that with Alexi. Even if we did, it wouldn't work. Yurichenko is surely having him watched. And his profile is too high. He'd never get out."

"So you're just going to let him fry?"

Again it was Mary who replied, "Sean, I care deeply for Alexi. There's just nothing we can do. The White House doesn't want any troubles with the Russians . . . that's just the way it is. Even if we could put together an operation to try to get him out, the White House would veto it."

"So that's it?"

"That's it," Johnson said, sounding ruthlessly unsentimental.

I smiled. I pulled my trusty tape recorder away from the earpiece. I flicked it off. Then I said, "Hey, guess what?"

"What?" Johnson asked.

"I just recorded this whole conversation, too. I know I shouldn't have, and I feel really bad about it, only I thought whoever listens to Martin's confession might enjoy listening to you admit you were using me, an officer of the court, as bait for killers. Not to mention your willingness to let a valuable asset die. I'll bet that'll do wonders for recruiting future assets. They'll be lining up at the door. Don't you think that's a nice touch?"

There was a moment of agonized silence. I was put on hold again. But that's okay; I'm not the kind of guy who gets his feathers all ruffled by life's little annoyances.

And while I waited, here's what I was thinking. The good news here was that Mary hadn't tried to have me murdered. That was a reassuring thing to know, after all. What lousier feeling is there than knowing the woman you used to love—had I really been that stupid?—hired some goons to turn you into compost?

But that's as far as the consolation went. Mary had played me like a harp from the beginning. I thought back to that opening session with her, when she sat on that flowered couch looking like the distraught wife and got me to beg her not to feel bad about dragging me into this. I thought about all those times we met where she denied knowing what the hell was going on. I was more than a sucker.

Johnson's voice finally came back on. "Drummond, we need to make a deal."

The man had good instincts and knew exactly what this call was about. I replied, "Same conditions as last time. I name the terms, you nod your head and say, 'Yes sir, and what else can I do for you?' If I hear a single hesitant pause . . . well, there won't be a second chance. Got that?"

"Yes sir, and what else can I do for you?" he responded, showing he was a careful listener who hadn't missed a single comma.

I outlined everything he and Mary were going to do for me, then hung up. I walked across the lobby and handed the phone back to the businessman, who beamed like an idiot.

I went back upstairs. Katrina was seated on the bed, watching MTV, of all things. "Well?" she asked, so anxious she couldn't even look me in the eye.

"It worked," I said. "You were right. They're going for it."

She just nodded. The idea for the scheme was Katrina's. That's the problem with spending so much time around professional spies: After a while their deceitfulness rubs off and you begin thinking likc they do.

Without saying anything, she pushed the button that killed the TV, then lay down and closed her eyes. I lay down on the bed next to her and was beginning to think about our next steps when my own exhaustion finally caught up. It's damned hard work torturing suspects and blackmailing the CIA. Or extorting. Or whatever.

CHAPTER THIRTY-SIX

KATRINA and I drove through the gate to CIA headquarters at seven the next morning. We'd been up since four, making copies of the two tapes, mailing one set to Imelda and the second to General Clapper, whom I trusted to do the right thing in the event anything happened to Katrina and me.

I called Clapper at home before we left the hotel room. I outlined what we'd discovered, and, as you might imagine, he wasn't all that happy that the CIA had used one of his officers and a temporary civilian employee as decoys.

Which isn't to say he was happy with me, either. He most definitely wasn't.

I then asked Clapper to recuse me and assign a new counsel. I'd become so personally involved in the case, recusal was a foregone conclusion. If I didn't voluntarily submit myself, some pissed-off judge would dismiss me, and I'd risk disbarment for malpractice. He said he'd take care of it. It was the only moment in the phone call that he sounded the least bit happy. Who could blame him?

I didn't tell him how I kidnapped Martin and persuaded him to confess. Some things would be too stupid for words, and full disclosure on my part fell cleanly under that heading. As I said earlier, smart lawyers don't lie; like clever moths around flames, they just don't get too close to the truth.

Mary and Johnson were actually waiting for us at the front entrance of their big building. Johnson shook hands and tried to act warm and convivial, which showed he wasn't stupid, because I held his fate in my hands. Mary leaned forward to give me a friendly peck on the cheek, and when I drew back she accepted it gracefully, like there was no harm in trying.

We went up in the elevator to a big conference room filled with men and women in crisp blue and gray suits. The room reeked of self-contentment, smugness, a clubby bonhomie. These were the same folks who'd spent ten years chasing a mole and were cocksure they'd nailed him and dragged him up to the altar of justice. The mood in that room was haughtiness. They had beartrapped the most elusive spy in history, the same squirrel who'd eluded so many of their pre-decessors.

That mood wasn't going to last long.

There were seats reserved for Katrina and me, even down to name placards, which showed Johnson was going a bit over the top to treat us like visiting dignitaries.

He stood up and introduced us to everybody, then put on a melodramatically grim smile and said, "Major Drummond, please play your tape."

I did. And the whole room sat spellbound, right to the end. Johnson let three or four pregnant seconds pass before he said, "That was the voice of Milt Martin, the former Assistant Secretary of State for the former Soviet republics."

"Jesus Christ," one guy muttered. "Oh shit," a blonde girl at the end of the table erupted. One guy actually pounded the table with his fist. It took another moment for the emotional chaos to subside.

A silver-haired guy who looked like an aging movie star roared, "That goddamn tape is for real?"

A coy grin popped onto Johnson's face. "Major Drummond, I'd like you to meet Richard Semblick, who was in charge of the team that nabbed General Morrison. He spent three years hunting for our mole, and it was on his recommendation that we focused on your client."

Semblick's face instantly turned pink, and I knew immediately what was going on here. Johnson and Mary were choreographing this meeting to cover their own butts. Johnson had that attitude like, Okay, all you putzes screwed up and made us bag the wrong guy, but thankfully I took care of matters myself, so all the rest of you inept idiots bow to my greatness.

I peeked at Mary's face, and her eyes were fixed on me. Her expression was beseeching, like, Drummond, please, fight your self-righteous instincts . . . play along with us and we'll play along with you, too.

I gave a fleeting thought to laying it all out, to explaining to everybody what lying phonies Mary and Johnson were, but that's all it was: a fleeting thought. We had a deal, and although they hadn't fully articulated their expectations, we were three-quarters of the way there and I couldn't afford to jump back to go.

I smiled. "Mr. Johnson's right. With his help, and Mary's inducement, we found the real mole. I couldn't have done it without them."

From a reductionist's standpoint, this was true—if they hadn't turned us into sitting ducks, with deadly killers hunting us down, I wouldn't have had the "inducement" to do it without them.

Johnson winked at me, like this was just so much fun, and he was just *so* damned glad I thought so too. He said, "We've initiated a nationwide manhunt for Martin, who was last seen near Garrison, New York. The FBI have notified all airports and seaports, and Martin's photo has been distributed at all border crossing points. Canada would be his obvious choice, but given that goddamn honker of his, he'll be easy to recognize."

This ignited loudly appreciative guffaws around the room, because every soul there was in overdrive, straining desperately hard to work themselves back into Johnson's good graces. Most had that sheepish expression little kids get when they poop in their drawers and everybody's looking at them like, Hey, what's that awful stench.

The realization was sinking in that the arrest and public roasting of Bill Morrison had been a king-size goof. Somebody on the Russian side had played them for a fool, and heads were going to have to roll, because this was the CIA after all, and Agency-bashing is maybe the favorite sport of the national press and Congress.

A fair number of the quicker-witted folks around that table were eyeing one another, obviously trying to strike instant alliances and make someone else be the "Weakest-Link-good-bye" guy.

The moment was ripe for me to say, "You can at least recoup some face. We know who Martin's controller was, right?"

"Yurichenko," said Johnson, picking up on his line in this passion play.

"Right. So, what if we were to go get Yurichenko's fair-haired boy? What if we were to bring Arbatov out for all the world to see?"

A roomful of people pondered that. At least half the folks here were going to spend the rest of their careers crammed into a janitor's closet in the basement trying to figure out how many angels you can fit on the head of a pin. They were vulnerable to any suggestion that would make them look less stupid than they really were.

"Plus," I quickly added, "you've obviously got a bigger problem."

"And which one would that be?" asked Mary, reading from her script.

"If you listened closely to that tape, you heard Martin confess that he told Yurichenko that Alexi Arbatov was a traitor. Martin may have told him that as long as ten years ago, when Morrison first disclosed it to him."

Katrina, who'd been struggling to disguise her disgust, suddenly said, "What Major Drummond is telling you is that you have to rescue Alexi. He has given you information for over a decade, and you therefore owe him a great deal."

Johnson did not even pause. "Here's the way I see it. We have a chance to repay Yurichenko. Okay, he turned one of our key people. Well, we turned one of his, too. In a zero-sum game everybody's equal."

This obviously was the deal we'd struck the night before—well, except for the fact that Katrina and I were going to be used as pawns by Mary and her boss to restore their own legitimacy. But hey, in the grand scheme, it's no big thing, right? If the law has taught me one thing, it's that there's no such thing as full justice. Consider yourself lucky if the meter simply tilts in your direction.

You could swear we were at a neck-snapping convention, the heads were nodding so furiously. Then there were a few tentative smiles. Then actual guffaws. Then the pros took over. They began talking back and forth as they tried to come up with a plan.

CHAPTER THIRTY-SEVEN

MOSCOW was pitch-dark and freezing when we landed. White snow covered the land and frost hung from the trees. We came in on a U.S. Air Force converted 747 carrying the Secretary of State, who was arriving for a swiftly arranged meeting with his Russian counterpart.

Katrina and I were dressed as U.S. Air Force enlisted troops and were described on the flight manifest as crewmen, Katrina as a steward, me as a radiotelephone operator. The Secretary of State was scheduled to be there only a few hours, which was tight, but coming and going under his diplomatic cover was the only way to get done what we needed to accomplish. Mary was along also, listed under an alias as a publicity aide to the Secretary, which was a thin cover, but she wasn't leaving the plane, as the Russians knew her on sight.

It had to be us three. Alexi knew Katrina and me, and Mary had been his contact all those years. We were the only ones who knew how to contact him, who he'd talk to—the only three he'd conceivably entrust with his fate.

The instant the Secretary's official welcoming ceremony was over and the cavalcades of black, official-looking cars had departed, we got to work. Another stream of cars began trickling in, and men and women camouflaged in workers' coveralls began streaming up the steps and clustering in the lounge next to the Secretary's sleeping suite. Within ten minutes, twenty CIA folks were packed in that compartment, and Mary began her briefing.

You'll never guess who was in charge of the ground team. My old buddy Jackler, the grand inquisitor himself, and he had Mary's former embassy crew working for him, since they were intimately familiar with Moscow and Russia's security procedures, which was essential for our purposes.

Jackler had apparently been warned to be nice to me, and he was—to a point. You could see it really hurt him, but he was trying. He was like that pit bull you keep chained in the basement. Politeness had been bred out of his gene pool. When we were done with the operations briefing he barked at everybody to get moving, and bodies began slamming into one another as they raced for the exit.

As soon as the last of the common field hands were gone, Jackler and Mary sidled over to Katrina and me. He growled, "You two need to have your friggin' heads examined. We don't do shit this way. You're flyin' by the seats of your pants."

Katrina said, "And is there another alternative?"

"Yeah. Send Arbatov a goddamned sympathy card. That's how the code works in these things."

"It isn't an option," Katrina said, eyeing him suspiciously.

"Lady, it's your ass. If this thing goes south, we can't help you. This is their country. You got any idea what Russian prisons are like?"

"I don't care."

Maybe she didn't, but I did—I cared a lot. I mean, I was all for getting Alexi out of there, but it sure would suck if our plan was foiled and all three of us ended up in Yurichenko's hands.

I gave Jackler my most badassed stare. "You better make sure it doesn't go south. See, I left copies of some very embarrassing tapes with some friends back in the States. If I don't come back, they've been told where to send those tapes, and trust me, that would be a disaster for you and all your buddies at Langley."

Jackler's eyes darted over at Mary. She simply shrugged, like, Yeah, I know it sucks, but that's the way it is.

Then Mary looked at me. She put a hand on my arm and dragged me away, into a corner. With her hand still on my arm, she leaned so close that I could feel her hair against my face and her breasts pressed against my arm. "Sean, please, be very, very careful. Our people have the meeting site staked out. If they give you the signal to abort, you and Katrina get out immediately. You understand that, right?"

"I understand that." Although I somehow suspected that that wasn't what this was really about.

"Listen . . . I, well, uh . . . I know you're disappointed in me."

She paused for me to answer. I was supposed to say something like, "Uh, yeah, I'm not too happy about the way all this went down, but crap happens; I'm over it now, and my heart still goes pitter-patter when I'm around you." I didn't say anything. I used Eddie's favorite stunt. I left the full onus of carrying this conversation on her shoulders.

"Anyway," she finally said, "I'm still serious about divorcing Bill. I contacted a lawyer yesterday. He's filing the papers."

"Yeah, well," I said.

She gave me that toe-tingling smile. "Open and shut, the lawyer said. He really loved those pictures of Bill slipping in and out of hotels with different women. There'll have to be a yearlong separation, but I'll have freedom to see who I want."

Those breasts pressed a little closer. Those blue eyes turned a little more imploring. "I don't want to lose you at this point, Sean. I, uh, I . . . well, I hope we can . . . maybe . . . well, maybe recapture what we once had."

I stared at her.

She pressed a forefinger against my lips, the way they do in those mushy movies. "Don't say anything," she murmured. Of course it was already evident I wasn't about to anyway. "I know you're confused right now. I don't blame you. There'll be plenty of time to sort things out later. Just come back safely, okay?"

"I plan to," I said, which was as neutral a signal as I could offer under the circumstances.

She stepped away and I looked over at Katrina, who was gazing back at me curiously, wondering what in the hell was going on here. I shrugged, then walked over and joined her. We departed with Jackler and climbed into a windowless van parked right at the base of the steps.

You could tell by Jackler's sour expression what he thought of this whole thing. Actually, his thoughts probably weren't any different from mine. Katrina was a civilian. If I was glaringly short of field crafts, she was ten gallons past empty. We were going into a complex, high-risk operation with a couple of complete hacks who could clumsily trigger a huge international incident with the one country the United States didn't want to piss off right at that pivot point in history.

But there really wasn't any other way this could work. It might not work anyway, but it was the only shot. We were pitting Alexi's affection for Viktor against his affection for Katrina, and it was still a flip of the coin. However, there's no disputing the influence of human plumbing in these situations.

Jackler put tiny microphones under Katrina's and my shirt collars and then ran a few quick tests to be sure the electronics worked. They did. One of Jackler's agents was driving. Another was riding shotgun in the passenger seat—literally riding shotgun, because he had a lethal-looking sawed-off model resting on his lap. I looked at my watch; 4:30 A.M. local time, right on the dot.

The drive took thirty-five minutes. A radio operator in the back with the rest of us kept receiving reports from various teams that were already maneuvering into position. The operation was still an hour off, but nobody was taking any chances of getting caught in traffic, or having an accident en route. Since it was my ass on the line, I highly approved of that. I've never been one who likes to hang out with type A anal-retentive assholes, but in situations like this you gain a whole new appreciation for them. Katrina sat calmly, while I drummed my fingers and peppered Jackler with incessant questions about precautions and failsafes in the event anything went wrong. He humored me. I was obviously keyed up and overanxious.

Katrina and I climbed out of the van a block down from the subway station. We looked around and there was hardly a soul there, unless you want to include a bunch of beggars and miserable-looking veterans, the normal shrubbery of Moscow streets. We rushed to the subway entrance and down the stairs till we found the sculpted she-bitch from hell, and we scraped our three stripes at the base of her foot.

Then we rushed back upstairs and to the ninth floor of the hotel that overlooked the kiosk. Neither of us said a word. We were both too immersed in our own thoughts to make small talk, which was the only kind of talk possible in moments like this.

At 5:45, he came out of the subway entrance and then walked nonchalantly toward the kiosk. He bought a magazine from the vendor, then stood for a moment, flipping through it and studying the pages. Katrina stopped breathing. If Alexi didn't head for the bakery, this was the last time she'd ever see him alive. I put a hand over her shoulder and held her.

Finally, Alexi casually walked away from the kiosk and headed straight down the sidewalk and hooked a left into the coffee shop. Katrina and I left the window and raced down to the lobby.

Just as we were going through the entrance, a short, chubby woman dressed like a street person shoved her way past us to get to the warmth inside the lobby. At the instant we passed her, she swiftly whispered, "Abort."

I was stunned. We were so close—there was no time to think about it, though. On the sidewalk I grabbed Katrina's arm and whispered, "That lady just said to abort."

Her brown eyes glanced at my face for a brief instant. Then she ripped her arm out of my grip and raced down the sidewalk to the bakery. I hadn't expected it and was caught flat-footed for a critical moment. I finally came to my senses and ran after her, but she dove into the bakery before I could stop her. That was always the problem with Katrina: She was too stubborn and willful by half.

She was seated at the table, kissing Alexi, when I entered. This time Alexi had ordered three of everything, I guess in the event we both showed up.

Alexi broke away and gave me a delighted smile. "Ah, Sean, how very good to see you."

Unfortunately, there wasn't time for pleasantries. In a very quiet tone, I said, "Alexi, appear normal, but listen closely. You've been followed. Viktor knows about you. He's known for years."

I chuckled like I'd just told some big joke, then picked up my coffee cup to take a sip, and Alexi did the same thing, although in his case to disguise what had to be his shock.

Katrina was whispering, "It's true, Alexi. We're here to get you out."

He put his coffee cup on the table, to his credit appearing perfectly unaffected. "You are making mistake, Katrina. Viktor cannot know about me. This is not possible."

"There's no mistake," she assured him. Under the table I pressed a tiny earphone into his hand. The earphone was connected by a wire to the tape recorder I also slipped him under the table. There was a moment of confusion until he figured out what the earphone was. Then he carefully reached up and placed it in his left ear, where nobody in the bakery could see it.

While he listened to a carefully condensed version of Martin's confession, I gave Katrina a hard stare. I whispered, "Do you know what you're doing?"

She smiled, like I was flirting with her. "Don't be going soft on me now."

"These people are pros. We're in big trouble."

She smiled harder. "We're not leaving without him."

I turned my head and did a few big phony sneezes, using the chance to spy around. Fifteen or so people were seated at tables and about twenty more were standing in line. It was impossible to tell who the followers were. There were probably fifteen young or middle-aged men—any of whom, or all of whom—could've been SVR agents. Or any of the women in the shop, for that matter.

Or maybe none of them were SVR people. Maybe Jackler just wanted to call it off. He hadn't seemed the least bit enthusiastic anyway, and by calling it off he could say, "Hey, we did everything you demanded, only the operation was compromised, so tough shit."

Katrina suddenly said, "My bladder's killing me. I have to go to the bathroom."

She reached under the table and gave my hand a hard

squeeze, and then left me with Alexi. I didn't say anything till he reached up and pulled the earphone out.

"This makes no sense," he whispered.

"Tell me about it," I complained.

"Where did Katrina go?" he asked.

"The bathroom. Wait ten more seconds, then go join her. She's going to tell you about our escape plan."

He looked indecisive, like he wasn't sure what to do next. Finally, he got up and went to the bathroom, leaving me alone at the table. I sipped from my coffee and pondered this whole thing. I'd had some lousy cases before, but nothing comparable to this. I'd nearly been killed three times, found out my dream woman was a manipulative, coldhearted witch, and I was clearly facing an ugly confrontation when I got back and tried to explain to my superiors how I killed six men, and tortured a suspect, and blackmailed the Central Intelligence Agency—and all for a client I could barely stand to look at.

Katrina was taking a long time. I was drumming my fingers on the table. I watched several men and several big, fat babushkas leave the bathroom area and waddle out. I let my eyes stray over to seven or eight younger men I figured were the best bets for SVR agents. I tried to detect if they were watching me. Two or three returned my stare, and I wrote them off. I mean, professional watchers never return your gaze, right? They act like they don't even know you're there. That narrowed my suspects down to about five guys, three of whom were seated at the same table, and I wondered if undercover agents traveled in packs.

I sipped my coffee and kept watching them. My staring made one of them nervous. He began playing with a napkin, and his eyes were darting around in distraction. I also noticed a bulge under his left arm. He either had a very ugly tumor or was packing heat, as they say.

Another minute passed before the door to the men's room opened. Alexi's head popped out and he looked around, then walked out. But before he could get to the table, I got up and walked toward him. I took his arm and tugged him toward the doorway. We almost made it, too. In fact, I'd just gotten the door opened when the three guys at the table leaped out of their seats and rushed toward us, yelling and hollering and reaching for their guns. I swung open the door and fled out onto the street, now only worried about saving my own ass. In situations like this, it really is every man for himself.

My best bet was the subway, and I sprinted as fast as my legs could carry me toward the entrance. I was less than twenty yards away when three guys carrying pistols came careening around a corner and cut me off. I spun to the right and lurched into the traffic, praying I could make it to the other side.

A black sedan came straight at me, and that option evaporated. I fell back, and a couple of pairs of hands jerked me off my feet.

I yelled, "I'm unarmed, I'm unarmed." I didn't want anyone getting any funny ideas.

Two very big thugs moved alongside me and took hold of both my arms and nearly carried me back toward the bakery, where four more goons were holding their traitor. A black paddy wagon immediately pulled up and we were both shoved inside, roughly, so that we landed on our bellies. Five SVR goons crawled in behind us and began slapping cuffs on our hands and ankles and gags on our mouths.

Nobody said anything. We felt the van jerk forward and remained quiet while we went wherever the hell we were going. This wasn't the way this thing was supposed to end. I was scheduled to be in a different van, headed toward the airport, where there was a big comfortable plane that would take me back to the good ol' U.S.A.

CHAPTER THIRTY-EIGHT

T took twenty minutes before the van jolted to a stop. One of the guards swung open the door, and we were both shoved out. We were then pushed and dragged inside a big, multi-storied building that didn't seem to have many windows. I didn't like that not-many-windows thing. Buildings that don't have a lot of windows don't have them for a reason.

We were led to some stairs in the back that went down to a basement. The inside of the building had an institutional look and air to it, like a hospital. Or, considering the circumstances, like a prison. We took a left at the bottom of the stairs and then walked down a hallway before we were shoved into a starkly empty room.

Our gags were removed, but neither of us said a word. We were both stunned. We just stood with our hands and ankles cuffed, staring at the white walls and contemplating our fates. We remained like this for nearly five minutes before a door opened behind us. I spun around and saw four really big goons enter, then the diminutive figure of Viktor Yurichenko.

Viktor immediately said, "Alexi, Alexi, it is so tragic that it has come to this. I am truly sorry it had to be this way."

Alexi said nothing, so Viktor angrily shouted, "But you've been a damn fool! You never should have dealt with the Americans."

When Alexi still didn't answer, Viktor walked around me, until he faced him. His eyes narrowed into angry slits, then he barked something in Russian that I didn't understand, but I didn't need to. It was probably the Russki version of "shit" or "damn it," and I started chuckling.

I tried to stop myself, but the chuckles kept bubbling out of my chest. Viktor walked in front of me and slapped me as hard as he could. The truth was that it wasn't all that hard, and I chuckled even harder, partly because this whole thing was funny as hell, and partly because I was so damned nervous, it was either laugh or faint.

Viktor yelled something in Russian at his goons, and two of them rushed over and forced my partner to bend over. Then one pulled off the wig, and the other began yanking at the elastic, skin-like rubber of the mask. It came off in chunks and pieces, and after about thirty seconds of tugging they had most of it off. Those modern Hollywood disguise kits, you can't believe how authentic-looking they can be.

I didn't know the guy under the mask, except that he was a federal prisoner chosen for this job because he had identical physical measurements to Alexi's. He'd been doing hard time for three counts of armed robbery and the CIA had cut him a deal. Since he was a three-time loser serving a life sentence, if he took this job and it worked, the President of the United States would get him a pardon.

At that moment he looked absolutely bewildered, since his role in this operation wasn't supposed to end this way. The CIA had positioned him in that bathroom for an entirely different purpose. The real Alexi was supposed to join Katrina in a stall in the ladies' room, they'd both don chubby babushka disguises, and then saunter out together. That touch was mine, of course. I mean, it had worked for me in the mall, right? I was supposed to leave right behind them.

Only that plan hadn't considered the fact that there'd be a bunch of SVR goons *inside* the bakery. The way that plan was supposed to end was that the convict disguised as Alexi would emerge from the men's room a few minutes after Katrina, Alexi, and I made our escape. He'd then hurry to the subway, get off after a few stops, dodge into a restroom, get out of his Alexi costume, then go to a linkup point where the CIA would meet him and get him back to the States and freedom.

But we all know what they say about the best-laid plans, right? The minute I knew the SVR had agents in the bakery, I realized it was time for plan B. Which was a bit of a problem, because there wasn't any plan B. With both Alexi and Katrina in the bathroom, I was the only one left that the SVR watchers could observe. When I saw Alexi and Katrina leave in their disguises, I had to buy them at least two or three minutes to make it to the CIA van idling three blocks away, so they could make their getaway. Had I gotten up and followed them out, the whole thing would've collapsed.

I felt pretty proud about the self-sacrifice I'd made to get them a chance at a new life. There's a certain nobility in that, right? It's like that classic Dickens line " 'Tis a far better thing I do," and all that crap. But as I stared at the enraged face of Viktor Yurichenko, I remembered how that same novel opened: "It was the best of times. It was the worst of times." "The worst of times" were on their way.

"Who are you?" Yurichenko growled at the prisoner.

I said, "Let him go. He's nobody. He was a federal prisoner hired to do this job. He had no idea what the operation was about, or even why he's here. He was promised freedom if he just hid in that bathroom and then walked out two minutes after he heard a knock on the door."

Viktor was now staring at me. Remember when I mentioned that Viktor sort of looked like a skinny Santa Claus, with those big smile creases around his eyes and mouth? Let's amend that. He now looked like a cranky old man with giant hemorrhoids that were killing him.

"A common prisoner?"

"Yes."

He looked over at one of his goons, and before I could say anything, there was a pistol shot and the poor guy slumped to the floor, the front of his forehead blown clear across to the far wall.

I yelled, "You bastard!"

Then suddenly I felt a searing pain on the back of my neck, and I crashed down onto the floor. I felt groggy, and rolled onto my back and looked up. A goon lifted me off the floor like a sack of feathers. He held me steady while another goon came over. This goon looked like his creator got confused about where his legs and arms were supposed to go, because he had short skinny legs and huge stumps for arms that hung from massive arched shoulders. I tried tensing my muscles to protect my organs, but it didn't seem to matter. The guy had fists like concrete blocks. He kept pounding me in the stomach, and every time he hit me, I could feel the pulverizing force right down to my toenails. This went on for about thirty seconds, which doesn't sound like a long time, but when you're a punching bag it's a *very* long time.

Then Viktor barked something and he backed away. I was almost past caring by that time. A few more punches and I would've suffocated.

I was moaning and trying to draw breath when Viktor lifted my chin and stared into my face. "They don't like it when you call me names," he said, very calmly. "I advise you not to do that again."

I mumbled something, but it was incomprehensible, because I'd literally been punched silly. I had vomited, and it was hanging off my lips. I could barely draw any breath.

Viktor said, "Felix has quite a punch, doesn't he?"

I think I nodded, and he asked, "Where is Alexi?"

"Gone," I gasped.

"Liar. He isn't gone. All our border crossings and airports have his photo. They know to stop him. How were you trying to get him out?"

I didn't say anything, so Viktor said a few words to his goons again, and we went through the punching-bag routine again, only Viktor must've ordered Felix to pull his punches a bit, because this time I didn't feel them all the way down to my toes. Only my knees.

Anyway, at least forty minutes had passed since Alexi and Katrina had left the bakery, so there wasn't any tangible reason to keep taking this beating. I finally moaned, "All right . . . all right."

Felix stepped back, and Viktor's smug face reappeared. "Where?"

"On, uh, on the Secretary of State's . . . uh, on his plane."

He barked something at another goon, who immediately sprinted out of the room. We stood for the next two minutes without anybody saying a word. To say that the air was thick with tension would be an understatement. I kept glancing down at the poor guy whose cranial fluid was making a big puddle on the floor.

Finally Viktor stared at me. "You sacrificed yourself for Alexi and the girl, yes?"

I didn't need to answer.

He chuckled and rocked back and forth on his heels. "How very, very stupid, Drummond. If Alexi escaped,

I will never forgive you." He peered more closely into my face. "You understand that, don't you? I won't kill you, but you'll wish I would. You'll pray every night to die. You'll become my solace."

Suddenly the door burst open and the goon rushed in. He said something in rapid-fire Russian and Viktor just glared at him. I was in big trouble.

I almost shuddered from the expression on his face— a mixture of bitterness, hurt, and fury that coursed straight up from his soul. I didn't have to guess what the news was. I already knew. The Secretary of State had canceled his appointment with the foreign minister and took off at 6:20. Alexi and Katrina had accompanied him, of course.

This was great for them. This was exceedingly bad for me.

I said, "It's done. Let it go."

He didn't say anything for a moment, I think because he was choking on his own bile. I doubt if he'd ever lost at anything, chess or espionage. Losing gracefully is an acquired skill. Defeats pile up on top of defeats and eventually you lose the outrage for the next one that comes along. Viktor obviously hadn't built up that immunity yet. I vaguely realized that if I didn't make him think of something else, he might break his word and have Felix come over and punch my nose through the back of my head.

I asked, "If he was a traitor, why do you care? He's got nothing more to tell us, right?"

The goon who held me tightened his grip, and Felix took a step in my direction.

Instead, Viktor's neck snapped up. "You don't understand, do you? Of course you don't. Alexi was like my blood. I treasured him. I raised him. I took him in when he was a sniveling little pig farmer's son. I, uh—" He suddenly stopped talking. He became emotionally tongue-tied, and I realized he really did look upon Alexi as his own child. Perhaps a wayward child, but don't most parents love their kids, warts and all?

Still, it didn't add up. A piece was missing, and I didn't know what it was.

I said, "You knew he was a traitor. For twelve years you knew. Why didn't you stop him?"

He stared at me with pure hatred. "Because it was useful, you idiot."

I was thoroughly baffled. "Useful? I . . . I don't get it."

"Of course you don't. What was Alexi reporting to your people?"

"About some cabal he thought was undermining Russia and causing wars and revolutions."

"A cabal?" Viktor asked.

"He said it helped undermine the Communists and get Yeltsin into the presidency. It helped him get reelected. It sparked the wars in Chechnya and Georgia and Azerbaijan."

He was chuckling long before I was done. "And you believed this garbage?"

"Uh, well . . ." I stammered.

"Of course you didn't," he snapped. "Surely your people had that figured out. Poor Alexi . . . so brilliant and attractive and, well, troubled in his head. Yes?"

I nodded.

Then he really chuckled. "For twelve years Alexi told your people these wild stories and the more he elaborated, the more crazy he sounded."

"But you believed him, too, didn't you? You helped Alexi search for this cabal. You infiltrated Yeltsin's organization, you dispatched Alexi to find them. You gave him resources and you were involved."

A look of amazement crossed his face. "Alexi told you this?"

"Yes."

The surprise gave way to curiosity. "Did he say he ever found these people?"

"No. But you know that . . . he was reporting back to you. You were involved in every step of the search."

"Oh really?"

"Alexi told me—you directed him to find these people. He reported everything to you."

"Ah, yes, that's true," he said, slapping his side, like what a stitch that was. "Alexi thought he came so close, so many times. Then, mysteriously, the evidence would disappear."

I was shaking my head, now completely confused. "What are you talking about?"

"He was always the good son, and he wanted his adopted father to see what he'd done. He so wanted me to be proud of him that he rushed in to tell me every time he got close. Unfortunately, he was about to destroy the most important work of my life. I had to prevent that, of course. So I sabotaged his operation."

"You mean, you—"

"Of course, you idiot. This cabal, as you call it, these are my people."

"But—"

"But nothing," he sneered, obviously knowing what I was about to say. "Let me ask you something."

I nodded.

"Do you know I put Kim Il Sung in power? I went into North Korea with him when the Great War ended. I disposed of his enemies and gave him the weapons to build a liberation army. I even persuaded Mao to send the Chinese army in to save him when your army chased him out of the South. Do you know I was the man who recruited Fidel Castro? I met him in Mexico when he was just an angry young punk with a big ego. I gave him the guns and told him how to run Batista off that island. Ho Chi Minh was another of my creations. I had his rivals assassinated and helped him rise to the top of the nationalist movement. I helped him run the French out, and orchestrated every inch of our support for his war against your army."

He paused to let me absorb all that. I had picked up bits of it in the intelligence files, but it wasn't the same as listening to him brag about everything he'd done. It isn't often you hear from a man who's changed the course of world history. It was chilling.

"And there were other leaders, other nations. The Congo, Ethiopia, Eastern Europe. I was the man who knew how to orchestrate revolutions and wars, to make sure the right man rose to the top. I was the kingmaker. That was Stalin's nickname for me. Khrushchev's also. Brezhnev thought I walked on water. Andropov, too."

"You must've been busy as hell," I said, wondering where this was going.

He gave me a sardonic look. "I woke up one day and realized something quite shocking, Drummond. I was working for idiots. I was the man building their empire, while they were destroying my homeland. They were stupid, venal men, all of them. Stalin nearly buried Russia. He made that idiotic bargain with Hitler and nearly got us all killed. Then Khrushchev, who was so clumsy in his dealings with your Kennedy, he nearly got us blown into a nuclear dustpile. And Brezhnev was nothing but a common thief. He wasn't even a smart thief. We were lurching from bad to worse. Do you know what it feels like to serve a system that produces such garbage for leaders?"

"No," I admitted, and I meant it, too.

He seemed to consider my answer, as though it were the naive babbling of a child. He sighed. "I was helping them destroy Russia. You Americans, you had the right idea. You ran your empire like an elite country club. You took only the rich and talented . . . Japan, Western Europe, Taiwan, Canada. We . . . well, we were taking in useless leeches. Eastern Europe, Vietnam, North Korea, Cuba, Yemen, Ethiopia—what do all those places have in common? They are all impoverished messes. They were needy orphans that drained our wealth and energy. We got nothing from them. Nothing. And our own people were becoming poorer and poorer. This is not how these things are supposed to work, is it?"

I shrugged. Having never been in the empire-building business, what the hell did I know?

"It had to end," he said, moving across the floor and waving his hands. "But how? Who had the skills to end it? I did, I suddenly realized. Poor Gorbachev, he never understood what was happening. Everything started going wrong. The Poles began striking under that mustachioed idiot Lech Walesa, and for some odd reason our intelligence services couldn't seem to stop them. Very strange, eh? All of our power, and we couldn't stamp out this rebellious movement. Then our great Red Army couldn't seem to win in Afghanistan. Think about that, Drummond. Do you really believe that the Russian army was *that* incompetent against a bunch of fourth-world tribesmen? Or that we couldn't have smashed Walesa and his people?" He chuckled. "We looked incompetent only because some very patriotic generals and officials deliberately made it seem that way. The whole point was to begin the fraying of the empire, to lose the war, to give Russia its own Vietnam. Then came the problems in Georgia, then Chechnya, then this man Yeltsin comes out of nowhere and threatens Gorbachev's grip."

"You were behind all that?" I asked, staggered by the scale of his plot, which was obviously more fantastic than Alexi had imagined.

"Of course. Oh, there were others, certainly . . . Many others, actually. Patriots who knew we had to sweep away the old system, to destroy the old order so we could rebuild."

"But Alexi? Why didn't you tell him? He was like your son, right?"

He stared down at the floor a moment, almost as though he was embarrassed by this admission. He said, "How could he have embraced what we had to do? He hadn't seen how the Marxist idiots misruled, hadn't experienced the cruel bite of their incompetence. He was too naive to understand at that time. Oh, I would've told him eventually." He paused and seemed to wonder if he'd made the right choice. Then his indecision evaporated. "But Alexi served a vital purpose."

"And what was that?"

"When he first came to me with his suspicions, I realized something. Everything was so vulnerable in the beginning. It could've been stopped so easily by forces inside Russia or by the West. We were so fragile in the beginning, secrecy was our only protection."

"So?"

"You still don't see it, Drummond?" he snapped, angered that I couldn't jump to what he considered obvious conclusions. Like a lot of ridiculously smart people, those of us with average intelligence taxed his patience. "Alexi was the first outsider to detect it. With his extraordinary intellect, he was the only one who noticed that history was not flowing on a logical path. I was quite proud of him, actually. So I decided to use Alexi as a watchdog. He would keep me and my people on our toes. It was perfectly safe, of course, because he kept me informed of everything. But if Alexi couldn't find us . . . well . . . then nobody could."

I was suddenly awed by the sheer deceitfulness of this man. To him the whole world was a chessboard to be ordered as he wanted. Even Alexi was just one more pawn to be shuffled from square to square.

"That's cold," I said, unable to help myself.

"Cold?" he asked, shaking his head. "No, Drummond. I gave Alexi a historic role. He who serves in ignorance still serves, yes? Knowing we had a worthy opponent made us much more cautious. Without Alexi we might have become sloppy." He paused and seemed curious. "Tell me something. How did you uncover poor Milt? What led you to him?"

"The second time you tried to kill us," I admitted.

"Ah." He nodded his head, obviously piecing the rest of the story together. He really was frighteningly brilliant. "I thought that was it. After the attempt in Moscow, I debated whether to try again. I just . . . well, I couldn't have you and that girl sniffing around Alexi. You have to understand, Drummond, when you set the board, the pieces have to move by the rules. You and that girl were upsetting the rationality. You, nosing around in things that weren't your business, and her becoming romantic with Alexi. What else could I do but eliminate you?"

I was thinking there were plenty of other things he could've done, but then I had very strong prejudices in this matter.

I said, "Yeah, well, we cross-indexed all the documents the CIA supposedly got from your vaults. When we found a few only Martin had seen, it all fell into place."

"Oh, that's very clever, Drummond. Poor Milt. You're probably wondering how we recruited him. Back when he was a college student majoring in

Russian studies, he visited here with a student group. It was the sixties, when so many of your young people were disenchanted by Vietnam, and Milt was very vocal about the rottenness of your country. We barely had to recruit him. Fate plays funny tricks, yes? Who could've imagined that his college roommate would go on to become President? The only use I ever saw for Milt was writing a few books and articles that were damaging for your CIA and foreign policy. We made a trade. I provided him the information and he became famous as a writer."

"Well, as we say in America, sometimes you fall into a pile of shit and find a brick of gold."

He gave me a very unpleasant look, and Felix took a step toward me. "Metaphysically speaking," I quickly added. "I mean, Martin was a really brilliant coup, wasn't he?"

"Brilliant?" Viktor said. "Milt was a coward. He refused to do anything unless I shielded him. So I gave him the template for a cut-out. The day Morrison walked into his office he knew he'd found the perfect doppelgänger. You remember, I hinted to you that Morrison brought this on himself. He was so ambitious, and so obsequious, he virtually volunteered himself."

"And Milt became invaluable?"

"You can't imagine," Viktor said, chuckling some more. "Poor Yeltsin, he couldn't believe the quality of the intelligence I gave him, the things I could get your government to do. Every time I provided him with your President's talking papers before they met, he would howl with laughter."

"Yeah, but you put him in power and you owned him anyway, right?"

"I would hardly say I owned Yeltsin, Drummond. He was certainly not the man I would've chosen for the job. His only qualifications were his availability and pliability. Not that it mattered. He was always a transitory figure. We never intended to build our new Russia around him."

"No?"

"Of course not. He never knew about us. He was a caretaker we leveraged into place to keep the chair warm until we could prepare one of our own to take over. Yeltsin would take the blame for the inevitable aftershocks of such abrupt change, and then we would offer the people a savior, a sober, take-charge type who promised to clean things up."

The shock of what he was saying literally hit me like a jackhammer. "You mean . . . ?"

He smiled. "You Americans are so blindly stupid, it's extraordinary you've gotten so rich and powerful. Where did our new president come from? He worked for me, in my bureau of the KGB. How else do you think he got the job?"

I was shaking my head in disbelief. "It will never work, Yurichenko. Eventually the world will learn. You can't keep it hidden forever."

He brought his hand up to his chin, the same way Alexi did. It was almost uncanny. "So what? It's gone too far to stop. Why would anybody even want to stop it? What would they worry about? Another empire? It's the farthest thing from our minds. The whole notion of empires is passé, wouldn't you say? They all fail, don't they?"

"But what you've done in Georgia and the other republics. The world won't permit that."

He was shaking his head. "We don't covet our neighbors, Drummond. We simply tell them what we want and force them to provide it. If they get rambunctious, like the Chechens and Georgians and Armenians, we make examples of them. But why would we want Uzbeks or Tadzhiks or Kazakhs back as part of our country? They'd all go right back to sucking off the tits of the Russian people. We simply want their oil and cotton at prices we set. You see how much better this is?"

He was asking rhetorically, of course. He knew damn well what I thought. In fact, he was chuckling, enjoying the amazement on my face, which was when I realized the only reason he'd explained all this to me. The old man was sadistically letting me know he'd pulled off the biggest scam in world history, and there wasn't a damned thing I could do about it. It was his little victory dance, his way of saying, "Okay, so you stole Alexi from me, but don't kid yourself that it was any big thing, because in the scheme of everything you're hearing it's a pimple on a gnat's ass. You sacrificed yourself for nothing, Drummond."

It was creative cruelty at its best. And the very fact that he was explaining all this in the first place was also a sly way of informing me he intended to embalm me in Russia's deepest, darkest corner, and never let me smell anything close to freedom again.

He suddenly turned to his goons and barked something in Russian. Then he turned and gave me that sweet, grandfatherly smile. "Well, Drummond, we will not be meeting again."

"Don't be so sure," I growled, and he gave me a curious look.

Then he turned around and walked out the door, leaving me to ponder a future that was going to really, really suck.

CHAPTER THIRTY-NINE

YOU'D think that by the twentieth of April there'd be a hint of warmth in the air. I mean, April is a few weeks into spring—the ground should've been thawed, the trees should've been budding, and maybe even a few wildflowers should've had enough chutzpah to poke their stems out of the ground. Siberia's different.

I blew hard on my hands and tried to warm them up before I spotted Igor heading in my direction. I quickly picked up my shovel and started doggedly hacking at the frozen earth. Igor had a thing for me, and I didn't want to exacerbate it. He hit me once or twice a day just on general principle, and if I gave him more than general principle to go on, he beat me silly. I don't know if Igor was even his real name. He was just so damned ugly that he had to be an Igor.

The other prisoners all kept their distance, I guess because they sensed there was something special about me, and they didn't want any of that specialness to rub off. I didn't blame them. I didn't speak their language, so we had nothing to talk about, nor did we have anything in common since they were mostly thieves, murderers, and Mafiya scum, whereas I was an American Bar Association member who'd seriously underestimated his own limitations. But it was more than that. The guards had instructions to treat me differently, to hurt me on a regular basis, although nothing too serious, because I was supposed to survive. I was supposed to live to a ripe old age in this frozen hellhole with nothing to look forward to except beatings and constant pain, until I either went stone-cold mad or killed myself.

I had thought December in Siberia was bitterly frosty, but by January I realized I didn't know the meaning of cold. And February was even worse. My piss froze before it hit the ground. I'm not kidding. These yellow icicles were striking the permafrost and shattering into tiny crystals.

I've never been particularly big on Russian cuisine, but you wouldn't believe all the things you can make with cabbage. There are cabbage broths and soups and salads, or just plain raw cabbage itself. Raw fish heads were the big treat, but they only threw those on our plates on Fridays. I tried to make friends by giving mine away, but for some odd reason that never seemed to work.

Anyway, Igor continued to head toward me, so I chipped away at the icy ground even more furiously. I whispered a prayer that he was heading toward somebody else. That's the thing about Siberian prisons. After a while, you get pretty damned selfish. They're pretty much dog-eat-dog places.

Every morning the guards came through the barracks and dragged out the corpses of poor buggers who had died of disease, or malnutrition, or had frozen to death in their sleep. And this being a prison, there were a few murders every week as well. We were each issued a single, threadbare wool blanket that had been used by generations of other prisoners. The trick was to try to collect two or three of them, so the multiple layers could protect you from the cold. The barracks were unheated, so in the morning you'd awaken covered by a layer of frost, so damned stiff you could barely climb out of bed. Your blanket would be gone, and you'd have to go through the rest of the barracks and find the culprit, and then you'd have to fight to get it back, because without it, you wouldn't last long. The training I'd had in the outfit was the only thing that saved me. After I beat up four or five of the biggest badasses in the barracks, nobody wanted to go near my blanket.

Suddenly Igor was right behind me, and I tensed for the inevitable assault. What would it be? A rifle butt in the kidneys or the kick on my backside that would send me flying? Nothing happened. I slowly turned around and faced him. He hooked a finger. I put down my shovel and followed him like an obedient puppy, coughing and hacking the whole way, because I seemed to have caught a very nasty cold.

We ended up at the headquarters, one of only two buildings at Camp 18 that had wood-burning stoves. The second we walked inside I felt like my skin had caught on fire. I hadn't been near heat in months, and the sudden sensation burned.

Three or four senior guards were huddled around a stove in the corner, and they all looked up when I entered. One got a pissed-off look and climbed off his stool.

"You are Drummond, yes?"

"Yes," I said, surprised to hear English. None of the other guards spoke English.

He pointed a hand toward a doorway. "You will go in there and take shower."

I didn't ask him why, because I'd been trained to comply immediately with every instruction. Given that it was me, it had taken a bit longer than normal to learn that lesson, and I had the scars to prove it.

I nearly passed out in the shower, my first in over five months. There was a small bar of coarse, sandy soap, and it took a lot of hard scrubbing to get all the dirt and grime off my body. I was actually bleeding in a few places, but what did I care?

I slipped back into my ratty, smelly clothes and walked out ten minutes later. The guards were all huddled around the stove again. The same guard got up, snapped cuffs on my wrists, then led me outside to a small truck with big tires. We climbed in the back and left. After about an hour, the truck stopped and we climbed out at an airfield, the same one I'd landed at five months earlier. Was it really only five months before? A big military Tupelov airplane was idling on the tarmac, and the guard led me stumbling toward the plane.

We took off a few minutes later, and while it was a long flight, I don't remember much of it, because I was floating in and out of la-la land. I'd wake up every few minutes hacking and coughing, and it dawned on me that it wasn't a cold but pneumonia. I hadn't recognized the chills and fever before because I was always chilly and shivering anyway.

We landed at a military airport I didn't recognize and left the plane for a military sedan. I had no idea what was going on nor did I ask. Russian prisons teach you that, too. Don't ask questions: You might not like the way the answer's delivered.

We drove into a big city I suspected was Moscow. Spring had made more of a dent here. At least there was no snow on the ground. I hadn't seen bare earth since I left.

We pulled to a stop in front of a big building that looked like it had once been a former palace of some sort. I climbed out of the sedan, but not until the guard ordered me to, because, like I said earlier, I'd been thoroughly housebroken. We entered the building and went up two flights of stairs. The guard walked ahead of me and opened a pair of double doors, then indicated with an arm wave that I was to enter.

The heat from the building gave me that uncomfortable burning sensation again. Four people were gathered around a long table. On one side sat Harold Johnson, my old friend from the CIA, and General Clapper, my old boss. On the other sat Viktor Yurichenko and an older man I didn't recognize.

Johnson and Clapper looked up when I entered.

Clapper's eyes popped open, because I'd changed somewhat since the last time we saw each other. I was skinnier, for one thing. Much skinnier. I'd guess I'd lost at least thirty pounds, and I wasn't heavy to begin with. I looked like a dazed bird that had forgotten to head south for the winter and paid dearly for it. For a second thing, like all Camp 18 prisoners, my head was shaved to the skin. For a third thing, being continuously outdoors in subzero temperatures isn't recommended by dermatologists. I had cold sores on my lips and my skin had cracked open in places, and the vitamin deficiency hindered the healing process. Finally, the steady beatings meant I was always sporting a black eye, or swollen lips, or a fresh bruise here and there.

"Jesus, Sean!" Clapper yelled. "What the hell have these bastards done to you?"

Johnson peered across the table at Yurichenko. "Viktor, this is unacceptable."

Yurichenko finally turned and looked at me also. "Russian prisons are harsh places, Harold. I don't make them this way."

Johnson nodded back, then he turned and looked at me again. "Sean, your boss and I are here to try to negotiate your release. This is a very delicate matter. You're being charged with three counts of murder and espionage. Those are serious crimes."

I stood perfectly still. The espionage charge was obviously the most problematic. I had helped get Alexi out of Russia—guilty as charged. The three counts of murder baffled me until I realized this had to do with me killing the three hit men who tried to take me out. Very clever.

"That's right, Sean," Clapper quickly added. "The other gentleman here is the equivalent of a Russian superior court judge. He can take your case to the president to arrange a pardon, or he can decide there's not enough evidence to have a trial."

Well, wasn't that interesting? I'd been in prison over five months, and now they were considering a trial. I stood mute, sensing I really had no role in this proceeding, that a great deal of discussion had already occurred, and I sure as hell didn't want to harm the chances of success. I wouldn't be standing here if they didn't have something cooked up.

Yurichenko was giving me his grandfatherly smile, the one intended to warm the cockles of your heart. I felt a chill. I dreamed of getting my hands around his neck and choking the bastard to death.

Johnson ignored me and turned back to face Viktor, evidently continuing the conversation I interrupted when I came in. "The point is, Viktor, our President would consider it a very big favor if you would drop this. He asked me to emphasize how very beneficial this would be for both sides."

Yurichenko was shaking his head, but mildly, like he wasn't quite sure how that logic worked. "But, Harold, you have nothing to trade. Please forgive me for being selfish, but I must see some quid pro quo. We are both pros in this game. We both know how it works. I cannot give you something for nothing."

"And do you have something in mind?"

"A simple trade-in-kind would be ample. I want

Alexi back. Return him, and you can have Drummond."

Johnson suddenly stared down at the tabletop, as though what he was about to say was very difficult. "We can't do that. It's not even negotiable. Besides, there's a bit of a problem here."

"And what would that be?"

"Before he came over here, Drummond made some tapes. They're embarrassing for both of us, but they're much more embarrassing and problematic for you. If those tapes get out, our relations would be grievously wounded. All these areas where we're cooperating— the missile reduction pact, NATO participation for Russia—it would all go up in smoke."

Viktor leaned back in his chair, obviously surprised. "Tapes? What is on these tapes?"

"The whole thing," Johnson grimly admitted, appearing greatly pained.

Yurichenko looked over at me. His eyes roved from my shoes to the bald tip of my skull. I was a most unlikely-looking suspect to have found a way to outsmart him. He seemed to be thinking furiously about how to handle this.

He asked Johnson, "And you really think these tapes would be a problem?"

Which actually was a clever way of saying, "Hey, I'm not really buying this. And you better not be bluffing or Drummond over there will think he just spent five months vacationing on the Riviera compared to what I'll do to him."

"Oh for Godsakes, Viktor. They detail attempted

murders by you inside our country, as well as the murder of an American officer in Moscow. On one of them, Martin admits to everything. He names you as his controller. He admits it was your idea to frame Morrison. Do you know what would happen if all that got out? If the American people learned that for eight years you were actually running our foreign policy toward your country, they'd go wild. The President asked me to tell you he'd be left with no choice. He'd have to cut off everything. He's not exaggerating, Viktor. You have no idea what those conservative pricks on the Hill are like. We're talking endless investigations here. This was your doing, not ours. It was your operation. You owe us something for keeping it quiet. That's the quid pro quo."

Viktor looked like somebody just threw a glass of ice water down the back of his shirt. It took him a moment to recover. "But there is still a problem, Harold. Even if we released Drummond, we have no guarantees it won't come out. Look at him. Imagine the anger in his head. The moment he stepped off the plane, he would tell everything."

Almost on command, Johnson and Clapper pivoted their necks and faced me. Clapper said, "That's why we insisted on having Drummond here for this meeting. He'll have to swear to give back those tapes and that he'll never utter a word about any of this." His eyebrows came down about two notches. "I'm sure you'll be willing to do that. Right, Sean?"

Now, here's the truth about what was running through my head at that very instant. The whole five months I spent in Siberia, I'd known this moment was coming. It was the only thing that kept me sane, that let me withstand the constant beatings, and the incredible loneliness, and the bitter cold. Those tapes were my only source of hope.

They were a ticking time bomb. They'd do incalculable damage to American-Russian relations. The American people don't like being played for suckers. They get real grumpy about that. And frankly, given what I now knew about Yurichenko's plot, that might even be the best thing that could happen. But was it worth the rest of my life?

I leaned my back against the wall. I was suddenly pensive.

Knowing me as he did, Clapper said, "Don't even think about it, Sean. There's no real choice for you. If you say no, those tapes will still never see the light of day. Trust me on this."

There was something in his tone, a slight intonation, as if he knew something I didn't know. Okay, I had to consider that. But the other thing I considered was that with or without those tapes, I could still accomplish a great deal of good by telling the CIA and, if they didn't listen, the American press, all about Viktor and his cabal. And frankly, that was much bigger news than another spy scandal anyway. That was the news that would blow the top off everything.

"Okay," I mumbled, and Johnson and Clapper relaxed back into their seats.

As if by some hidden cue, the door behind me opened and the guard yanked me back out of the room, so the grown-ups could be left in privacy to discuss whatever the hell it was they needed to close the deal.

I was led back to the sedan and then driven to a local jail, where I was given my own cell. I lay down, closed my eyes, and tried to sleep. I couldn't, though. Between my hacking coughs and my troubled thoughts I was still wide awake at three in the morning, when two guards and two Americans in dark gray suits came to get me. I stared out the windows at Moscow's streets the whole drive to the airport. The usual assortment of beggars and crippled vets were roaming around, all those poor bastards who never realized they were the pawns on the chessboard whose fates were being decided by men like Viktor Yurichenko. I actually had tears in my eyes as they loaded me on an American C-130 and it took off.

CHAPTER FORTY

I SPENT a miserable week in the military hospital in Landstuhl, Germany, while the docs probed and checked every square inch of my body for infections and diseases I might've picked up at Camp 18. I had a blood infection, but they cleared that up in a few days. They emptied pharmacies full of drugs into my system for the pneumonia. The whole week they also kept intravenous tubes hooked into my arms so they could restore my vitamin balance, or my blood cell count, or maybe my sperm count. Nobody told me, so how the hell was I supposed to know?

In between my medical treatments, two of those

glum-faced Agency guys kept coming into my room to debrief me. I went over everything. I told them about Viktor's admissions, and about Milt Martin, and then about life at Camp 18. They taped every word and listened patiently, but I had no idea what they thought. Like most debriefers, they were as uncommunicative as brick walls. Every time I asked them what had happened in the past five months they just stared blankly and said they weren't allowed to talk about it.

After the hospital released me, I actually took a civilian flight back to the States. The first thing I did after I was seated was bribe the stewardess into giving me six extra bottles of scotch. I deserved a little reward. Although unfortunately, my body was so battered and depleted that I was in a coma after the third one.

I woke up with an incredible headache and a stewardess shaking my arm. The plane was empty of passengers; it was just me and the cleaning crew. I stumbled down the aisle, feeling spectacularly sorry for myself. Was this any way to treat a returning hero?

I made it through customs in record time, and just as I was leaving the sealed-off area, I spotted a short black woman in civvies flapping her arms and running toward me. If I didn't know her better, I'd swear she was excited to see me.

She walked right up and threw her arms around me, hugging me tightly, like a mother taking care of a child she knew had suffered some grievous misfortune. We stayed like that nearly a quarter of a minute, and it felt wonderful.

Then she backed away and her face got scrunched

up. "You look like shit."

"Well, hell, Imelda," I said, "it sucked pretty bad."

She shook her head and sort of half smiled. "Don't you try any of that bitchin' and moanin' crap on me. I ain't got no time for wimps."

"But I—"

"But you nothin'," she said, still smiling.

"Thanks anyway. I mean it, Imelda. Thank you. I owe you my life."

She shrugged as if it was no big thing. "I gave 'em the tapes last week. General Clapper said it was part of the deal."

"It was," I admitted. "They give you a hard time?"

"Them bastards can't spell hard time. They tried to turn up the heat pretty good for a while. Them people also sneaked into the office and my apartment, lookin' for them tapes. Like I'd leave 'em in plain sight that way. Hummph."

I put a hand on her arm. You have to know Imelda. If she said they tried to give her a pretty hard time, that meant they threatened to rip out her fingernails and kill every last member of her family.

I knew when I sent her the tapes, I'd just taken out the best life insurance a man could have. When I was still missing after a week, I knew Imelda would contact the right people and threaten the hell out of them with exposure. She'd know just how to handle it, too. Thirty years as an Army sergeant is the equivalent of a Ph.D. in making others suffer.

I kind of felt sorry for the Agency. They had never run into the likes of Imelda Pepperfield. She doesn't respond well to pressure. Which is another understatement, because squeezing Imelda is like punching a porcupine. It ends up hurting you a lot more than it hurts her.

I finally said, "Imelda, I hate to sound ungrateful, but what took so damned long?"

She looked down at the floor in evident embarrassment. "It was part of the deal. Them CIA people said you couldn't come back till they was ready."

I filed that one away, as I patted her on the arm. "Don't worry about it. Really. I was having a great time. I was cursing when they dragged me out of the special resort they sent me to. I'd made all kinds of friends. I miss them already."

Anyway, she led me out to the parking lot where her black Mazda Miata was parked. I'd never reckoned Imelda as the cutesy Miata type, but then nobody's ever exactly what you think they are, are they? We stayed on the Dulles Toll Road till we got to the Tysons Corner exit. She took the exit, and I asked where she was going, and she just shrugged. The next thing I knew we were pulling up to the front of Morton's Steakhouse. A guy in a silly-looking uniform took her car and gave her a ticket.

When we entered, Imelda murmured something to the maitre d', while I stood frozen in the entrance, literally swooning from the aroma of cooking steaks and lobsters and prime rib. The food here probably wasn't nearly as good as Camp 18's, but I thought, What the hell . . . why not give the place a chance?

Oddly enough, two stiff-looking types in dark suits

were standing beside the entrance to the private room we were led to. I snarled at both of them as we walked in. For some odd reason I'd developed a real grudge against intelligence people.

Katrina came running at me. She threw her arms around my shoulders and kissed me right on the lips. Then she backed away, and Alexi was there with his hand held out.

"God, it's great to see you two," I blurted, and it really was. We shook hands like a couple of old pals.

"You're, uh, you are still Alexi, aren't you?" I asked.

"No, I am now Bill Clinton."

"Bill Clinton?" I asked. "What asshole thought up that cover name?"

"Is only big joke," he chuckled. "I am developing American sense of humor."

"Who's teaching you? The CIA?"

This one passed right by him. Maybe it wasn't funny anyway. Maybe I needed a bit of work on my sense of humor, too. Five months in Siberia can cause you to lose a few steps.

He very seriously said, "Unfortunately, I am also being told I cannot give you real names. Tonight, Katrina and I will be moved to a new location to assume these new identities. Is all set up, because Viktor has people trying to find us. Mary says nobody can know of our new identities, not even you."

Katrina was rolling her eyes. "You should see the shit we went through to have this dinner with you. What's with these people?"

"It's this whole concept of friendship. Very mysterious to them, trust me."

Did I sound bitter or what?

Katrina said, "They've been treating us like little kids. We've been living in safe houses for months, while Alexi was getting debriefed."

"I'll bet that was fun."

"Fun, my ass," she replied, pushing a strand of hair off her forehead as she looked me over from head to toe. "But we obviously got the better part of the deal. You look like shit. Why didn't you follow us out of that bakery? We waited until Jackler insisted we couldn't wait any longer."

I briefly thought of telling her the truth. I considered saying, "Hey, remember when that lady said to abort, and you blew her off? Oh, and you blew me off when I reminded you? Well, guess what? These last five months of my life, that was the result."

I didn't, though. I wasn't about to. The truth was, I'd just spent five months being ridiculously envious of Alexi. Corny as I know this sounds, Katrina was the kind of girl I should've fallen in love with, because she believed in her man, and because she was willing to risk her life for him. I, on the other hand, had been in love with a manipulative schemer who chose a complete jerk over me and still had the gall to bring me back into the picture, so she could use me like a dishrag.

So instead, I said, "There was this really cute girl over at the next table, and she, uh . . . ah, Christ, you don't want to hear about it."

She looked at me like I was crazy as hell.

I gave them both a big smile. "So are you two getting married or something silly like that?"

Alexi grinned proudly. "I asked Katrina two months ago."

"And she told you no, right? She said she'd fallen head over heels for this very dashing, extraordinarily handsome Army lawyer, and she could never settle for a lesser man."

Alexi obviously had a long way to go before he'd understand American sarcasm. "Uh, no, Sean, this was not what she was saying."

Katrina took his arm and shot me a bullet of a look. "He's joking, Alexi. And for Godsakes, don't copy his sense of humor."

"Ah, I see," said Alexi, trying to manufacture a polite laugh.

"So have you set a date?" I asked.

"We must wait until we are resettled and have new identities."

"Well, I'm very pleased for both of you. I really am."

And I really was. Real life doesn't always produce storybook endings the way movies do. And I felt a certain grim satisfaction in being the Cupid who gave these two a chance—I just never realized that Cupid had to go through so much shit to make these romances work.

We sat down and a waiter immediately appeared. I ordered a steak and a prime rib and a lobster, with three or four side orders, and four desserts, and made an obscene pig out of myself. The CIA was paying for this dinner. I wanted to make it a night they'd remember for a long time.

Between shoveling forkfuls of food down my throat, I told Alexi and Katrina all about Viktor and his cabal, and Alexi said he and the CIA had already figured it out. The second he escaped, they had put two and two together and it all fell into place. I tried to fill in a few details they hadn't guessed, and he looked surprised, but I suspect he was only being polite. He knew Viktor better than anybody. And with that brain of Alexi's, he probably guessed things Viktor had done that even I didn't know about.

He finally said, "So you have heard what happened to Milton Martin?"

"No, my barracks at Camp 18 didn't have a satellite dish," I replied, stuffing another slice of steak through my lips. "The next one over did, but it was filled with real selfish bastards who wouldn't let us come over and watch."

"A week after Katrina and I arrived, Martin jumped off a thirty-story building in Manhattan."

"He jumped?"

"There was suicide note left on rooftop saying he was most unhappy with life and professionally disappointed. Was of course phony. Viktor was eliminating loose ends. Martin had completed his purpose, yes? Was of no more use to Russia . . . and was time to eliminate source of possible embarrassment."

"Gee, I'm sorry to hear that," I said, wondering if maybe Yurichenko and the CIA had cooked up some kind of deal to keep Martin from becoming the newest sensation. "I hope the concrete he landed on was damned hard."

By eleven o'clock my three plates were empty, and I'd finished my dessert. I'd also generously helped Imelda and Katrina finish theirs, and the third champagne bottle was empty. I was drunk, and hugging and kissing both of them, and saying all kinds of goofy shit, and was right on the verge of puking my guts out.

One of the security agents knocked on the door and stuck his head in. He politely said it was time for Alexi and Katrina to go, because they had a late flight to catch. We exchanged more hugs and kisses, knowing we'd never see one another again.

Imelda drove me back to my apartment. When I let myself in, I noticed that somebody had paid my rent and electricity and phone bills, because everything was in working order. It had to be Imelda, of course. She never misses a beat. Of course, there'd be a big IOU on my desk in the morning. With compounded interest, too, since, like I said, she never misses a beat.

I slept in till ten, when I heard a knocking on my door. I was in my pajama bottoms when I opened it.

Mary was standing there with that awesome smile. "Hey skinny, welcome back."

"I, uh, well, it, uh . . . thank you."

She walked in without asking. She looked better than I'd ever seen her, and I noted that being separated from Bill obviously agreed with her. Her cheeks had a healthy glow, and she had on another miniskirt and a blouse tight enough to show what great uptoppers and shapely legs God loaned her. Her eyes shifted around my apartment, which was small enough to fit into the maid's bathroom in Homer's house.

"Nice place," she said.

"Bullshit," I replied. "It's an armpit. This a personal or professional visit?"

"A bit of both," she said, then leaned against a wall and studied me with those luminous blue eyes. "How bad was it over there?"

"Bad enough. Let's just say I doubt they have much of a recidivism problem. The odds against surviving that first prison tour just ain't that high."

"I'm sorry," she said, and she did look sorry. "When you didn't come back to the plane, I was frantic. There just wasn't anything I could do, Sean."

"It wasn't your fault. I didn't blame you."

"We tried to abort."

"I know."

We'd exhausted that subject, and I was fairly sure she'd already read through my debriefing materials, so she knew everything that had happened. She walked over to a bookshelf and began staring at titles—the point was, she wasn't looking at me.

Her voice sounded nervous. "You're not going to believe this."

"You'd be surprised what I'd believe these days."

"I received a promotion. After the operation ended, I was made an SES 2. I'm Johnson's new deputy."

I shook my head, but not in disbelief. "Well that's really something."

"Nobody was more surprised than me," she said, pretending that it was true, which it obviously wasn't. She'd turned on her own husband to get ahead, and when that had fallen apart, she'd covered her own ass better than anybody. She had great instincts and wonderful reflexes. Why wouldn't they promote her?

"So how's your husband?" I asked, since there was still this five-month gap in my knowledge of anything that had happened outside the frozen wasteland called Camp 18.

"He's fine. After you left, a new lawyer was appointed."

"Yeah, I know. How'd he do?"

"You left him a birthday gift. We brought Eddie Golden over to the headquarters and made him listen to your tape. We were very blunt. We told him we could no longer support the charges of treason or murder. He wasn't happy."

"I'll bet," I said, trying to swallow my disappointment at missing that particular meeting. Of all the unfair things about this case, that was the most painful. I'd earned the right to see the blood drain from Eddie's face as he realized what a horse's ass he looked like after all those leaks and briefings to the press about Morrison. That's the thing about laying it all out for the public the way he had. When your face appears on the cover of *People* magazine, you better deliver.

"After that," Mary continued, "a deal was worked out. Bill was allowed to retire as a major general in return for his confession on adultery."

"As a major general? But he was only on the list. He never even wore the stars."

She sort of dipped her head. "We wanted the deal very badly, and Bill was furious about this whole thing.

We all agreed he had a right to be mad. We were willing to offer him a concession or two."

I was suddenly suspicious. "And why'd you want a deal so badly?"

She stopped looking at my bookshelf. She stared out the window instead, anywhere but at my accusatory eyes. "Because of the way we had to explain this, Sean. The story we eventually released was that we thought we had an impeccable source in Moscow. He made some grand claims and we believed him. We paid him a great deal of money to turn over certain documents we thought were authentic. Only later did we learn that he was a forger and the documents were fake. There was no traitor."

"You're shitting me!" I yelled.

She acted like I hadn't said anything. "It was embarrassing for the Agency to have to admit it had been gulled by a common thief, but we stomached it. It was a damned sight better than the real story."

"And why is it better?"

She finally turned around and faced me. "Because for fifty years, we and the Russians were pointing tens of thousands of nuclear warheads at each other. Because the current situation might not be perfect, but it's a massive improvement over the past. We're talking about cutting our nuclear arsenals in half. They're working with us on ending terrorism. Together, we're looking at hundreds of ways to cooperate and make the world safer and more peaceful. A whole new partnership is being born. Don't you get it?"

"And what about Viktor and his plot? That doesn't

bother you?"

"Sean, for somebody so smart, you can miss the most obvious things. Look at it practically. He ended Communism. He ushered in a democracy. Do you think we and the Russians would be having the discussions we're having today if the old system was still in place? He's made the world a much better and safer place. We're not going to complain about how he did it. That's ancient history. The important thing is the future."

I stared hard at her for a few moments. She stared right back. And slowly, reluctantly, even painfully, it dawned on me. I didn't want to admit it, but it was true. If you looked at it practically, she was right. His motive and means might've been pathetic, but in the grand scheme of things, that was irrelevant.

Mary turned back and lifted a book off the shelf. She opened it halfway and acted like she was glancing at the pages. "The point is, Sean, we got you back, and we expect you to honor your deal. Everybody's happy, so don't upset the apple cart."

"Well, there's still a bit of a problem."

"And what's that?"

"It's the little matter of the five months you all left me rotting in a Russian prison camp. Imelda told you to get me out of there a week after I disappeared. Why didn't you?"

She was still staring inside that book. "Oh, that. Don't blame the Agency. And don't blame Sergeant Pepperfield, either. Trust me, we don't ever want to have to deal with that woman again." She looked up from the book and finally looked directly at me. "It was you. You gave us no choice."

"How's that?" I asked, sounding angry, because I was.

"Sean, this thing had to be cleaned up. The wrangling with Golden and with Bill, and getting the right story out to the public, that took time. We considered the stakes, and your stubbornness, and decided it was best to leave you there until everything was taken care of."

"It was that cold?"

She ignored this. "We had to be sure that even once you were back you couldn't climb up on some self-righteous horse and do any damage. If you walk out that door right now and hold a press conference, it won't work. The bodies have all been buried, Alexi and Katrina have disappeared, and we have the last of the tapes. Don't be angry, Sean, just accept it. Put it behind you."

This was obviously the point of her visit. She'd been sent over here by her bosses to ascertain whether I'd be cooperative or not. They were still using her to use me. I spent another moment acting like a potted plant, long enough that she knew she had me. Her intuition about me always had been right on the mark. She closed the book and slipped it back on the shelf. She finally turned and faced me.

"I've given a lot of thought to us. It would never work, would it?"

"No, I don't guess it would," I admitted. "But one question."

"What?"

461

"Why'd you marry that bastard in the first place? Why did you dump me?"

I don't think she expected me to ask that. She looked confused for a brief span. Then no longer confused, just mildly embarrassed. "Sean, marrying you was *never* in the cards. I'm sorry. We're too . . . different."

She patted me on the cheek and left, closing the door quietly behind her. I stared at the doorknob. The truth is, sometimes what you think is true really is the furthest thing from it. Like Yurichenko. If you stare through the prism from one angle, he's a monstrously bad man. But if you turn that prism just slightly to the right, he deserves a Nobel Peace Prize.

I'd always thought losing Mary was the worst thing that ever happened to me. When a woman is that beautiful, it makes it damned hard to turn that prism. You don't really want to find the imperfections.

I had only one more thing to do. I made a few calls and then took a shower, got dressed, and drove to my office. Then I drove across the river and into Washington, over to Eddie's imposing office building. I took the elevator up to the twelfth floor and was gratified to see there were no more guards with Uzis. Eddie's artifices were being taken away. Too bad—Eddie lived for the trappings.

I walked down the same hallways I'd been down all those months before. There was no noise or activity in the offices. Boxes were stacked everywhere, apparently waiting to be picked up and trucked to a secure storage facility where nobody would be allowed to see them for fifty years. The whole place had that mood of a carnival that was closing down and getting ready to move on to the next town.

The ringmaster was seated in the conference room when I opened the door and looked in.

"Afternoon, Drummond," he said, staring at me curiously, obviously wondering why I'd asked him to meet me here.

I grinned. "Hey, Eddie. Tough luck the way this whole thing turned out, huh?"

"It wasn't my fault," he immediately snapped. "They tossed me the wrong man. It was their fuckup, not mine."

"That's one way to look at it. I just wanted to drop by and leave you something to remember me by." I tossed the baseball bat at his feet. It had been snapped in half.

He was still sputtering curses when I walked out. See, the thing with life is, you win a few and you lose a few, and if you don't relish the few you win, well, then you go crazy. I've always been an optimist at heart, anyway. I mean, there's plenty of girls other than Mary, right? And my stomach was still filled with all that Morton's steak and lobster that the U.S. government even paid for. Plus I was back to sleeping in my own bed, without anybody stealing my blanket. Now I ask you: How could it get any better than that?

Center Point Publishing
600 Brooks Road • PO Box 1
Thorndike ME 04986-0001 USA

(207) 568-3717

US & Canada:
1 800 929-9108